AFRICA IN THE MODERN WORLD

General Editor GWENDOLEN M. CARTER

ETHIOPIA

The Modernization
of Autocracy

ROBERT L. HESS

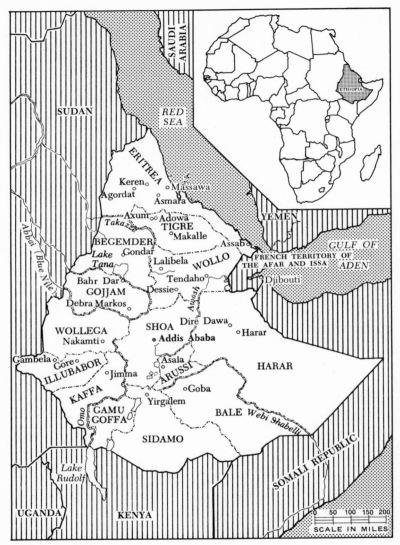

Map 1. Ethiopia

ETHIOPIA

The Modernization of Autocracy

ROBERT L. HESS

UNIVERSITY OF ILLINOIS
AT CHICAGO CIRCLE

Cornell University Press

ITHACA AND LONDON

International Standard Book Number 0-8014-0573-4

Library of Congress Catalog Card Number 79-120290

PRINTED IN THE UNITED STATES OF AMERICA
BY VAIL-BALLOU PRESS, INC.

For F. A. H.

Foreword

The subtitle of this book, *The Modernization of Autocracy,* epitomizes the character of contemporary Ethiopia and suggests an element of its uniqueness. Alone among African states, Ethiopia maintains an imperial dynasty with its remarkable emperor, Haile Selassie I, the ultimate source of decisions. Where other independent African states organized mass political parties to oppose colonial control, Ethiopia, with a long history of independence, apart from the short-lived Italian occupation of 1936–1941, has remained a "no-party" state whose nascent parliamentary system has been sponsored from above. The striking modern architecture of its capital city, Addis Ababa, contrasts sharply with traditional forms of agriculture and dwellings not far from its center. Even so, the instruments of modernization are not without effect on the character of Ethiopian life and policies.

While literacy rates are still among the lowest on the continent, the number of secondary schools has expanded considerably, aided by substantial contingents of Peace Corps volunteers. Haile Sellassie I University produces an annual crop of graduates whose work-service year has acquainted them with village needs. The still newer Law School, so far staffed largely by expatriates, is training a group of young Ethiopians to cope with the manifest problems of administering the French Civil Law Code in a society still operating for the most part with customary law norms. Younger administrators, many of whom have had training and experience abroad, have ambitious plans that are beginning to have an impact despite cumbersome processes and often lethargic superiors.

Yet in the face of what needs to be done to reform agricultural practices, rural communications, and health, the pace of change is agonizingly slow. Developments that appeared promising five years ago are now less encouraging compared with the advances in countries, like Kenya, whose soil is no more fertile. Ethiopia is paying a heavy price for its loss during the Italian occupation of gifted administrators who might have bridged the wide gap between the vigorous younger members of the imperial structure and the elders still in command, whose vitality and foresight are often so inferior to those of the Emperor himself.

Inevitably the issue of succession is discussed, at least in private. No one would consider disputing the eminence and role of the Emperor in Ethiopia any more than one would the supreme position of President Tubman in Liberia. But both countries, strongly traditional, autocratic yet slowly modernizing, have perforce the same question confronting them because of the age of their central figure. In Ethiopia, with its much larger population and still sharper internal divisions, the issue is still more disturbing.

By treating both Ethiopia's long and rich historical background and its contemporary problems, Robert Hess has brought out the essential links between the past and the present, which all too many contemporary treatises on African countries fail to do. Moreover, he discusses in detail important events of the 1960's—ministerial reforms, tax innovations, the 1960 coup, the student riots—about which relatively little is known. He has also indicated significant new trends in Ethiopian political life and has tried to look beyond the present into the uncertainties of the future. For those who want still more information, his bibliography lists a wide selection of recent publications.

Inevitably so comprehensive yet concise an account offers judgments that will provoke questions, comments, and possibly even anger in some quarters. To attempt to avoid criticism is generally to remain colorless. The stuff of politics, which deals with personalities and the interpretation of events, is controversial. What an author can do is to make available his perceptions and the judgments that he draws from them in the hope not only of informing and of stimulating interest but also of encouraging additional research and dialogue.

Americans need to know much more about Ethiopia. The American government provides that country with more foreign aid per capita than it does any other in Africa. Addis Ababa is the center of the Economic Commission for Africa and the Organization of African Unity, and Emperor Haile Selassie I has taken an active personal diplomatic role in many tangled African issues, including the recent Nigeria-Biafra civil war. This book should help to broaden understanding and inspire interest in a particularly beautiful, richly historical, and significant country.

GWENDOLEN M. CARTER

Northwestern University
May 1970

Acknowledgments

This study is the outgrowth of research in Ethiopia in 1963 for the preparation of a monograph on Ethiopia for *National Unity and Regionalism in Eight African States,* edited by Gwendolen M. Carter (Ithaca, N.Y.: Cornell University Press, 1966). Since that time I have expanded the original study, revisited Ethiopia, and continued my research in order to give the present work contemporary significance as well as scholarly interest.

I am grateful to Gwendolen M. Carter and Richard Greenfield, who carefully read an earlier version of this study and freely gave of their time and suggestions for improvement, and to William A. Shack, whose criticism of the manuscript I value highly. In Ethiopia, I was received graciously by Richard Pankhurst of the Institute of Ethiopian Studies, who helped facilitate my work there. I am especially indebted to Alemayyehu Moges, who tutored me in Amharic, and to Stephen Loewenstein, then of the Law School at the Haile Sellassie I University. For long hours of their time and patience in answering my many questions about contemporary Ethiopia, I express my appreciation to Ambassador Edward Korry, and to John Buche and Thomas Walsh of Washington, D.C. A young and enthusiastic economist, Richard Jolly, introduced me to the activities of the United Nations Economic Commission for Africa and served as a sounding board in the formulation of many of my ideas. In 1966, Christopher Clapham, then preparing his dissertation on Ethiopian politics, briefed me on the changes that have taken place within

Parliament. I am equally indebted to Peter Schwab of Adelphi University for materials on recent attempts at tax reform and to Gerhard Loewenberg of the State University of Iowa for his acute insights into comparative politics. For information on the activities of the Ethiopian Students Association in North America, I owe thanks to Hagos G. Yesus, an articulate representative of the student intellectuals. A word of thanks is due the Imperial Government of Ethiopia for its hospitality in 1966 during the Third International Conference of Ethiopian Studies and to the many Ethiopians, critical of their government's policies and willing to discuss their grievances with me, whose names I cannot mention.

The University of Illinois at Chicago Circle has given me generous financial assistance in my researches. I consider myself fortunate also to have the encouragement of my friend and colleague Robert V. Remini. My research assistant, Susan Roy, and the secretarial staff of the Department of History, Emilie Binder, Barbara Hodges, Lillie Brewton, and Allie Clift, gave unstintingly and cheerfully of their time. A graduate student of mine who served with the Peace Corps in Ethiopia, James Baylor, provided useful information about the role of the United States in Ethiopia. Lastly, a tribute to my wife, who shares my enthusiasm for history and for teaching.

Robert L. Hess

Glencoe, Illinois
June 1970

Contents

Illustrations

MAPS

PLATES

Introduction

Ethiopia or Abyssinia? The official name of this northeast African country is Ityopya, or Ethiopia, a word of obscure origin. The ancient Greeks called all areas inhabited by dark-skinned peoples Aithiopia; the term means "Land of the Burnt Face," after the legend that Phoebus' golden chariot passed too close to the tropics and thereby left the peoples of the torrid zone permanently sun-tanned. The Ethiopians, who call themselves Ityopyawan, claim that the term is etymologically derived from Ethiops, an alleged descendant of Noah's son Ham. Medieval Europeans, however, borrowed from Greek geography and applied the terms Ethiopia and Ethiopian to sub-Saharan Africa, southern Arabia, and India, most specifically to the ancient empire of Kush, just south of Egypt, from whence comes the biblical Cush and the outdated anthropological Cushite.

Abyssinia was introduced into European usage by the Portuguese, most likely by way of the Arabic *Habesh*. Because the word has pejorative connotations of "mixed blood" in Arabic, the Ethiopians prefer not to use the term or its European derivatives. Yet the equivalent term in the Amharic and Geez languages, *Habasha,* is frequently employed by the Amhara and the Tigreans to refer to themselves as a collective entity. Historically, Abyssinia as the Portuguese first knew it was limited to the northwest quarter of what is now modern Ethiopia.

Ethiopia has long exerted a powerful influence on the imagination of both scholars and laymen. Archaeologists and classicists have attempted to unravel the mysteries of the origin of the ancient Ethiopian kingdom of Axum, its South Arabian connections, its relationship with the Greek world of the eastern Mediterranean two millennia ago, its trade connections with Egypt, Nubia, Persia, and India, and its role as a possible transmitter of metallurgical and irrigation techniques, domestication of plants and animals, and ideas of divine kingship to other areas of Africa. For medieval and Renaissance Europeans, Ethiopia was the land of Prester John, the object of centuries of speculation, and the goal of expeditions by the Portuguese almost five hundred years ago. For modern Ethiopians their country is the land of the Queen of Sheba and of the Conquering Lion of Judah.

Church historians have concerned themselves with the unique nature of the sixteen-hundred-year-old Ethiopian Christian Church, one of the most isolated branches of Christianity. Linguists have found much to study in the Semitic languages spoken in Ethiopia, and much research remains to be done on the Cushitic and other languages of the country. The historian has the problem of unearthing the past and pulling together the pieces of Ethiopian history into a coherent whole. He is fortunate to have the written records so rare in African historical research, chronicles dating from the thirteenth century and tantalizing inscriptions dating back to the fourth century, as well as fragments of pre-Axumite inscriptions that give evidence of not only an early form of writing but also the development of an advanced civilization more than two thousand years ago. Only relatively recently have social scientists begun to work in projects related to Ethiopia, and much remains to be done in the areas of sociology, social anthropology, and economics. Even more is to be discovered by the political scientist. This study cannot pretend in any way to be definitive, for Ethiopian and non-Ethiopian scholars alike still have much to contribute toward an understanding of the history and nature of one of the world's oldest and least-known states.

Ethiopia has survived as a political entity since the early days of Axum, a city-state contemporaneous with Imperial Rome, and has a dynasty that dates its origins from about 1000 B.C. This dynasty has been the single most important factor in the emergence of Ethiopia as a modern state in the past century. Today the center of politics in Ethiopia is held by an Emperor who is venerated by his people and admired by the world for his courageous stand at the League of Nations in 1936. In a world of dwindling monarchies, Haile Selassie I [1] is almost an anachronism, and yet he is one of the acknowledged leaders of the movement for African unity. On the African continent itself, Ethiopia's Emperor arouses mixed feelings. Outside Ethiopia, he is admired as the leader of the one African nation that successfully fought off European colonialism in the nineteenth century and evoked international sympathy (if not action) for its resistance to Italian Fascist imperialism in the twentieth. Within Ethiopia, he has

[1] There is no universally accepted style for the transliteration of Amharic names into English. For convenience I have used a modified version of the system followed by the Institute of Ethiopian Studies. Exceptions are made, however, in the case of Ethiopian names already familiar to English readers. Thus, the Emperor's name appears as Haile Selassie, rather than Haile Sellassie, a form more current in Ethiopia than outside the country (and the correct form for Haile Sellassie I University). The Emperor should never be referred to as Selassie; Haile Selassie is the Emperor's throne name, a compound meaning "Power of the Trinity."

Ethiopians do not usually have family names. An individual is referred to by his first name, or names in the case of compounds; the second name is always that of the father. Thus, Haile Selassie's name, Tafari Makonnen, means Tafari, son of Makonnen.

given rise to concern over the autocracy of his government and the repression of new ideas and political opposition. All too often those new ideas and the opposition represent the major trend of developments in other African states. Thus, the future of Ethiopia is no less a subject for speculation than its past and a topic as fascinating as its present.

ETHIOPIA

The Modernization
of Autocracy

Negus kamotu bamān yimmāggotu

When the Emperor dies, whom
can one ask for justice?
—Ethiopian proverb

CHAPTER 1

Among the
Blameless Ethiopians

Ethiopia occupied a special place in the cosmology of the ancient Greeks. According to Homer, the ancient gods often journeyed to the farthest reaches of the Hellenic world to enjoy the hospitality of a people who, unlike corrupt Mediterranean man and his gods, were renowned for their grace and virtue: the "blameless Ethiopians." [1] Modern Ethiopia may be far removed in time and space from the Ethiopia of classical Western mythology, but, like its legendary namesake, it too occupies a special position. Modern African statesmen frequently journey to this once remote land to enjoy the hospitality of a monarch whose capital is now renowned as the headquarters for two of Africa's most important institutions, the Organization of African Unity and the United Nations Economic Commission for Africa.

If the Olympian deities were seeking a land with beauty to rival Mount Olympus, they should have visited not only legendary Ethiopia, but also the remarkably beautiful land of contrast and diversity that is modern Ethiopia. The richness of the vegetation in the highlands, the haunting loneliness of the stark deserts, the ugly black lava outcrops of Dankalia, the striking contrast between the lofty mountains of the northwest and the vertical walls of the Rift Valley,

---

[1] "For Zeus went to the blameless Aithiopians at the Ocean yesterday to feast, and the rest of the gods went with him. On the twelfth day he will be coming back to Olympos" (*The Iliad*, Book One, lines 423–425).

which cuts through the center of the country, the teeming
wildlife of the lowlands, and the tortuous gorge of the Blue
Nile as it knifes its way from island-studded Lake Tana to
the Sudanese border provide Ethiopia with a natural setting
that some have compared to the scenic beauties of Mexico
and the majestic wonder of Switzerland.[2]

Modern Ethiopia covers some 457,000 square miles, equal
to the combined areas of France and Germany. It lies at the
core of the great eastern Horn of Africa, which it shares with
the adjacent—and rarely friendly—Somali Republic and
with the French Territory of the Afar and Issa, formerly
French Somaliland. Together these territories form a geo-
graphic unit bounded on the southeast by the Indian Ocean,
on the north and northeast by the Red Sea and the Gulf of
Aden, on the west by the Sudanese lowlands, and on the
south by Kenya. This vast region is characterized by strong
contrasts between its rugged mountains, its fertile plateau,
and its hot and often arid lowlands. For convenience, the
Ethiopian portion of the Horn may be divided into three
broad regions: the western plateau, the eastern plateau, and
the Rift Valley and Danakil plains.

The best-known part of the country is probably the western plateau, which comprises about 40 per cent of the area
of Ethiopia.[3] The western plateau—especially its northern
half—was the heartland of Christian Ethiopia, the Abyssinia
of the Age of Discovery. It runs from the mountains of

[2] G. C. Last, "Introductory Notes on the Geography of Ethiopia,"
Ethiopia Observer, VI, no. 2 (1962), pp. 82–134.

[3] See Y. Abul-Haggag, *A Contribution to the Physiography of Northern Ethiopia* (London: The Athlone Press, University of London, 1961)
and Frederick J. Simoons, *Northwest Ethiopia: Peoples and Economy*
(Madison: University of Wisconsin Press, 1960); see also E. Migliorini,
L'Africa (Turin: Unione Tipografico-Editrice Torinese, 1955), pp.
461–542.

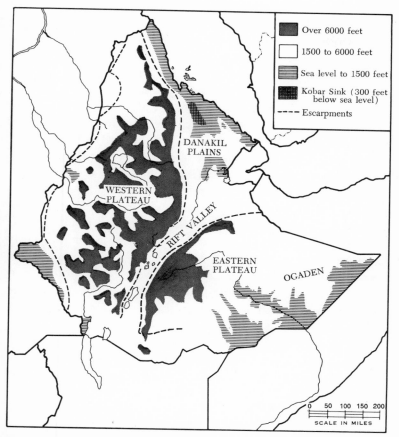

	Over 6000 feet
	1500 to 6000 feet
	Sea level to 1500 feet
	Kobar Sink (300 feet below sea level)
- - -	Escarpments

DANAKIL
PLAINS

WESTERN
PLATEAU

RIFT VALLEY

EASTERN
PLATEAU

OGADEN

0   50   100   150   200
SCALE IN MILES

Map 2. The natural features of Ethiopia

Semien in the north just south of the Red Sea as far as Lake Rudolf on the Kenyan border. From the Red Sea the plateau presents an imposing wall of mountains that was virtually impenetrable to invasion until the twentieth century. With a general elevation of from 6,000 to 10,000 feet above sea level, the plateau boasts one of the highest average altitudes of any country and some of the highest mountains on the African continent. Ras Dashan in the Semien Range, the highest peak in Ethiopia, soars to an altitude of more than 15,000 feet. Equally impressive are Mount Abuna Yosef (13,750 feet) and Mount Berhan (13,450 feet). A characteristic feature of the mountains of northwest Ethiopia is the frequently encountered, mesa-like amba, a flat-topped mountain with a sheer drop on all sides and an excellent potential as a natural fortress or a place to exile political opponents. This extensive highland area is sharply divided in many parts by steep valleys, and escarpments that fall away precipitously for from 1,500 to even 3,000 feet or more are common. This western highland may very well also be the most fertile portion of East Africa. In some places in Shoa, for example, the topsoil is more than fifteen feet thick, despite centuries of erosion.

The eastern plateau, which can also be called Muslim Ethiopia, has sometimes been termed the Somali plateau, for it is part of a larger plateau that extends from the 14,000-foot mountains of Arussi and Bale Provinces in a northeasterly direction through the Somali Republic to Cape Guardafui, the easternmost tip of Africa. Sloping gradually toward the Indian Ocean, this plateau is also broken and irregularly elevated, but unlike the western plateau, its valleys are not gorges, its average altitude is considerably lower, and for the most part the area is poorly watered.

The two great plateau regions are divided by the impressive Rift Valley.[4] Not so well known as its more southerly extension in Kenya and Tanzania, the Ethiopian Rift Valley is well defined and limited by the two plateau areas. The escarpment between valley and plateau is generally a steep edge frequently broken by smaller valleys, and transportation and communication between these regions have always been difficult. In the south the Rift Valley cuts through a series of basins in which lie numerous lakes of unparalleled beauty. Only Lake Abaya (formerly Lake Margherita) is sizable (420 square miles), while the smaller lakes like Chamo, Zwai, Shala, Langano, Abyata, and Awasa range from about 200 to less than 50 square miles. To the northeast of the lake region the valley fans out into the semidesert plains of Dankalia, dipping to more than 300 feet below sea level in the potassium-rich Danakil depression. Then the Rift system continues northward along the geological line of the Red Sea, the Gulf of Aqaba, the Dead Sea, and the Jordan Valley, as far as Syria.

Because of these differing geographical areas and the great variations in altitude, the climate of Ethiopia varies widely. Toward the Somali border and in the Danakil lowlands, a hot, dry climate produces semidesert conditions. In the southwest near the Sudan border, the lower basin of the Baro River, a tributary of the White Nile, is hot, swampy, and malarial. In the lower-lying deep valleys of the Takazze and the Abbai (Blue Nile), conditions also approach those of the tropics, while Massawa on the Red Sea has the dubious honor of being one of the hottest places on earth, with temperatures reaching an infernal 140 degrees Fahrenheit. There one does not find the cool bracing air of the highlands, where, for the most part, the average temperature is be-

[4] G. C. Last, "Some Notes on the Scenery of the Ethiopian Rift Valley," *Ethiopia Observer,* V, no. 3 (1961), pp. 194–202.

tween 60 and 80 degrees. Thus, although the country lies
within the tropics, not far north of the equator, the elevation
of the land more than compensates for this position, and the
fertile plateau regions enjoy a healthful and invigorating
climate. On the two plateaus the average temperature varies
little throughout the year. Between June and September
comes the rainy season when most roads become impassable
as the monsoons pour down their heavy burden of water and
provide not only the needs of Ethiopia, but those of the
whole Nile Valley.

Ethiopians distinguish three climatic zones according to
altitude with terms that have been in use for at least a
millenium.[5] The *dega* zone is defined as any area over 8,000
feet in elevation. Here the temperature in the warmest
months rarely rises above 60 degrees (F.), and the air is thin.
Thus the alpine dega is suitable only for grazing and for
growth of sturdy cereals. The *woina dega,* literally "the wine
highland," has an elevation between 5,000 and 8,000 feet
above sea level, and mean temperatures range between 60
and 68 degrees (F.). In this temperate zone, where nights are
cool, it is hard to believe that Ethiopia lies between 200 and
1,000 miles north of the equator. The *quolla* zone, below
5,000 feet, includes all lowlands, whether the deserts of Dankalia, the coastal region of Eritrea, the waterless tracts of the
Ogaden, the deep and lush valleys of the Takazze and the
Abbai, or the tropical lowlands along the borders shared with
Sudan and Kenya. This hot zone is closer to the popular
Western image of torrid tropical Africa, but it is not typi-
cally Ethiopian.

The complex geography of Ethiopia has helped shape
Ethiopian society, history, and politics. In some respects geography has been a special friend of Ethiopia, for the two

[5] G. A. Lipsky *et al., Ethiopia, Its Peoples, Its Society, Its Culture*
(New Haven: HRAF Press, 1962), pp. 30–31.

plateaus have often served as mountain citadels and the ambas of the western plateau have offered refuge and asylum for beleaguered rulers. The steep escarpment and the desert-like coastal plain served, until the twentieth century, as natural barriers to large-scale military penetration. To the west the plains lead into the Sudanese desert; to the east lies the arid steppe country of the Somali. Furthermore, no navigable river leads into Ethiopia and the highlands from outside.[6] These natural obstacles worked in the past to sustain Ethiopia's political isolation and made it difficult for Ethiopia to maintain contact with the world beyond its immediate neighbors. Within Ethiopia a divisive topography has had to be overcome in order to create unity, for the country's internal regions are separated from one another by great gorges, often a mile deep and several miles wide. In times of political disintegration, this has fostered traditions of regional independence and the greatest political diversity. The highly rugged terrain of Ethiopia, by permitting each provincial region a degree of insularity, has been at the heart of many of the centrifugal tendencies that resist an imposed unity from the center.

Yet one should not be misled by the challenges of geography, for Ethiopia was rarely completely isolated from contact with Jerusalem, Alexandria, and, of course, its neighbors across the Red Sea. Moreover, striking evidence of the vitality of Ethiopia is the fact that the regions of the country have for centuries maintained a network of trade across political, religious, and tribal borders, kept alive the concept of a greater Ethiopia much as the concept of the Holy Roman Empire survived in Europe despite long traditions of internecine warfare, and gradually evolved a distinctive civilization that from the north has spread over much

[6] Until 1962 steamers from the Sudan called at Gambela on the Baro River to pick up coffee and skins.

of the country and promises to absorb and assimilate all of the disparate elements of the population into a national amalgam.

But who are the Ethiopians? Not a simple ethnic group, to be sure. Even the most casual visitor to Ethiopia soon perceives the bewildering complexity of the population of Africa's third most populous country. Classical authorities notwithstanding, the least scientific or satisfactory way to categorize the population is by skin color or moral virtues. The usual approach to the Ethiopian population is analysis by religion, language, and ethnic origin. But no single approach to Ethiopia's more than 23 million people is completely satisfactory because the various categories overlap.

The original inhabitants of northwestern Ethiopia, where the Ethiopian state was first formed, were probably the ancestors of the Agaw who have survived in scattered pockets in the northern provinces of Begemder, Gojjam, Wollo, and Eritrea. Today there remain two major areas of concentration of these Cushitic peoples: one to the northeast of Lake Tana (Kemant, Kayla, Kamta, Khamir), the other to the southwest (Aweya). Their name has survived in the district of Agawmeder near Lake Tana. They number about 100,000, or less than one-half of one per cent of the population.

During the first millenium B.C., immigrants from southern Arabia filtered across the Red Sea into what are now the provinces of Eritrea and Tigre. Attracted by trade and the similarity of this region's climate and topography to their homeland, these newcomers were related to the ancient Sabaeans, the people of Biblical Sheba, or Saba. They spoke a number of Semitic languages, and one of them, Geez (or ancient Ethiopic), became the dominant language of this area. As they developed first a number of city-states and then a kingdom centered on Axum, they must have intermarried with the aboriginal population. From this mixture of peoples evolved the Amhara and the Tigreans, two related peoples who together are known as the Abyssinians in the older European literature dealing with Ethiopia.

The Christian Amhara and the Tigreans dominated the Ethiopian state. Over the centuries they extended their control over the other peoples of Ethiopia and planted colonies throughout the country, especially military and administrative settlements in Muslim and pagan areas. Although their culture is strikingly similar, the Tigreans often regard themselves as culturally purer and superior to their Amhara cousins, who have intermarried to a greater extent with other elements of the population. At present the Amhara comprise about 20 per cent of the population of Ethiopia, while the Tigreans number about 9 per cent.[7]

Approximately one thousand years ago the Amhara and Tigreans penetrated into the southern half of the western plateau. They did not complete its conquest, however, until the nineteenth century. The original inhabitants, the Sidamo, were a Cushitic people. Archaeological investigations indicate that this area is rich in remains of material culture suggestive of a high level of agricultural technology and civilization that may have served as a link between Ethiopia, the Nile, and Africa to the south. Among their ethnic derivants are the Ghimira, the Maji, the Ometo, and the Sidamo proper; collectively all these peoples have been referred to by outsiders as Sidama. By the fourteenth century the western Sidama had established a number of kingdoms, including Kaffa (from which the word *coffee* is derived) and Janjero; both kingdoms had a life span of more than five hundred

[7] Lipsky, *Ethiopia*, pp. 52–61. Amazingly, no systematic study of Tigrean culture has ever been done.

years before they were absorbed into the Ethiopian state.
The Sidama peoples number more than 2 million, or about
9 per cent of the total population.

From one of the earliest Tigrean military colonies planted
in the area southwest of Addis Ababa there descended the
Gurage, who intermarried with the Sidamo and with later
immigrants from the north. Maintaining their own language
and ethnic identity, the Seven Houses, or tribal groupings,
of the Gurage today count approximately 500,000 people, or
2.5 per cent of Ethiopia's population.[8]

To the east of their state, as the Amhara and Tigreans
descended the escarpment from their highlands, they came
into contact with a number of nomadic or seminomadic peoples, the ancestors of the Danakil (known also as the Afar
and Adali) and the Saho. Occupying a hot desert of lava outcrops and scrub bushland that Europeans have referred to
as the "hell-hole of creation," they number about 250,000 in
Ethiopia and 60,000 in the neighboring French Territory of
the Afar and Issa. Until recently they had a reputation as
fierce warriors who mutilated their victims in order to bring
their fiancées the trophy expected of all men before they can
marry. Once bitter enemies of the Christian Amhara and
Tigreans, the Muslim Danakil were nevertheless indispensable trading partners; they controlled the major trade routes
from Shoa to the coast and were a major supplier of salt,
which was in short supply in the plateau country. The Saho,
who number about 50,000, are of mixed Danakil, Arab, and
Tigrean origin. Located to the north and west of the Danakil
in Eritrea, the Saho are generally nomadic, although some of
them have become agriculturalists. These peoples were not

[8] The most complete study of the Gurage is W. A. Shack, *The Gurage,
A People of the Ensete Culture* (London: Oxford University Press for
the International African Institute, 1966).

incorporated into the Ethiopian state until the late nineteenth and early twentieth century.[9]

To the east of the Danakil, across the Rift Valley on the eastern plateau, Semitic peoples from southern Arabia settled and gave rise to the once-independent city-state of Harar, which became the most important urban center in eastern Ethiopia. The 35,000 Harari who are their descendants form a distinct cultural group that has preserved its identity though surrounded by other peoples.

North, east, and south of Harar are located the Somali, a nomadic people who for four hundred years have looked to Harar for religious inspiration. They are part of the Somali nation found also in the Somali Republic, the French Territory of the Afar and Issa, and the Northern Frontier District of Kenya. Spiritual heirs to the Muslim traditions of struggle against the Christian Amhara, who occupied their land in the last quarter of the nineteenth century, they have separatist tendencies that are reinforced by Somali nationalism emanating from the neighboring Somali Republic. Estimates of the number of Somali in Ethiopia have varied from 350,000 to more than 1,000,000.[10]

[9] The Danakil and Saho are dealt with in I. M. Lewis, *Peoples of the Horn of Africa* (London: International African Institute, 1955), pp. 155–176. The classic studies of the Danakil are R. Franchetti, *Nella Dancalia etiopica: Spedizione italiana, 1928–29* (Milan: Mondadori, 1935) and L. M. Nesbit, *Desert and Forest, the Exploration of Abyssinian Danakil* (London: Jonathan Cape, 1937). The most recent population figures are found in V. Thompson and R. Adloff, *Djibouti and the Horn of Africa* (Stanford: Stanford University Press, 1968), p. 24.

[10] I. M. Lewis, *Peoples of the Horn of Africa*, p. 50; Lipsky, *Ethiopia*, p. 45. Lewis, who has done extensive research on the Somali, has also written *A Pastoral Democracy: A Study of Pastoralism and Politics among the Northern Somali of the Horn of Africa* (London: Oxford University Press, 1961) and *The Modern History of Somaliland* (London: Weidenfield and Nicolson, 1965).

Four hundred years ago, while the Amhara and Tigreans of the western plateau and the Danakil and Somali of the Rift Valley and eastern plateau fought a long series of debilitating wars, the Galla penetrated into Ethiopia, occupying lands that once belonged to each of these peoples. Today they are found in twelve of Ethiopia's fourteen provinces. As they fanned out across the country, they separated into three major areas of concentration: in the southwest (Wollega, Illubabor, and Kaffa Provinces), in the north (Wollo Province), and in the southeast (Bale Province). The first two groups settled down to an agricultural existence, while the Galla Borana of the more arid regions of the southeast remained nomads. Some Galla converted to Christianity and readily absorbed Amhara culture. Shoa, in particular, though generally regarded as an Amhara province, has a strong Galla background. In contrast, the Galla of the southeast resisted alien influences and maintain much of their traditional culture. Most important, however, is the fact that the Galla, who number approximately 9 million, are the largest single ethnic group in the country, comprising 40 per cent of the total population.[11]

In the lowlands to the northwest of the Amhara-Tigrean state range a number of additional nomadic groups. The Beni Amer, a Beja tribe thought by some to be the descendants of the same Beja whom Herodotus mentioned as threatening the southern borders of Pharaonic Egypt in the fifth century B.C., are the main group. Today they number more than 60,000 in Ethiopia and have close connections with the 100,000 Beni Amer in the Sudan. The nomadic Habab, Ad

[11] A compilation of information on the Galla is to be found in G. W. B. Huntingford, *The Galla of Ethiopia* (London: International African Institute, 1956). The vitality of Galla customs is discussed in Asmarom Legesse, "Class Systems based on Time," *Journal of Ethiopian Studies,* I, no. 2 (1963), pp. 14–29.

Takle, and Ad Tamaryam, like the Beni Amer, have been influenced over the centuries by immigrants from southern Arabia. As recently as the early nineteenth century small groups of nomadic Arabs were still crossing the Red Sea into this area. Most of these tribes acknowledged a degree of Ethiopian suzerainty in the nineteenth century; in the twentieth century they have resisted Ethiopian attempts to extend administrative control over their territories.

Along the western marches of modern Ethiopia are located a number of Negroid peoples, who comprise 3 to 5 per cent of the total population of Ethiopia. They are among the last peoples to have been added to the empire of the Amhara and Tigreans. In the nineteenth century they were enslaved in large numbers by the Amhara, as well as by the Sudanese Arabs and the Beja. The largest of these tribes are the Baria and Kunama of Eritrea, who together number about 45,000; the Berta, Beni Shangul, Koma, and Mao of Wollega Province, for whom current population figures are not available; and the Annuak (30,000) and Guma of Illubabor Province. They are generally despised by the highland peoples, who invariably refer to them in derogatory terms, employing a word for black never used in describing the blackest Amhara.[12] The Amhara-Tigrean prejudice against Negroid peoples is shared by the Somali and Agaw and to a lesser extent by all the other Cushitic peoples. The Amhara refer collectively to all these Negroid peoples as *barya,* which quite literally means "slave," or *Shankalla,* a pejorative name derived from the Beni Shangul, a Negroid people of Dar Fung in the Sudan; they have figured in the chronicles of Ethiopia since the fifteenth century. Prejudices notwithstanding, there has been considerable miscegenation between the Amhara and all the peoples with whom they have come in contact.

[12] Lipsky, *Ethiopia,* p. 325.

Along the Webi Shabelli River in Bale and Harar Provinces, there are a few small enclaves of Bantu groups, presumably the remnant of a population settled in that area before the advent of the Somali. Virtually nothing is known about them, however.

The linguistic map of Ethiopia is as complicated as its ethnic map.[13] Three major language groups—Semitic, Cushitic, and eastern Sudanic—and a host of minor groups are represented. Of the estimated seventy languages and two hundred dialects spoken in Ethiopia, all but eight or nine are spoken by relatively small numbers of closely grouped peoples.

By far the most important language is Amharic, the Semitic language of the Amhara, which has become the official national language. Amharic is derived from Geez, or ancient Ethiopic, a South Arabian language related to Arabic and Hebrew; Geez is still used as the liturgical language of the Ethiopian Orthodox Church. During the last hundred years, as increasing numbers of non-Amhara have come to speak Amharic, the language, which had already absorbed many elements of languages spoken by the Cushitic peoples of the western highlands, has undergone a process of simplification. Its historical development is suggestive of some parallels with the English language. Just as Norman French invaded Anglo-Saxon England and gave rise to a hybrid language with significant vocabulary accretions and shifts in syntactical formation, so South Arabian Geez invaded Cushitic Ethiopia and produced a language whose vocabulary and grammar are manifestly Semitic, but whose syntax is often strongly Cushitic.

[13] Lipsky, *Ethiopia,* pp. 52–61.

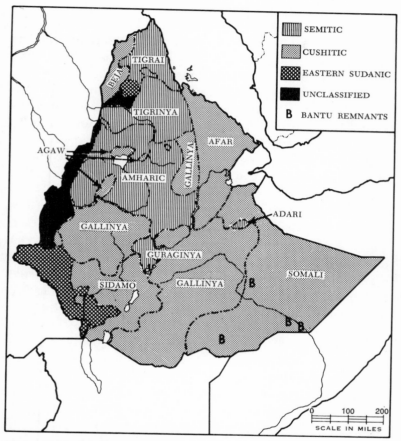

Map 3. Ethiopian languages

Amharic and its ancient Ethiopic predecessor have a written form that dates back to at least 250 B.C. In Geez and Amharic there is an extensive traditional literature that includes religious tracts, lives of saints, historical chronicles, and poetry, and in Amharic there is a burgeoning modern literature in such new forms as the novel, plays, and short stories, as well as the older satirical and deliberately ambiguous political poetry upon which Amhara dote.[14] The Amharic alphabet, or more accurately syllabary, is written in a script of thirty-three different consonants, each of which has seven vowel forms. Today almost half of the population of Ethiopia speak Amharic; this takes us far beyond the reaches of the Amhara proper, who account for not much more than one-fifth of the total population.

The second most important Semitic language is Tigrinya, the language of the Tigreans, spoken in the provinces of Tigre, Eritrea, and Begemder. In many respects Tigrinya is more closely related to Geez than is Amharic, just as geographically the Tigreans are closer to the center of ancient Ethiopian civilization. Unlike Amharic, however, Tigrinya has a comparatively sparse literature, despite the fact that Tigrinya can be written in the Geez-derived script. A partial explanation is that Geez is intelligible to many Tigreans without great effort and study. Although related, Tigrinya and Amharic are not mutually intelligible.

A third Semitic language, Guraginya, the language of the Gurage, has a history like that of Amharic and Tigrinya. Although the Amharic script is suitable for transcribing its sounds, Guraginya is not often reduced to writing. Recently, however, English translations have been made of both traditional and modern Guraginya literature.

[14] E. Cerulli, *Storia della letteratura etiopica* (Milan: Nuova Accademia, 1962); I. Guidi, *Storia della letteratura etiopica* (Rome: Istituto per l'Oriente, 1932).

Other Semitic languages include Adari, Gafat, Argobba, Tigrai, and Arabic. Adari is the language of the city of Harar; it is written in an Arabic script. Adari is now a small island of Semitic speech in a sea of Cushitic languages, but the high development of Adari literature indicates that at one time the language held wider sway in eastern Ethiopia. Gafat and Argobba are two examples of Semitic languages distantly related to Amharic; both have been dying out in the last century. Tigrai, also known as Hasi and lowland Tigrinya, is spoken by an estimated 200,000 pastoral nomads of northern and western Eritrea. It has no significant literature; these people equate literacy with a knowledge of Arabic.

The Arabic language, the liturgical language of the Muslim population of Ethiopia, is spoken by the numerous Yemeni Arabs who have crossed the narrow Red Sea to trade and settle in Ethiopia. Most of them are to be found in Eritrea, where perhaps 25 per cent of the province's total population has some acquaintance with the language. Arabic is spoken also in Harar and Jimma, two important Muslim centers.[15]

The Cushitic language group is represented in Ethiopia by Gallinya (Galla), Somali, Sidamo, Agaw, Afar (Danakil), Beja, and several lesser languages. These languages are distantly related to ancient Egyptian and Berber. Relatively little is known about the Cushitic languages of Ethiopia, but a language survey of the country is now in progress and this new research into these languages is most welcome.

The most important Cushitic language, Gallinya, is spoken by the greatest number of speakers in Ethiopia and probably has the widest distribution of any language in the country. The language has not yet been studied in any great detail,

[15] See also W. Leslau, *An Annotated Bibliography of the Semitic Languages of Ethiopia* (The Hague: Mouton, 1965).

but it appears that it is devoid of distinctive dialects and that all Galla can understand one another. Gallinya has a rich and extensive oral literature including songs of war, chronicles, love songs, and proverbs; the Galla share with the Amhara and Tigreans a fondness for ambiguity and puns in politically oriented poetry. Occasionally Gallinya has been written in both the Amharic and the Arabic scripts, but the development of Gallinya as a written language has not been encouraged in Ethiopia.

Somali, the second most important Cushitic language in Ethiopia, also has an unusually rich oral literature. Literacy among the Muslim Somali has also meant the use of Arabic as a written language, and consequently the reduction of Somali to a written form has been slow in coming. In the adjacent Somali Republic, Somali is occasionally written in Arabic characters or, more rarely, in Latin characters. A Somali script, developed in the 1920's by a Somali scholar who sought to overcome the inadequacies of the Arabic and Latin alphabets, has not yet been widely accepted.

Another important group of Cushitic languages is the Sidamo, which has apparently influenced the development of both Guraginya and Gallinya. The Sidamo languages are divided into a great number of dialects, including Hadya, Kambatta, Tembaro, Alaba, Sidamo proper, Darasa, and Qabenna. Scholars differ as to the exact relation to Sidamo of the Ometo (dialects: Wollamo, Gofa, Basketo, Kachama, Zaysee), Janjero, Kaffa-Shinash, Ghimira, and Konso-Geleba groups of the Cushitic languages.

The original language of the western Ethiopian plateau was probably Agaw. Over the past three millenia Agaw has continually lost ground to the Semitic languages. Little is known of this language, though it is suspected that upon further investigation important connections may be discovered with the Amharic language, which it probably greatly influenced in the early stages of its development. Many of the Agaw have learned Amharic and have been absorbed by that dominant group.

Afar and Beja are spoken by nomadic Muslim peoples who, like the Somali, prefer to use Arabic as their written language.

All too little is known about the eastern Sudanic languages spoken along the western borders of Ethiopia. Baria, however, is known to be related to languages spoken along the Nile in the Sudan; indeed, ninth-century Arab chronicles place both the Baria and the Kunama, whose language has not been classified, in the neighborhood of modern Khartoum. The Berta of Ethiopia speak a single dialect, while other Berta in the Sudan speak a number of different dialects or languages. Nilotic languages are represented by the Annuak and the Didinga-Murle groups, both of which straddle the Ethiopian-Sudanese border.

The simplest map of Ethiopia is probably that of religion. A circle drawn around the western highlands would, for the most part, delimit the Christian heartland of Ethiopia. The eastern plateau, the Rift Valley and its extension into the Danakil plains, and western Eritrea are solidly Muslim. Along the southern and western borders there are large pagan populations. Yet even in Christian Ethiopia there are significant pockets of Muslims and other non-Christians; Islam has also made inroads in the southwest.

Since no official religious census has ever been taken in Ethiopia, it is impossible to tell with any degree of accuracy what proportion of the population is Muslim, Christian, or pagan. Estimates of the Christian population run from 30 to 67 per cent; 40 per cent is probably the closest approxi-

mation.[16] It is quite possible that the Muslim population
ranges from 45 to 55 per cent. Yet Ethiopia has a distinctly
Christian history, and religion has played a special role in
its past.

Ethiopian Christianity, dating back to the fourth century,
is often inaccurately called Coptic. Although the Ethiopian
Church established an early connection with the Coptic
Church in Alexandria, their relationship through the centuries has been tenuous. The two churches share a common
theology that sets them off from the Protestant, Roman Catholic, and Greek Orthodox Churches. Since the Council of
Chalcedon in 451, the Alexandrian and Ethiopian churches
have adhered to the doctrine of Monophysitism, a belief in
the single nature of Christ, as opposed to the more common
Christian belief in the dual (human and divine) nature. In
addition to this theological unity, the head of the Church
in Ethiopia and usually the only bishop, the *Abuna,* was traditionally an Egyptian monk appointed by the Patriarch of
Alexandria. This custom, which dates back to the fourth
century, was changed in 1929, when additional bishops were
appointed, and came to an end on July 13, 1948, when the
Coptic patriarchate yielded its ancient prerogatives to permit
the Ethiopian bishops to elect an Ethiopian Abuna from
among themselves. Apart from these two elements, the Ethiopian Orthodox Church, as it is officially called, developed
its own Geez liturgy and unique religious practices that
clearly distinguish it from all other forms of Christianity.

The Church once owned as much as one-third of the lands
of Ethiopia; it exerted a powerful influence on the local level
and occasionally played a decisive role in Ethiopian politics.
In general, the Church has been one of the most conservative
forces in Ethiopian society and still enjoys immense prestige

[16] Lipsky, *Ethiopia,* pp. 101–102.

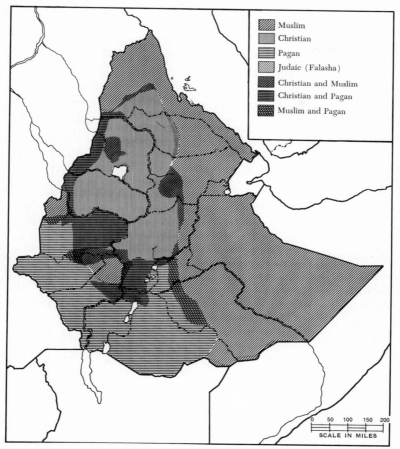

Map 4. The religions of Ethiopia

in the rural areas of the western plateau. Like so many other
areas of Ethiopian society, the Church has also experienced
a change in its relationship to the State in the past half century. Once the rallying point for national unity, the role of
Ethiopian Orthodox Christianity has greatly diminished in
modern, pluralist Ethiopia, although several attempts have
been made to revitalize the Church.

Islam in Ethiopia was never as well organized institu-
tionally as Christianity, yet in the twentieth century it has
been more of a vital force than the Ethiopian Orthodox
Church. Islam has spread among the pagans of Ethiopia, and
Muhammad's banner has been raised to unify Muslim Eritreans and Muslim Somali against a Christian-dominated
government. Christian converts to Islam are not unknown;
the Jabarti, or Muslims of northwest Ethiopia, may have
originated in this manner. It is impossible to say whether
Islam or Somali nationalism is more of a catalyst for hostility
to the regime in the Ogaden. Certainly in the past two strong
Muslim movements, that of Ahmed Grañ in the sixteenth
century and of Muhammad Abdullah Hassan in the first two
decades of the twentieth century, unified large numbers of
Muslims in a struggle against Christian Ethiopians.[17] Memories of both men are said to be vivid in the Ogaden today.

In the northwest the Falasha, a people apparently of Agaw
origin, practice an archaic form of Judaism, with many bor-
rowings from their Christian neighbors. The traditional
religions of the border peoples, where Islam has not yet in-
filtrated, have changed little, for the Ethiopian Church has
not been a vigorous proselytizer. Where pagans have been
converted to Christianity, it has been through emulation of

[17] J. S. Trimingham, *Islam in Ethiopia* (London: Oxford University
Press, 1952), pp. 76–97; R. L. Hess, "The Poor Man of God: Muhammad
Abdullah Hassan," *Leadership in Eastern Africa,* N. R. Bennett, ed.
(Boston: Boston University Press, 1968), pp. 65–108.

the dominant Amhara or through the work of foreign missionaries.

A number of Christian missionary groups have been active in Ethiopia, but they have not met with much success. In Eritrea the Roman Catholic Church has made a few tens of thousands of converts, but not many elsewhere. The government forbids any foreign groups to proselytize in Ethiopian Orthodox areas, where missionary work is limited to medical stations and schools. Among the Muslims little headway has been made, either by the Ethiopian Orthodox Church or the European and American religious groups. Among pagan elements, the Sudan Interior Mission, the United Presbyterians' Mission, two Swedish groups, an American Lutheran Mission, and a Seventh-Day Adventist Mission are active.[18]

From this brief description of the complexities of Ethiopia's demography, it is evident that modern Ethiopia, with its welter of ethnic and linguistic groups and its mixture of religions, is a polyethnic, multireligious empire very different in nature from the original state of the Amhara and Tigreans. Regional differences, accentuated by geography, are further widened by tribal, linguistic, and religious diversity, yet the dominant Amhara have tried to assimilate more than seventy ethnic groups to a modified model of Amhara culture. The process began more than two thousand years ago when the first South Arabian tribes conquered the northern part of the western plateau and began to absorb the Agaw. It was nearly reversed three hundred years ago when the Amhara confronted the vastly more numerous Galla, who,

[18] Nevertheless, modern missionary literature is very enthusiastic about prospects for proselytizing in pagan Ethiopia. See, for example, M. Forsberg, *Land Beyond the Nile* (New York: Harper, 1958) and Sudan Interior Mission, *Root from Dry Ground: The Story of the Sudan Interior Mission* (Toronto: Sudan Interior Mission, 1962).

however, in the long run proved to be assimilable. In the
twentieth century, with the aim of modernizing the State and
with the aid of foreign advisers, the process has continued as
the government expanded national schools and administrative agencies into Sidama, Galla, Somali, and "Shankalla"
regions. The task has been easier because of the lack of political unity between the various subject ethnic groups.

Despite these changes in the nature of the empire, the
Amhara and Tigrean peasantry have remained intensely
conservative, proud of their Christian ancestry and ancient
traditions, and suspicious of innovation.[19] In the countryside
little has changed, and rural Ethiopia of the late twentieth
century differs little in its social patterns and social attitudes
from the Ethiopia of five hundred years ago. Religion still
dominates the life cycle, and the peasants' life has a stability
tinted with a fatalistic view of nature and the world. For the
peasant, ownership of land is of singular importance, not
only for social status, but also as a bond with his revered
ancestors. The peasant also respects force, hierarchy, and
authority, whether of his elders, his landlord and local officials, or of his highly venerated Emperor. To rise in social
status he can hope only to acquire small parcels of land
through litigation often based on genealogical precedence or
to be rewarded for his services or his loyalty by a wealthy
landowner. Formerly, in time of war, when Ethiopian society
was more mobile, the peasant was rewarded for his military
prowess by imperial land grants. The ideal of the Amhara-
Tigre peasantry even today is that of the highly individu-
alistic warrior-farmer.[20] The conservative Ethiopians of the
countryside consider other occupations, such as merchant,

[19] D. N. Levine, *Wax and Gold: Tradition and Innovation in Ethiopian Culture* (Chicago: University of Chicago Press, 1965), pp. 55–58.
[20] Lipsky, *Ethiopia*, pp. 64–66.

artisan, or laborer, degrading, despite the fact that Amhara and Tigreans do perform these occupations today in the urban centers.

The Amhara and Tigreans have traditionally had very strong opinions about the other subjects of their empire. They despised the "Shankalla" as pagans and slaves. Perhaps slightly above these were the Agaw, who were tanners, smiths, potters, and masons, occupations suitable only for pariahs, according to the Amhara-Tigre scale of values. The Gurage, too, are despised because of their occupation as merchants or porters, and also because of their food habits. Like the Sidama peoples, whom the Amhara-Tigreans also consider inferior, the Gurage eat *Ensete edulis,* or the "false banana" plant, a food crop considered inedible by the Amhara and Tigreans, who thrive upon cereals (barley and teff, a highly nutritious grain unique to Ethiopia) and meat.

It is less easy to generalize about Amhara-Tigrean attitudes toward the Galla. Those Galla who have become Christians and have learned Amharic have been completely accepted into Amhara society. Indeed, many such Galla are highly placed in the government and the army and are well connected to the royal family and the nobility through marriage. Those Galla who are Muslim nomads have sparse contacts with the Amhara and Tigrean peasantry of the plateau. As Muslims, like the Danakil and the Somali, they do not fit directly into the traditionalist Christian's concept of Ethiopian national life.

One last set of attitudes should be mentioned. Traditionalist Amhara, Tigreans, Somali, and Galla alike are distrustful of white foreigners, at times to the point of xenophobia. A brief walk down the main street of any small town can elicit mutterings of *ferenji, ferenji* ("Frank," or "foreigner"). Only in Addis Ababa and a few other large urban centers is the

Ethiopian exposed to cosmopolitan contact with non-Ethiopians.

Among the significant communities of foreigners resident in Ethiopia are the Italian, American, Greek, Armenian, Indian, and Arab. According to the Ethiopian government, more than 60,000 foreigners were registered as alien residents of Ethiopia in 1965. These figures do not include foreigners who do not have the status of alien residents. The total number of *ferenji* is probably closer to 100,000.[21]

Longest in the country have been the Arabs, most of whom came from Yemen or elsewhere in southern Arabia. The Arabs are more widespread and probably more numerous than any other foreign group and have traveled with considerable ease about the country for generations. Yemeni Arabs are scattered throughout Christian and Muslim Ethiopia, although the greatest concentration is in Eritrea. Never popular among the Amhara and Tigreans, the Arabs have nevertheless been the chief merchants (slave traders in the nineteenth century), small traders, and importers of foreign objects into northwestern Ethiopia for centuries. No estimates of the *total* Arab population of Ethiopia are available; more than 40,000 Yemeni and Saudi Arabians, however, have resident status.

Armenians have resided in Ethiopia since at least the fifteenth century. Even though many were Monophysite Christians and had taken Ethiopian wives, Armenian merchants are looked down upon because of their occupation. The Greeks, who like the Armenians number a few thousands, probably first came to Ethiopia after persecutions

[21] Ethiopia, Ministry of Finance, *Statistical Abstract, 1965*, p. 34. According to the Ethiopian government, 62,650 foreigners were registered as residents of Ethiopia in 1965. This included 25,164 Yemeni, 16,921 Saudi Arabians, 3,819 British subjects, 2,530 Frenchmen, 2,383 Indians, 2,256 Greeks, 1,773 Americans, 1,344 Italians, and 1,229 Swedes.

by the Turks in Smyrna (Izmir) in the seventeenth century. Like the Armenians, they too are despised as middlemen retailers noted for their avarice and exploitation, but some have intermarried. Nor are the Indians, still fewer in number, particularly highly regarded, except for a small group of secondary-school teachers and military advisers. No folk memory seems to survive of the fact that the fourth-century Ethiopian court spoke Greek, as evidenced by coins and inscriptions, or that sixteenth-century emperors employed Armenians as envoys to Europe, or that seventeenth-century emperors employed Indian masons to construct the palaces at Gondar, as recorded in the imperial chronicles. Probably because of these long contacts with Arabs, Armenians, Greeks, and Indians, and possibly because of Arabic usage of the word to refer originally to the *faranj*, or Frankish Crusaders, the Ethiopians apply the term ferenji not to these foreigners, but only to Europeans (except Greeks) and Americans.

The largest European community, the Italian, once numbered more than 100,000. Today not more than 8,000 remain in Eritrea. Italian influence in Ethiopia has been strong for more than seventy-five years, but the amount of Italian heard throughout the country is declining rapidly.[22]

The Americans are for the most part connected with missionary activities, the strategic communications base at Kagnew outside Asmara, or technical aid missions, such as the Military Assistance Advisory Group, the Agency for International Development, the Agricultural College near Harar, the Peace Corps, the Haile Sellassie I University, and the Public Health Center at Gondar. The American presence has been felt only since 1948; there may be as many as 6,000 Americans in Ethiopia today.

Small numbers of Yugoslav, Czech, Russian, Swedish, Nor-

[22] A. Del Boca, *La guerra d'Abissinia, 1935–1941* (Milan: Feltrinelli, 1966), pp. 247–249.

wegian, British, German, and Israeli technical advisers also
are to be found. French influence, so apparent in the aristocracy and the court forty years ago, has begun to revive.

With the relatively large influx of foreigners since World
War II, a segment of the Ethiopian population has accus-
tomed itself to contact with the *ferenji*. Educated Ethiopians
can use the term almost jokingly with the foreigners they
come to know well.

Although the bulk of the people still live in villages and
hamlets and have little contact with foreigners, the growth
of a number of urban centers has brought an increasing number of Ethiopians into contact with the modern world. Addis
Ababa, with its population of more than 637,000, is probably
the largest city in Africa between Cairo and Johannesburg.[23]
Until recently it was nothing more than a sprawling collection of villages and scattered modern buildings, but now it
has the outlines of a planned modern city. The city was
founded in the 1880's by Menelik II. In 1910 it had a population of 100,000, which grew to about 400,000 according to
a 1960 census. By African standards, this was hardly a phe-
nomenal increase. Since 1960, however, the population has
increased more rapidly as more Ethiopians have been attracted to the new way of life offered by the city.

Elsewhere in Ethiopia, urban growth has been much
slower than in other parts of Africa. The second largest city
in the country is Asmara, the capital of the former Italian
colony of Eritrea. Once a prosperous city, it is still vaguely
suggestive of a southern Italian city, with its palmetto-lined
boulevards, sidewalk cafés, and espresso bars. Until 1965 it

[23] R. K. P. Pankhurst, "Menelik and the Foundation of Addis Ababa,"
Journal of African History, II, no. 1 (1961), pp. 103–117, and "The
Foundation and Early History of Addis Ababa," *Ethiopia Observer*,
VI, no. 1 (1962), pp. 33–61; *Statesman's Yearbook, 1968*, p. 969.

slowly declined in population and spirit, as large numbers of Italians left for Italy or for more prosperous areas of Ethiopia. Since then, rural Eritreans (especially Christians) have gravitated toward Asmara. Its population now is about 150,000.

Dire Dawa, a town of approximately 50,000 inhabitants, ranks next. Its broad streets lined with walls covered with bougainvillea behind which are handsome small villas are strongly reminiscent of the Italian-built center of Mogadishu in Somalia. Dire Dawa, the most important stop on the railway between Addis Ababa and Djibouti on the Gulf of Aden, is a town of relatively recent origin; its sidewalks of inlaid brick further attest to the European influence brought in by the railroad. The fourth largest town, Dessie, has a population of more than 40,000 and is growing in importance because it is an administrative center situated near the junc-. tion of the main highways to Addis Ababa from the port of Assab and from Asmara and the north. It has already surpassed Harar's population of about 38,000. Other towns of significant size are Gondar (30,000), Jimma (30,000), Makalle (23,000), Debra Zeit (22,000), and Debra Markos (21,000). It is doubtful that there are more than ten other towns in Ethiopia with a permanent population greater than 12,000.[24]

Thus, the overwhelming majority of the population is still rural and widely scattered over the rugged terrain. That population is as varied as the Ethiopian landscape, for the peoples of Ethiopia are far from homogeneous. A modern nation is yet to be hammered out of Ethiopia's diverse religious, linguistic, and ethnic multitudes.

[24] R. K. P. Pankhurst, "Notes on the Demographic History of Ethiopian Towns and Villages," *Ethiopia Observer*, IX, no. 1 (1965), pp. 60–83; *Statistical Abstract, 1965*, pp. 25–30; *Statesman's Yearbook, 1968*, p. 969.

CHAPTER 2

Two Thousand Years
of History

Ethiopia's long and varied history has left its mark on current developments in the eastern Horn of Africa. Few states can boast a history that goes back more than two thousand years. Centuries of relative isolation and encirclement by the Muslim world have given Ethiopia distinct characteristics, including a dynasty that traces its origins to the Old Testament's account of the visit of the Queen of Sheba to Solomon's court in Jerusalem. After the rise of Islam, Ethiopia lost touch with the Mediterranean and Near Eastern worlds from which it derived much of its early civilization. In the following centuries Ethiopian kings constructed an empire that has slowly evolved into its present form.

Ethiopians are proud that some sixteen hundred years ago there thrived on the highlands of northern Ethiopia a kingdom, centered in Axum, that had trading connections with the interior, possibly as far as the modern Sudan, with the Red Sea and the kingdoms of southern Arabia, and with Greek-speaking merchants who ranged far from their Mediterranean homelands.

The South Arabian connection of Axum was strongly expressed in language, architecture, and religion. The best-known examples of Axumite architecture, the carved steles of Axum, attest to the high development of early Ethiopia. These monumental columns were carved with representations of doors and windows and crowned with the crescent-sun symbol of the pagan religion apparently common to both South Arabia and Axum (see Plate 1).

Not only did the South Arabian religion cross the Red Sea to Axum, but there is some indirect evidence that Judaism and Christianity both may have entered Ethiopia at an early date. Like the South Arabian sun-moon cult, Ethiopian Judaism must have come from Yemen, where Judaism at one time flourished among South Arabian tribes. In all probability one Agaw group, the Falasha, was converted to this form of Judaism some two thousand years ago.[1] Similarly, there are grounds to believe that Christianity may have arrived earlier than the fourth century, as Ethiopian tradition claims.

After adoption of Christianity as the religion of the Axumite court approximately at the time of Constantine's reign, Ethiopia was far from isolated from the rest of the Christian world. Not only did Axum have dealings with the Coptic Church of Alexandria, but one Ethiopian king concluded an agreement with the Byzantine Emperor Justin I in the third decade of the sixth century providing for cooperation in war against the persecutors of Christians in southern Arabia. To judge from Greek, Syrian, South Arabian, and later Arabic records, the Axumites won a great victory and extended their kingdom to the other side of the Red Sea, the area from which their ancestors had come a thousand years earlier. Later, Justinian the Great proposed an Axumite-Byzantine alliance against the Persians for the purpose of expanding the silk trade with India, but nothing seems to have come of this proposal.[2] Persian intervention eventually

---

[1] R. L. Hess, "Toward a History of the Falasha," *Eastern African History*, D. F. McCall, N. R. Bennett, and J. Butler, eds. (New York: Frederick A. Praeger, 1969), p. 111.

[2] A. A. Vasiliev, *Histoire de l'Empire Byzantin* (Paris: A. Picard, 1932), I, 183.

destroyed Axumite power in southern Arabia and may also have contributed to the decline in Axumite power on the Red Sea.

The rise of Islam had a tremendous influence on the course of Ethiopian history, and the threat of Muslim encirclement dominates much of Ethiopian history. The Muslims gained control of the Red Sea in the late seventh century and initiated the long period of Ethiopia's isolation from the rest of the civilized Middle East. In the early years of Islam, Ethiopia occupied a special position in recognition of the asylum that Axumite kings had given to some of Muhammad's exiled followers.[3] Ethiopia was spared the *jihad* (Islamic holy war) for several hundred years; not until the tenth century did Muslim-Christian rivalry assume fierce proportions. But with trade disrupted first by pirates and later by readjustments in trade routes, Axum slowly declined, and the outside world heard little of Ethiopia for the next five centuries.

Paradoxically, although Axum was declining in commercial prosperity, the kingdom was at the same time expanding, just as the Roman Empire did in its last centuries. The Axumites spread southward and conquered the northern half of the plateau in the eighth century. Thus, as Ethiopia turned away from the outside world, the center of gravity of the Christian kingdom in Ethiopia shifted southward across the Takazze River in the conquest of non-Semitic and non-Christian peoples that continued until the end of the nineteenth century.

The expanding Axumite kingdom, now more interested in conquest than trade, gradually experienced an inner transformation. The conquerors imposed their Semitic language

[3] J. S. Trimingham, *Islam in Ethiopia* (London: Oxford University Press, 1952), pp. 44–46.

and Christian religion on the conquered Agaw. The new people were not readily assimilated into the old culture, which instead absorbed elements of Agaw culture. In one respect or another the dominant culture of Ethiopia has been absorbing elements of the culture of its subject peoples ever since.

Southward expansion involved a new threat to Axum from the conquered peoples who maintained their older traditions. Failure to pacify the Agaw led to the fall of Axum; the dynamics of expansionism proved to be more of a threat than the drying-up of the Red Sea trade. The first sign of trouble came from the Judaized Agaw, the Falasha, who in the tenth century undertook a campaign of destruction, burning churches everywhere and finally devastating the city of Axum itself. Despite their destruction of the power of Axum, the Falasha were unable to replace their predecessors with a permanent state, and their power soon evaporated. The Axumites were not able to regain their former power, and a Christianized Agaw dynasty, the Zagwe, restored peace and order and for three centuries ruled over the area once controlled by the Axumite kingdom.[4]

With the Zagwe era the center of political gravity shifted to Lasta, and a new capital was established at Roha, some 160 miles south of old Axum. Claimants to the throne of Axum regarded the Zagwe as usurpers and managed to maintain their independence in Shoa, some one hundred miles farther south.

The Zagwe were not able to gain control of the coastal areas, and, like Axum in its late period and modern Ethiopia before 1951, their kingdom was landlocked. They also found political rivals in a series of Muslim states to the east of the

---

[4] Jean Doresse, *L'empire du Prêtre-Jean* (Paris: Plon, 1957), II, 181.

high plateau, where a resurgent Islam had made rapid progress since the tenth century. Muslim principalities like Adal,
Ifat, and Dawaro prospered in the lower country east of Shoa
and Lasta as well as in the eastern plateau on the other side
of the Rift Valley. Beyond Shoa in the south some of the
Sidamo peoples also converted to Islam. From the tenth century to the present, the Amhara and Tigreans have regarded
their Ethiopia as an island of Christianity in a sea of turbu-
lent Islam.

Though ringed by enemies, the Zagwe nevertheless experienced a certain degree of prosperity as evidenced by the
remarkable architecture of their capital, where a group of
twelve monolithic churches and chapels were hewn out of
the living rock. The Christian kings of Lasta preserved the
ancient Ethiopic language and the religion of the Axumites,
as well as a connection with the Coptic Church in Egypt. All
this indicates that in many respects the Zagwe period was not
a break in Ethiopian history but a bridge between the Axumites and the Solomonic monarchs who followed. Additional
support of this contention may be inferred from the fact that
the Zagwe "usurper," Lalibela (*ca.* 1200), is regarded as a
saint by the Ethiopian Orthodox Church, and that Roha, his
capital, has ever since been known as the town of Lalibela.[5]

Like the Axumites, the Zagwe were unable to consolidate
their holdings into one truly unified kingdom, the accomplishment of which had to wait until the nineteenth and
twentieth centuries. Not only was there the constant challenge of those who claimed to be the legitimate descendants
of the last of the Axumite rulers, as well as the potential
threat of the Muslims to the east, but certain elements of

[5] E. A. Wallis Budge, *A History of Ethiopia* (London: Methuen,
1928), pp. 279–283.

paganism survived among the Agaw, cultural distinctions remained, and linguistic differences continued. No doubt in order to give an aura of legitimacy to their rule and to provide some sort of rallying point for unity, the Zagwe rulers put forth the claim that they were descended from Israelite nobility.

Several possible explanations for this claim may be given. The Falasha uprising, with its Judaic elements, may have impressed later Zagwe kings, who surely were aware of the Jewish origins of Christianity. What better way to legitimize their position than to be both Christian and the heirs of the political leaders of the older dispensation? Or the possibility that some of the early Zagwe kings were Jewish (Falasha) may have suggested a genealogical continuity from a Judaic, hence Israelite, source. Alternatively, the Zagwe may have cultivated this tradition of descent as a response to the challenge of the Amhara rulers of Shoa, who traced their origins not only to the old Axumite dynasty but also to the Solomonic dynasty of ancient Israel. The last hypothesis is strengthened by evidence that the Zagwe voluntarily yielded their place to the Solomonic dynasty, for the Zagwe dynasty ended with Lalibela's grandson in 1270.

Myth has always played a large part in the construction of a national political history, and Ethiopia is no exception. To understand political realities in Ethiopia it is first necessary to discuss the story of the Queen of Sheba and what is officially described in Ethiopia today as the Solomonic Restoration.

Since the late thirteenth century the history of Ethiopia has in many respects been the history of the Shoan dynasty, which replaced the Zagwe and through which the present Emperor traces his descent. It has not ruled uninterruptedly, nor has it had a sure line of succession, but by and large the main outlines of the last 700 years of Ethiopian history have corresponded with the fortunes of the dynasty.

Most Europeans and Americans are probably acquainted with the story of the visit of the Queen of Sheba to the court of Solomon as sketchily set down in the Old Testament. It is less well known that the Queen of the South has been the subject of an extensive literature. She figures also in the Koran and in Arabic folklore, in Jewish legend, and in Ethiopian tradition, particularly in the *Kebra Negast* (Glory of Kings), one of the most important literary works in the ancient Ethiopic language.[6] Ethiopians believe that Sheba, or Saba, was located on their side of the Red Sea within the boundaries of old Axum. To bolster their claim they point to the archaeological excavation at Sabea, near the ancient home of one group of Axum's immigrants from South Arabia. There is not enough conclusive evidence to allow positive identification of any one place as Sheba, but this is largely irrelevant for an appreciation of the importance of the story for Ethiopian traditions.

According to these traditions, a suitable time after her departure from Jerusalem, Makeda, the Queen of Sheba, gave birth to Solomon's son, whom she named Menelik. When the boy matured, his mother sent him to Judaea to visit his father, who attempted to persuade Menelik, his firstborn, to remain in Jerusalem as heir apparent. Menelik's first loyalty, however, was to his mother and to their Ethiopian homeland. Unable to deter Menelik, Solomon gave him permission to leave. On the eve of his son's departure Solomon dreamed that the glory of Israel departed to another land. As his father slept, Menelik was preparing to return

[6] E. S. Pankhurst and R. K. P. Pankhurst, "Special Issue on the Queen of Sheba," *Ethiopia Observer*, I, no. 6 (1957), pp. 178–204.

to Ethiopia in the company of a large number of Israelites, the firstborn of the priests and nobility, whom Solomon had ordered to accompany his eldest son. Before their departure, however, the son of the high priest absconded with the Ark of the Covenant. Upon his return to his mother's homeland, Menelik became king and the eldest sons of Israel became his councillors and officers.

The importance of this legend for an understanding of Ethiopian history cannot be overestimated. Here we see a host of claims. With Menelik's return Judaism came to Ethiopia; hence the Ethiopians were not pagans before the advent of Christianity. The Ethiopian nobility was descended from the Israelite aristocracy; on this the Zagwe based their claim of legitimacy. The Ark of the Covenant came to Ethiopia with Menelik; hence the Ethiopians are God's chosen people, replacing the sinful Israelites. Lastly, the Ethiopian dynasty to the time of the Zagwe usurpation was descended from Menelik and Solomon, a claim that could not be matched in Christian Ethiopia by any rivals for the throne. By extension and emendation, the House of Menelik was of the root of Jesse. In other words, genealogically Menelik's descendants were distant cousins of Jesus; all were members of the House of David, a significant factor in the sanctification of kingship in a Christian country surrounded by Muslim rulers who claimed descent from Muhammad.

The chronicles of Ethiopia allege that the Zagwe dynasty freely relinquished the throne to Yekuno Amlak, a descendant of the last of the Axumite kings and of the House of Menelik, through the mediation of the Church. That the Zagwe should voluntarily yield the throne is not easily understood. One possible explanation is that by 1270 the Solomonic genealogy was generally accepted as valid; it is quite possible that the Shoan dynasty successfully used the Menelik story as an ideological weapon. Moreover, there is no conclusive evidence of the existence of the legend before the thirteenth century. A second explanation may lie in the inability of the Zagwe rulers after Lalibela to cope with the encroachments of the Muslim states to the east; there is some evidence that formerly Christian lands had been conquered by these Muslims. Lastly, the role it played suggests that for reasons of its own the Church threw its power behind the Solomonic pretenders. Each of these explanations may be partially valid.

Tradition recounts that a treaty between the Zagwe and the Solomonids granted the Zagwe hereditary rule over Wag, north of Lasta—no doubt a secure patrimony in contrast to the endangered empire they had ruled. By this same treaty the Church was allotted one-third of the kingdom for its support.[7] Here there are suggestions of an alliance between the Church, which obtained a degree of independence and wealth comparable to that of the Church in feudal Europe, and the Emperor, who gained the throne and effectively saw to it that the Church could not become a tool of factions within Ethiopia. The eighteenth-century Scottish traveler James Bruce reported that this arrangement continued in his time.[8]

In the course of the fourteenth century two elements of modern Ethiopia emerged and became clearly discernible: ethnic diversity and Christian-Muslim coexistence within the empire. At first the Solomonic kings struck back against their Muslim neighbors, especially to the northeast of Shoa. As

[7] Budge, *History of Ethiopia*, p. 216.

[8] James Bruce, *Travels To Discover the Source of the Nile in the Years 1768, 1769, 1770, 1771, 1772, and 1773* (Edinburgh: James Ballantyne, 1804), II, 458–459.

they reconquered the once-Christian lands of the escarpment and subdued their enemies, the emperors assigned the new provinces to Muslim governors. At the height of their success against Ifat, Dawaro, and Fatijar, the Christian monarchs of Ethiopia imposed their overlordship on these Muslim states. By 1415 only the Muslim state of Adal remained a potential threat.[9]

Through military conquest the empire once again changed its nature. No longer was Ethiopia a Christian kingdom with pagan or Judaic Agaw minorities, but now large Muslim populations to the east owed their allegiance to the Ethiopian monarchs, and Muslim governors administered both Christian and Muslim lands of the escarpment. In their relations with both the reconquered lands and the defeated sovereign Muslim states, the Ethiopians evolved a semifeudal political system with Christian overlords and Muslim and Christian vassals.

By the late fifteenth century Ethiopia reached a new peak in its development. Strong emperors like Zara Yaqob (1434–1468) gave Ethiopia the leadership necessary to organize military action against a strong enemy. The empire continued to expand southward and eastward at the expense of pagan and Muslim peoples.[10]

The capital, located at one town or another in Shoa, was the scene of court intrigues. Rivalries within the royal family and between the military nobility and the royal family became the rule rather than the exception. The chronicles indicate that early in the reign of Zara Yaqob there was a genuine resurgence of paganism to the northwest of Shoa.

---

[9] Trimingham, *Islam in Ethiopia,* pp. 69–76.

[10] J. Perruchon, *Les chroniques de Zara Ya'eqob et de Ba'eda Maryam, Rois d'Ethiopie de 1434 à 1478* (Paris: Bouillon, 1893).

The nobility then spread the rumor that the royal princes were dabbling in paganism, whereupon Zara Yaqob put most of his sons to death and delegated his daughters to govern the provinces. The intermingling of religion and politics also became manifest when a group of governors in the northwest rebelled against the Emperor, allegedly converted to Judaism, and briefly posed the threat of a Falasha revival. Yet despite the rivalry of the nobility and the threats posed by paganism, the Falasha, and the Muslims, the emperors enjoyed an immense prestige.[11]

The strength of the royal ruler consisted of several elements. The Solomonic dynasty was firmly entrenched as the only legitimate dynasty; the monarchs styled themselves Kings of Israel. The bulk of the army, moreover, was loyal to the death; military rank and noble privilege were identical, and both came from the emperor. Thirdly, the Church fully supported the Emperor, and Christianity had become a rallying point in an empire beleaguered by Muslims. In short, the monarch had the blessing of God and his person was regarded as sacred. His coronation at Axum was a religious ceremony befitting an Old Testament monarch. For the most part the Emperor did not appear in public unless veiled from the gaze of commoners, a practice that the Ethiopians may have borrowed from the Cushitic peoples whom they conquered. The Emperor was the main patron of the Church and in every sense the defender of the faith. Thus he assigned all the revenues of Shoa to the famous monastery of Debra Libanos.

It was Emperor Zara Yaqob, not the Church, who moved to wipe out paganism. By imperial order all Ethiopians were compelled to take an oath and to wear amulets readily iden-

---

[11] Hess, "Toward a History of the Falasha," pp. 113–115.

tifying them as Christians. The Emperor also decided purely religious issues and dealt ruthlessly with all opposition. Several religious tracts issued from his pen, and he attempted to reform the faith and purge it of extraneous elements.[12] By order of Zara Yaqob, the Nativity and other feasts were celebrated monthly, a feature unique to the Ethiopian Orthodox Church; both Saturday as the Sabbath and Sunday as the Lord's Day were strictly observed. Religious loyalty and political loyalty became identical for most of his subjects.

The chronicles indicate that much attention was paid to the complex organization of the empire. It was not completely safe to entrust the rule of outlying provinces to members of the royal family, who might use the office as a means to overthrow the monarch. Hence, surviving members of the royal family were confined to remote mountain areas, and the court too lived in isolation. The empire itself was composed of both kingdoms whose rulers, though appointed by the emperor, tended to come from the same families, and administered provinces or conquered territories. The most important of the kingdoms, whose rulers were often related to the emperor, were Gojjam, Tigre, Amhara, and, of course, Shoa. Generally, the emperor was also king of Shoa. The conquered territories, Ifat, Fatijar, Dawaro, and others, were either former Muslim states, occasionally governed by the hereditary Muslim ruler, or reconquered areas, like the Bahr Nagash (Eritrea) along the Red Sea. Until fairly recent times many of these areas continued to play an important part as recognizable political entities with strong regional interests.

Although isolated from major contacts with the Christian world by geography and political circumstances, Ethiopia did

[12] *Il Libro della Luce del Negus Zar'a Ya'qob (Mashafa Berhan)*, C. Conti Rossini, trans. (Louvain: Corpus Scriptorum Christianorum Orientalium, 1965).

have some infrequent contacts beyond the Muslim world. Certainly Christian pilgrims and Crusaders alike must have been aware of the presence of the exotic Ethiopians in Jerusalem after 1187.[13] There is inconclusive evidence that European monks and traders visited Ethiopia as early as the mid-thirteenth century, but scholars dispute whether or not the missionaries saw Ethiopia proper, inasmuch as medieval Europeans indiscriminately labeled most of sub-Saharan Africa and southern Asia "Ethiopia." In the reign of Zara Yaqob at least one European missionary did reach Ethiopia, for the chronicles describe a theological debate between Ethiopian monks and a European.

By the end of the fifteenth century more than a dozen Europeans, for the most part Italian traders, had reached Ethiopia, only to find that the emperors, who welcomed the technological skills of the foreigners, refused to permit them to leave the realm. Thus, while Ethiopia came to know of Europe, Europeans learned little about Ethiopia before the beginning of the sixteenth century. In the meantime, legend once more played an important part, and the romantic element of Ethiopian history reappears: to the story of the Queen of Sheba was joined the fable of Prester John.

Sometime in the twelfth century western Europe received word of a great defeat suffered by the Muslims at the hands of an unknown ruler to the east of the Muslim world. There was much speculation, and the belief spread that the potential allies of the Crusaders were the descendants of eastern Christians, perhaps Indians converted by the Apostle Thomas or Nestorians. Then, about 1165, the Byzantine Emperor received a letter from a mysterious Christian king who described himself as ruler over seventy-two kingdoms

[13] E. Cerulli, *Etiopi in Palestina: storia della comunità etiopica di Gerusalemme* (Rome: La Libreria dello Stato, 1943), I, 8–9.

stretching from Ethiopia to India. The letter, it is obvious, was a forgery. Nevertheless, the story spread of the eastern Christian ruler who was also a priest (*presbyter,* or *prester*). European tongues twisted the story sufficiently so that by the early fifteenth century the legend of Prester John was fully developed.

The story might have died out if at the same time Europeans had not begun to receive faint word of the existence of Christian Ethiopia. The Crusaders were the first to send the report home of their encounters with Ethiopian monks, priests, and pilgrims in the Holy Land. After the arrival in Rome and Avignon of an Ethiopian embassy from Jerusalem in 1306, European cartographers began to locate Ethiopia more precisely. That the Ethiopians were also combating the Muslims excited the Europeans' imaginations, which were further stimulated in 1428 when Yeshaq I proposed a marriage alliance to Alfonso of Aragon.[14] Considering the strain in Ethiopian-Muslim relations by the end of the fifteenth century, we must realize that it was greatly to Ethiopia's advantage that the Europeans believed the African kingdom to have been the land of Prester John. For the first time since the seventh century, Ethiopia would again have close relations with another Christian state.

After the death of Henry the Navigator, Portuguese interest in the route to the Indies and in the war with the Muslims merged with the Prester John story. Accordingly, in 1487, João II conceived the idea of a two-pronged expedition to the court of Prester John. From Portugal Bartholomeo Diaz sailed southward to round Africa. Less known is the other half of the king's plan: Pero da Covilhão was instructed

---

[14] Doresse, *L'empire du Prêtre-Jean,* II, 235–236; Leo Hansberry, "Ethiopian Ambassadors to Latin Courts and Latin Emissaries to Prester John," *Ethiopia Observer,* IX, no. 2 (1965), p. 90.

to reach Ethiopia via Egypt and the Red Sea. But the Portuguese never learned the outcome of da Covilhão's mission.
After landing at Zeila, he reached the court of the Emperor,
and like other Europeans then resident in Ethiopia, he was
compelled to remain in the country.[15]

Meanwhile, Ethiopia's position became increasingly peril-
ous as the Ottoman Turks extended their power down the
Red Sea and took nominal possession of the coastal regions.
Although the Ethiopians had no quarrel with the Ottomans,
the Turkish presence was ominous for several reasons. Turkish military success had considerably raised Muslim morale,
and the Muslim state of Adal prepared for a new round of
warfare with Christian Ethiopia. Arabic sources also indicate
that there was a religious revival within Muslim Adal; the
fervor of Somali converts added to the probability of renewed
conflict.[16] Moreover, in the Turks the Muslims of Adal found
a valuable ally who could turn the balance in their favor
through the introduction of firearms. These new weapons
greatly reduced the effectiveness of the Ethiopian spear and
bow.

To offset the Adal-Turkish entente, the dowager Empress
Eleni, who served as regent until Lebna Dengel came of
age, contacted the Portuguese in 1509 and asked for an alliance against the common enemy. The Portuguese were
now more concerned with the riches of the Indies, and when
the Empress' envoy finally was able to return to Ethiopia in
1520, he was accompanied by an ineffectual Portuguese diplomatic mission. They too joined the ranks of the permanent
European community of Ethiopia.

[15] E. Sanceau, *The Land of Prester John, a Chronicle of Portuguese
Exploration* (New York: Alfred A. Knopf, 1944), pp. 13–19.

[16] The major Arabic source for this period is Chihab ed-Din Ahmed
ben Abd el-Qader (Arab-Faqih), *Histoire de la conquête de l'Abyssinie,*
René Basset, trans. (6 vols., Paris: Ernest Leroux, 1897–1901).

In the meantime the Muslim enemies of Ethiopia, encouraged by the Turkish occupation of Arabia, launched an attack on the Christian kingdom. Lebna Dengel held off the Muslims, and a truce was put into effect. But in 1527, a year after the Emperor agreed to the departure of the Portuguese, the Muslims of Adal, under the dynamic leadership of Ahmed Grañ, decided on all-out warfare.[17] A jihad was proclaimed for the purpose of conquering all Ethiopia. Ahmed Grañ's campaigns inexorably penetrated westward. Lebna Dengel's forces were no match for Turkish cannons and muskets. By 1531 the Muslims occupied Dawaro and Shoa; two years later the historic kingdoms of Amhara and Lasta fell. In 1535, Tigre was vanquished, and Lebna Dengel and those chiefs who had not deserted to the Muslims sought refuge in the mountainous northwest. Totally defeated, Lebna Dengel died in 1540. The chronicles claim that nine-tenths of the population were converted to Islam.[18] Surely this was the blackest hour in Ethiopian history.

Had it not been for the Portuguese, Christian Ethiopia might have disappeared from the map. In desperation Lebna Dengel had instructed one of the Portuguese who had arrived in 1520 to seek Portuguese aid before it was too late. This time the Portuguese acted decisively, and in 1541, fourteen years after the Muslims had begun their jihad, four hundred Portuguese soldiers, armed with muskets, landed at Massawa.[19] They fought their way into the interior to the camp

[17] Trimingham, *Islam in Ethiopia,* pp. 76–97.

[18] *Chronique de Galawdewos (Claudius), Roi d'Ethiopie,* W. E. Conzelman, trans. (Paris: Bouillon, 1895), p. 123.

[19] The Portuguese intervention is dramatically described by a contemporary, Miguel de Castanhoso, in *Dos feitos de D. Christovam Da Gama em Ethiopia* (Lisbon: Imprensa Nacional, 1898), translated by R. S. Whiteway as *The Portuguese Expedition to Abyssinia in 1541–1543* (London: Hakluyt Society, 1902).

of the harassed new Emperor Galawdewos (Claudius), whose few hundred followers welcomed the Portuguese intervention. Soon Tigre and the Bahr Nagash rallied to his cause, and after heavy losses the allied unexpectedly killed Ahmed Grañ in battle early in 1543. With the death of their leader the Muslims retreated eastward, and Galawdewos temporarily reoccupied much of his father's kingdom.

The Ethiopians were gravely weakened by the long years of warfare, however, and had the Muslims been united enough to mount and sustain a new offensive, a disastrous defeat would have ensued. The Somali allies of Adal had abandoned the cause, and a shattered Ethiopia was safe from another attack for the moment. But weak Ethiopia could not prevent the Turks from occupying Massawa and much of the coastal plain. Ethiopia was preserved, but the Turkish presence ensured Ethiopian isolation after this brief period of contact with the outside world.

From time to time other Europeans entered Ethiopia, but for religious rather than political motives. In 1557, and again in 1603, groups of Jesuits entered the country.[20] Pero Pais, one of the leaders of the second Jesuit group, succeeded in converting Lebna Dengel's great-grandson, the Emperor Susenyos (1607–1632), to Roman Catholicism.[21] Pais' successor, Alfonso Mendes, decided to press forward and forcibly Romanize Ethiopian Christianity. Persecution of Monophysite believers became the order of the day at a time when Ethiopia could ill afford the luxury of religious dissension.

[20] The main European source for this period is Manoel de Almeida, *The History of Ethiopia or Abassia,* found in *Some Records of Ethiopia, 1593–1646,* C. F. Beckingham and G. W. B. Huntingford, trans. (London: Hakluyt Society, 1954).

[21] Pero Pais, *História da Etiópia* (3 vols., Oporto: Livraria Civilização, 1945–1946).

Susenyos, who had seized the throne, saw diminishing prospects of political unity. His immediate predecessor had been deposed as a result of the religious issue, and Susenyos could not risk a revolt from rivals for the throne who might use the cause of the Ethiopian Orthodox Church for their own purposes. What he feared occurred, and the empire was rent by politico-religious revolts. Finally Susenyos admitted defeat, restored the old faith, and abdicated in favor of his son Fasilidas. The Jesuits were expelled from Ethiopia in 1632, and the good will toward the Europeans who had saved Ethiopia from the Muslims was completely dissipated after a century of contact with later Europeans.

Ethiopia and Adal had fought to a stalemate, and both sides were weak from the long years of fighting. Unexpectedly, a major threat to Christian and Muslim alike appeared in the mid-sixteenth century. From the south Ethiopia and Adal were faced with a common invader: Galla tribesmen, who rushed into an Ethiopia debilitated by two decades of warfare.[22] Within twenty years they had devastated Harar and posed a greater threat to the Muslims than the Christians had ever done. The Cushitic nomads wrested from the Ethiopians control of the fertile provinces along their eastern borders. Soon the Christians in turn found that the pagan Galla were a more persistent problem than the Muslims had ever been.

The Galla swept through the area, occupying much of southern and eastern Shoa, the heartland of Solomonic

[22] E. Cerulli, "Documenti arabi per la storia dell'Etiopia," *Rendiconti della Reale Accademia dei Lincei,* ser. vi, IV (1931), p. 57; *Chrónica de Susenyos,* F.-M. Esteves Pereira, trans. (Lisbon, 1900), p. 60; *Historia Gentis Galla,* I. Guidi, trans. (Louvain: Corpus Scriptorum Christianorum Orientalium, 1961).

Ethiopia, as well as areas to the north and west. The Galla chiefs helped to place Susenyos on the throne, and in the religious civil wars of the seventeenth century hostile Galla took the opportunity to seize more land. By the end of the century they occupied more than a third of the empire. The Galla gradually settled down to an agricultural existence wherever they could (the Borana and the Arussi in the south and southeast remained pastoralists) and added to the ethnic diversity of Ethiopia, which would never again contain a majority of Amhara-Tigreans. The task of assimilating the Galla has continued to the present. If the Galla had not been so divided among themselves, the history of Ethiopia might have become the history of a Galla kingdom.

In the internecine warfare that divided Ethiopia in the early seventeenth century, the power of the monarchy declined. Portuguese interference in Ethiopian affairs had encouraged other members of the royal family to make their bid for the throne, and peaceful succession depended on royal strength. The Galla, in constant contact with the Amhara, played their part in Ethiopian politics. Susenyos married a Galla princess, and the blood of the Solomonic line mingled with that of the newcomers. The reign of his son Fasilidas (1632–1667) marked the last period of glory for Ethiopia until the late nineteenth century.

Under Fasilidas a brief revival took place (see Plate 14). Since Shoa was greatly subject to Galla influence, the Emperor established his capital to the north of Lake Tana at Gondar. Not since the Solomonic restoration had there been a permanent capital, yet Gondar remained the capital for more than a century. To repair the damage to churches caused by the civil wars and to emphasize the importance of his capital, the new Emperor imported all sorts of craftsmen, some from as far away as Egypt and India, and Gondar became a town dominated by a group of fortress-like castles, monuments to this Ethiopian renaissance (see Plates 3 and 8). Axum was rebuilt, while Gondar became the seat of an Amharic revival; poetry, music, architecture, painting, and literature all thrived at the court of Fasilidas.[23]

After the death of Fasilidas, however, the position of the monarch was slowly undermined in a process that led to the end of an effective central government. The door to change had been opened through marriage with the Galla, whose influence increased at the capital. Gradually, too, the power of the Amhara and Galla nobles grew at the expense of the monarch. As the star of the Galla nobility rose, the old Amhara nobility became increasingly restless. By 1753 the empire was on the verge of disintegration. Galla princesses and advisers tried to outmaneuver Amhara nobles for influence at court, and within ten years Gallinya rather than Amharic was the main language at court. Within another ten years the empire was on the brink of civil war not only between the party of the Galla nobles, who had made a puppet of the Emperor, and the party of the Amhara nobles, who wished their own puppet on the throne, but also among the various nobles of the kingdoms of Amhara and Tigre who aspired to the throne themselves.[24]

From 1769 to 1855, central power almost completely disappeared. At the nadir of imperial fortunes, five men claimed the throne. As in the Holy Roman Empire, power devolved

[23] D. N. Levine, *Wax and Gold: Tradition and Innovation in Ethiopian Culture* (Chicago: University of Chicago Press, 1965), pp. 21–28. The main Ethiopian sources for the period are *Annales Iohannis I, Iyasu I, Bakaffa*, I. Guidi, trans. (2 vols., Louvain: Corpus Scriptorum Christianorum Orientalium, 1954–1962).

[24] Bruce was an eyewitness to the disintegration of the empire (*Travels To Discover the Source of the Nile*, VI, 54–182).

to the nobles and regional rulers. The central government disintegrated, and Ethiopia divided into a number of small kingdoms as old local ruling families asserted themselves and appointed governors converted their offices into hereditary positions.[25] From the late eighteenth century until the mid-nineteenth century the Ethiopian Empire ceased to exist. It is more accurate to speak of the various kingdoms *in* Ethiopia, for Ethiopia had become a mere geographical expression.

[25] In this time of troubles, which lasted for eighty-six years, seventeen different men held the office of emperor during twenty-six reigns. One emperor, Tekla Giorgis, was restored to the throne on at least five occasions. The Ethiopians call this period *Zamana Masafint,* "the Era of the Judges." See *The Royal Chronicle of Abyssinia, 1769–1840,* H. Weld Blundell, trans. (Cambridge: Cambridge University Press, 1922) and Mordechai Abir, *Ethiopia: The Era of the Princes* (New York: Frederick A. Praeger, 1968).

CHAPTER 3

Reconstitution
of the Empire

Since 1855, Ethiopia has had four strong innovating emperors—Theodore II, Yohannes IV, Menelik II, and Haile Selassie I—each of whom has striven to create a national unity that would override earlier religious, ethnic, and regional differences. Theodore and Yohannes did not meet with great success, but they set the pattern for the more successful attempts by Menelik and Haile Selassie.

With the dissolution of law and order in the early nineteenth century, bandit groups, or *shifta,* appeared in the central highlands of the western plateau. So strong did one of the shifta leaders become that in 1855 he successfully claimed the throne as Theodore II. The new Emperor won his position after defeating the local rulers of Gojjam and Begemder, but he still had to contend with Shoa and Tigre. Military victories eliminated Shoa as an enemy, and Menelik, the young King of Shoa, was taken to Theodore's capital as a prisoner. To legitimize his position Theodore won the Church to his side and fabricated a genealogy depicting himself as a descendant of the Solomonic dynasty.[1]

[1] Ethiopian interest in Theodore has revived in recent years, and that emperor has been the subject of an historical novel by Girmachew Tekla Hawaryat, *Tewodros, Tarikawi Drama* (Addis Ababa, 1956) and of a play by Tsegaye Gabre Medhin, *Tewodros,* published in *Ethiopia Observer,* IX, no. 3 (1965). The only biography of Theodore is S. Rubenson, *King of Kings Tewodros of Ethiopia* (Addis Ababa: Haile Sellassie I University, 1966), based in part on two Ethiopian chronicles: Zaneb,

Unlike his predecessors, Theodore sought to endow his empire with permanent administrative institutions. To do this he hoped to replace local rulers with paid governors loyal to himself and not to regional interests and connections. It was an admirable plan for administrative reform, but the deeply entrenched Amhara and Tigrean aristocracy prevented him from implementing it. Modernization of the administrative apparatus had to wait until the time of Menelik and Haile Selassie.

Unable to depend on administrative reform, Theodore relied on military strength to consolidate his empire. Thus Theodore at first welcomed the advent of foreigners with useful technological skills. Soon his capital at Magdala contained a large number of Europeans, including missionaries, who were pressed into the manufacture of armaments. Some of these Europeans became his trusted advisers. Theodore also hoped to import weapons from Europe and departed from Ethiopia's centuries-old diplomatic isolation by proposing a treaty of commerce and friendship with Great Britain. But a series of errors on both sides soon led to a diplomatic embroilment, and a British punitive expedition was dispatched in 1867 to rescue those Europeans forcibly detained in Theodore's capital.[2]

Ya-Tewodros Tarik, translated by Enno Littmann as *The Chronicle of King Theodore* (Princeton: Princeton University Press, 1902) and by M. M. Moreno as "La cronaca di re Teodoro attribuita al dabtara Zaneb," *Rassegna di studi etiopici,* II (1942), pp. 143–180; and Wolde Maryam, *Tarik za-Tewodros,* translated by C. Mondon-Vidailhet as *Chronique de Théodoros, Roi des Rois d'Ethiopie (1853–1868)* (2 vols., Paris: Librairie Orientale et Americaine, 1904).

[2] J. R. Hooker, "The Foreign Office and the 'Abyssinian Captives,'" *Journal of African History,* II (1961), pp. 245–258. The official history of the British expedition is C. R. Markham, *A History of the Abyssinian Expedition* (2 vols., London: Macmillan, 1869).

The crisis with Great Britain proved to be Theodore's undoing, for a large number of disaffected Ethiopians welcomed the British. The route of march lay through Tigre, and the Tigreans seized the opportunity to help overthrow an unpopular monarch. The Church too did its part, and priests urged all Ethiopians to fight against an Emperor who had unjustly confiscated church lands and had rewarded his faithful retainers by giving them shares. Lastly, only the Church could release from their vow those who had sworn loyalty to the Emperor. The British were the catalytic agent for the overthrow of the Emperor by all the dissident elements of Ethiopia: the Church, the Tigrean lords, and the lesser nobility. As the British approached the capital, Theodore shot himself, whereupon the British easily occupied the capital, freed the captives, and promptly returned to the coast.

The outcome of the British withdrawal was readily predictable. Once again civil warfare rent Ethiopia for a number of years, until in 1871 a Tigrean *ras* (prince) whose firepower had given him a distinct advantage over all other claimants was crowned as Emperor Yohannes IV. As emperor, Yohannes continued Theodore's policies of restricting the power of the nobility.[3] Yohannes wanted to control the nobility and lay the basis for a state that could be called modern, but struggles with regional lords, Europeans, and Sudanese Muslims prevented him from achieving his goals.

---

[3] Yohannes' reign has been neglected by scholars. His foreign policy is dealt with indirectly in G. Douin, *Histoire du règne du Khédive Ismail; III, L'empire africain* (Rome: Istituto Poligrafico dello Stato, 1941). See also E. A. De Cosson, *The Cradle of the Blue Nile: A Visit to the Court of King John of Ethiopia* (London: John Murray, 1877) and J. de Coursac, *Le règne de Yohannes* (Romans: Imprimerie Jeanne d'Arc, 1926).

The only real rival for Yohannes' throne was Menelik, King of Shoa, who had survived imprisonment by Theodore at Magdala.[4] Menelik's claim to the throne was as good as that of Yohannes; both could claim Solomonic descent and the loyalty of large segments of the population. The regional rivalry of Tigre and Shoa was halted by a truce, however, and peace was sealed by a marriage alliance between Yohannes' son and Menelik's daughter. Moreover, Yohannes recognized the able King of Shoa as his successor to the imperial throne. The price was high, but it was worth it to the Emperor, who was aware that all too often in the past legitimate heirs to the throne had been deposed by rival claimants.

During the course of Yohannes' long reign the Italians established themselves on the Red Sea coast. At first they had only the desolate beachhead at Assab, where an Italian priest had bought land from a local sheik in 1869 as a coaling station for the Rubattino Shipping Company. In 1885, with British encouragement, the Italians occupied the seaport of Massawa, formerly held by Turkish and Egyptian garrisons.[5] Soon they expanded from their coastal beachheads across the uninviting coastal desert to the border of Tigre. When they attempted to occupy more salubrious lands, they were met by the forces of Yohannes' general, Ras Alula, who feared that they intended to scale the escarpment and occupy the cool and fertile highlands around his provincial capital, Asmara. Ras Alula soundly defeated the Italians at the Battle

[4] The "official" history of Menelik's reign is Guèbre Selassie, *Chronique du règne de Ménélik II, Roi des Rois d'Ethiopie* (3 vols., Paris: Maisonneuve, 1930–1932).

[5] The Italian decision to embark upon an imperialist program in the Red Sea is discussed in Carlo Giglio, *L'impresa di Massaua (1884-1885)* (Rome: Istituto Italiano per l'Africa, 1955).

of Dogali in 1887, the first major setback received by any European power at the hands of an African army, though only a sample of what was to happen nine years later at Adowa.[6]

Frustrated in their military ambitions, the Italians resorted to diplomacy and tried to exploit Tigrean-Shoan regional rivalry. Knowing full well that Menelik needed arms and munitions, the Italians proposed a treaty of commerce and friendship in hopes of using Menelik against Yohannes. For Menelik the proposal was fortuitous. As long as Tigre was well armed with European rifles and as long as Yohannes' son had hopes of gaining the imperial throne, Menelik was at a disadvantage and could not be certain that he would be the next emperor. Accordingly, Menelik concluded a treaty between Shoa and Italy, an adequate illustration of Shoan regional sovereignty and of the failure of Yohannes to create a unitary Ethiopian state to replace the very loose imperial arrangement.[7]

With Menelik a hostile friend and the Italians encroaching from the north, Yohannes found still another enemy in the Sudan. The Turks and Egyptians had withdrawn in 1884 from their garrisons on the coast and to the east. After supporting the Italian seizure of Massawa, the British, who were about to extend a protectorate over part of the Somali, took

[6] Italy's first major colonial setback is described in Francesco Crispi, *La prima guerra d'Africa: documenti e memorie* (Milan: Garzanti, 1939), pp. 89–97; and Camillo Antona-Traversi, *Sahati e Dogali, 25 e 26 gennaio 1887* (Rome: Antona-Traversi, 1887).

[7] Italian diplomatic concern with Shoa is documented in Carlo Rossetti, *Storia diplomatica della Etiopia durante il regno di Menelik II* (Turin: Società Tipografico-editrice Nazionale, 1910) and in C. Conti Rossini, *Italia ed Etiopia dal Trattato d'Uccialli alla battaglia di Adua* (Rome: Istituto per l'Oriente, 1935).

Zeila and Berbera as strategic ports opposite Aden. At the same time, France occupied Tadjoura, Obock, and Djibouti. To Menelik, King of Shoa, fell Harar and most of the eastern highlands in 1887. In that one year the territory of Shoa must have doubled, a forewarning of renewed Shoan ascendancy. To the west, however, the Turks and Egyptians had been replaced in the Sudan by the Mahdists, whose religious enthusiasm posed a real threat to Christian Ethiopia. Yohannes, of course, also regarded the turmoil in the Sudan as an opportunity to expand his Ethiopian empire westward into the lowlands, where there were prospects of gold, slaves, and direct access to the navigable Nile. In response to incursions by the Mahdi's dervishes, he led his warriors toward the lowlands. At Metemma a Mahdist bullet killed the Emperor and brought Menelik to the throne sooner than might have been anticipated.

Although the Scottish traveler James Bruce penetrated to the court at Gondar in the 1770's and another British traveler, Henry Salt, visited Tigre in the early years of the last century and was followed by a few Protestant and Catholic missionaries in the 1830's, not until the 1840's did there begin a thin but continuous and increasing trickle of European visitors to the chiefs, kings, and later emperors of Ethiopia. Ethiopian affairs, always complicated by the problems of regionalism and contacts with Islam, became more complex with the addition of the European factor.

Before the great wave of European imperialism in the late nineteenth century, the visitors to Ethiopia were travelers who shared that century's enthusiasm for exploration of unknown parts of the world, missionaries who in their pietistic zeal often naively misunderstood the nature of the country and failed to recognize the anomaly of their position as missionaries in a Christian country, and envoys hopeful of concluding advantageous commercial agreements with local potentates. The first two groups greatly stimulated European interest in Ethiopia, particularly in Tigre and Shoa. By the end of Theodore's reign there had appeared more than a score of books detailing the geography, ethnology, trade, and religious potential of Ethiopia. All these people, missionaries included, helped to introduce elements of Western technology, especially the technology of firearms, into Ethiopia.

In the last third of the century the number of European visitors increased, and European interest in the area of Ethiopia expanded from an investigation of commercial and missionary prospects into a study of colonial potential. To this genesis of colonial interest in Ethiopia, missionaries, travelers, explorers, and merchants of many European nationalities all made their contributions. Most noticeable of all were the Italians.[8]

At first the Ethiopians treated the Europeans as a pawn in their own internal affairs. Thus, at the time he became emperor, Menelik solidified his position by immediately concluding with Italy the famous Treaty of Uccialli, whereby he hoped to gain the support of a European ally as a special friend. The Italians, however, interpreted their role as special friend to mean the extension of an Italian protectorate over Ethiopia. Since 1885 they had hoped to obtain from the Sultan of Zanzibar the southern part of Somalia as an avenue of penetration inland to the rich lands of Kaffa, Sidamo, and Borana, then independent countries lying to the south of Shoa.[9] In 1889 they proclaimed to the rest of the world that

[8] Attesting to Italian interest in Ethiopia is the outpouring of articles and books listed in G. Fumagalli, *Bibliografia etiopica* (Milan: Hoepli, 1893).

[9] R. L. Hess, *Italian Colonialism in Somalia* (Chicago: University of Chicago Press, 1966), pp. 13–38.

the Treaty of Uccialli gave them a legitimate protectorate over Ethiopia. They did not realize at the time the considerable discrepancy between the Italian and the Amharic versions of the treaty.

Meanwhile, in the face of possible European aggression, Menelik's armies imposed his authority over an area much larger than that ruled by any of his predecessors for almost four hundred years. Not only were the traditional kingdoms of Gojjam, Begemder-Amhara, Tigre, and Shoa his, but also the newly won lands to the east around Harar. His armies scored even greater victories as they occupied the Somali country to within 180 miles of the Indian Ocean. Concurrently, other Ethiopian armies marched southward to destroy the ancient kingdom of Kaffa and to conquer the Sidamo and the Galla Borana. Thus, by the beginning of this century, Ethiopia, with the exception of Italian Eritrea, had reached its present borders.

Menelik's modernized army, equipped with French weapons, was soon ready to curb the threat of the rival Italian expansionism and convince the Italians by force that the Treaty of Uccialli did not make Ethiopia an Italian protectorate. The Italians accepted Menelik's interpretation of the treaty only after their disastrous defeat at Adowa on March 1, 1896, one of the most famous battles in the annals of modern imperialism.[10] Ethiopia's independence was secured, Ethiopian prestige was unique on the African continent, and Italy was so embittered by defeat on the battleground that forty years later Italians still sought revenge for Adowa. Moreover, no other African people could

---

[10] Augustus Wylde, *Modern Abyssinia* (London: Methuen, 1901), pp. 196–225; Roberto Battaglia, *La prima guerra d'Africa* (Turin: Einaudi, 1958), pp. 733–786.

boast of so successful a military confrontation with a major European power.

Ethiopia's aloofness from the outside world thus came to an end precisely at the same time that Menelik was consolidating imperial power and authority within an enlarged Ethiopia. From his capital of Addis Ababa, founded only a few short years before he became emperor, Menelik directed the process of changing Ethiopia from a traditional to a modern polity. The victory at Adowa thus dramatized not only Ethiopia's military prowess but also the promise of a new Ethiopia. Europe suddenly became aware of Ethiopia, and in Paris *La Liberté* exuberantly declared, "All European countries will be obliged to make a place for this new brother who steps forth ready to play in the dark continent the role of Japan in the Far East." [11]

Like the rulers of Japan and Thailand, Menelik learned from his experience with Europeans that in order to maintain its independence in the face of European imperialism, Ethiopia must learn much from the imposing body of Western technology. Such knowledge would also be of great usefulness in ruling an empire whose size had doubled in a very short time. For these reasons Menelik employed European advisers to modernize his army, to introduce modern communications and transportation, and to graft onto the traditional semifeudal government more modern bureaucratic institutions. In the decade after Adowa, Ethiopia took its first steps in this direction, and one European delegation after another made its way to the court at Addis Ababa to help in the process of modernization and to attempt to influence Menelik in its favor. Each of the European powers

[11] R. K. P. Pankhurst, "How the News was Received in England," *Ethiopia Observer,* I, no. 11 (1957), p. 366.

thought it could extract from Menelik concessions like those obtained by Europeans throughout the colonial world.

Menelik was willing to grant a concession for the construction of a railway from French Djibouti to Addis Ababa, as he was for the introduction of telecommunications, roads, technical assistance, and advisers.[12] Yet this willingness was not a sign of weakness. Rather, a strong case can be made that Menelik had an excellent sense of diplomacy and that in this clever ruler all European diplomats, not only those of Italy, met their match. If anything, the Europeans became a pawn in his plans for maintaining the independence and integrity of Ethiopia, for expanding the empire, and, significantly, for modernizing the State.

For ten years after the victory at Adowa, Menelik had little to fear from European powers. His main concern, rightly, was with rival authorities at home whose strength was based on family and regional connections. Like the emperors of the old Ethiopia, he had to deal with regional leaders like Ras Mikael of Wollo. But Menelik the innovator also had tradition on his side. Only the emperor could create the *neguses* (kings), and here there was ample precedent. Theodore had created neither neguses nor *rases* (princes). Yohannes IV had created only two neguses (one was Menelik in Shoa, the other Tekla Haymanot in Gojjam); both of these appointments, of course, represented weaknesses vis-à-vis those two regions. Menelik, however, created no new neguses.

By Ethiopian tradition, only the emperor or a negus could

[12] E. S. Pankhurst, "The Beginning of Modern Transport in Ethiopia: The Franco-Ethiopian Railway and Its History," *Ethiopia Observer*, I, no. 12 (1958), pp. 376–390.

create a ras. Menelik created many rases, but whereas formerly appointments of rases had often been an indication of weakness on the part of the emperor (as in the case of Galawdewos) and only confirmed existing power relationships, Menelik's appointments signified imperial control over these princes. In particular, he chose to ignore the claims of families who, if not by heredity, at least by tradition, had always filled the office of ras. In this manner he could be sure of loyalty to the Emperor and perhaps to the State, as he raised to high office Galla from newly conquered regions. Menelik also employed the traditional marriage connections of the Ethiopian aristocracy to strengthen his political position; he chose as his fourth wife the formidable Empress Taitu, who was of Galla origin and commanded the loyalty of large sections of the Galla. A cousin was married to one of the most important men of Lasta and thus ensured the loyalty of that province. Another cousin, Ras Makonnen, controlled Harar and the Ogaden. A third cousin, Ras Wolde Giorgis, who was married to a sister of Taitu, was particularly influential in the area of Gondar. One of Menelik's daughters married Ras Mikael of Wollo, and so it went.

To replace recalcitrant regional leaders and to complement the ranks of the loyal nobility, Menelik instituted the beginnings of centralized ministerial government, staffed by the forerunners of a modern elite.[13] By 1906 an impartial observer would have agreed that he had been largely successful in his attempts to create this new type of government.

[13] Guèbre Selassie, *Chronique du règne de Ménélik II*, II, 527–528; R. K. P. Pankhurst, "Misoneism and Innovation in Ethiopian History," *Ethiopia Observer*, VIII, no. 4 (1964), p. 305; also H. Marcus, "Menilek II," *Leadership in Eastern Africa*, N. R. Bennett, ed. (Boston: Boston University Press, 1968), pp. 58–59.

This success proved to be short-lived, however, for it depended on one man.

In 1906, Menelik suffered the first of several strokes. As
the Emperor became physically weaker, all the old elements
of instability reappeared in Ethiopia: court intrigues, attempted coups, and rivalries among regional leaders and
families for political influence. It seemed certain that Menelik's work would be undermined. He himself was too weak
to rule; the Empress tried to manipulate factions, but as
long as the question of Menelik's successor was undecided,
there cauld be no real stability. Finally, in June, 1908, Menelik's grandson, Lij Iasu, was named his successor. Lij Iasu
proved to be an unfortunate choice, for within a matter of a
few years he began dallying with Muslim elements. Perhaps
this was his best means of countering the influence of the
Tigreans and obtaining the support of Harar, for Makonnen,
who had won the loyalty of the Harari, had died in 1906.
Nevertheless, it did not bode well for the future of Menelik's
Ethiopia.

After Menelik's death at the end of 1913, Lij Iasu became
emperor.[14] The European powers, contemplating the prospect of the disintegration of Ethiopia, began to vie for
influence at the imperial court. The German and Turkish
diplomats in particular were successful in winning the attention of the young Lij Iasu. Local British consular agents
suggested to the Colonial Office that they consider extending
a protectorate over Ethiopia. The French hoped that their
large economic interests would develop into political inter-

[14] For accounts of Lij Iasu's brief reign, see R. Greenfield, *Ethiopia,
A New Political History* (New York: Frederick A. Praeger, 1965), pp.
131–145; and L. Mosley, *Haile Selassie: The Conquering Lion* (Englewood Cliffs, N.J.: Prentice-Hall, 1965), pp. 60–85.

ests. The Italian Colonial Minister drew up a grandiose plan for winning allied support for the extension of an Italian protectorate over Ethiopia. Thus, the Italian interest in Ethiopia, more or less moribund since the defeat at Adowa, was reborn.[15]

With European hopes rising, Lij Iasu publicly announced his conversion to Islam. Nothing could have been more startling. For many, especially the Amhara and Tigreans, Christianity and Ethiopia had become identical. This action by Lij Iasu was too much for all the traditional, and many of the modernizing, elements of Ethiopia, and in 1916 they joined to overthrow the Muslim Emperor. The Church, of course, played an important role; the Abuna released all Ethiopians from their oath of loyalty to the Emperor. The nobility, most of whom were Christian Amhara, also acted quickly. The Tigreans, moreover, saw an opportunity to extend their power. Leaders of the coup included Ras Wolde Giorgis, Ras Kassa Hailu of Gojjam, the Abuna Mattewos, various Shoan nobles, Ras Tafari Makonnen, son of Menelik's cousin Makonnen, and Menelik's Minister of War, Habte Giorgis. Thus, the nobility, the Church, and the army joined to overthrow Lij Iasu.

Although the coup was successful, the various groups could not agree on a program for Ethiopia. The nobles would have preferred that power once again be decentralized, but this was no solution; there were too many rivalries among them to permit it. Finally, it was agreed that Menelik's daughter Zawditu would reign as empress, but not

[15] For evidence that Italian interest in Ethiopia was *not* moribund from the defeat at Adowa until the advent of Mussolini, see R. L. Hess, "Italy and Africa: Colonial Ambitions in the First World War," *Journal of African History*, IV, no. 1 (1963), pp. 105–126.

rule. The nobility hoped that one of their number could act as regent, and so they chose a young man whom they probably regarded as malleable, Ras Tafari of Harar, a distant cousin of Menelik. Habte Giorgis, a noted general popular among the older nobility, remained as war minister. Thus, Ethiopia was ruled by a triumvirate: Ras Tafari as regent did not have complete powers, Zawditu as empress commanded great loyalty but little real power, and Habte Giorgis was able to control the army in the interests of the nobility.

In the years from 1916 to 1930, the Regent gradually extended his power. Ras Tafari put down several rebellions as he built up his own small military force. The deaths of both Habte Giorgis and the Abuna Mattewos in 1926 greatly simplified his task. Each unsuccessful rebellion increased the Regent's powers. Finally, after suppressing an uprising by Dejazmatch Balcha, a conservative noble who allegedly conspired with Zawditu to overthrow the Regent, Ras Tafari found himself in the position he desired. Zawditu had no alternative to yielding to the wishes of Ras Tafari. Not only did she name him negus, but it is claimed that she also nominated him heir apparent. In 1930, after one last uprising by Zawditu's former husband, Ras Gugsa Wolie, and after the subsequent death of the Empress, Tafari Makonnen triumphantly ascended the throne of Ethiopia and chose the throne name of Haile Selassie I.[16]

In his years as regent, Haile Selassie demonstrated great political ability and astuteness. He shared many of the characteristics of Menelik, although their temperaments greatly differed. He was not bound by the traditional way of doing

[16] Greenfield, *Ethiopia,* pp. 156–164; Mosley, *Haile Selassie,* pp. 131–151; C. Sandford, *The Lion of Judah Hath Prevailed* (London: J. M. Dent, 1955), pp. 44–45.

things. He also had some characteristics not to be found in Menelik. As a boy he had been educated by French Jesuits in Harar. There he had learned not only French, but also much about Europe and its accomplishments. For personal and state reasons, as regent he had resumed the process of modernization suspended for more than a decade after the death of Menelik. In his vulnerable position, Ras Tafari realized that if Ethiopia were to develop under his leadership, he must have men whom he could trust. He could not rely on the old nobility: this was a foregone conclusion. Consequently, he imitated Menelik, who founded the first public schools in Ethiopia, and established new schools and launched a program of sending promising young Ethiopians abroad for study in France, England, the United States, and elsewhere. Significantly, some young Ethiopians were sent to the French military academy at Saint-Cyr.

One of the goals of this program of modernization was the establishment of a new type of political stability. Yet despite the fact that the program may have been aimed at solidifying the position of the Regent, it had repercussions for Ethiopia as a state. In 1923, Ethiopia had become a member of the League of Nations. Subsequently, in 1924 the Regent found it necessary to emancipate all slaves in Ethiopia in order to render Ethiopia less susceptible to criticism from abroad. In that same year the Regent made his first trip outside Ethiopia (except for a trip the previous year to Aden, where he daringly flew in an airplane). His tour of England, France, Germany, Italy, Greece, and Egypt gave him added impetus for plans to modernize Ethiopia upon his return. From then on, an increasing number of foreign advisers went to Ethiopia to give assistance in technical matters. After his coronation in 1930 this process speeded up. Certainly Ethiopia was far from modernized, but the Emperor fully realized that the program had become necessary for an additional reason. Not only did modernization aid political stability and development, but it was also necessary for dealing effectively with European states.

The Ethiopians had good reason to suspect that there would be trouble sooner or later from Fascist Italy and its colonies, Eritrea and Somalia, which bordered landlocked Ethiopia. One way to cope with the possibility was to import modern arms, which began to arrive in larger quantities after 1930. In still another departure from tradition, in 1931 the Emperor granted Ethiopia a constitution providing for a bicameral parliament and a cabinet with responsible ministers. In its form the document was a praiseworthy liberal constitution, but Ethiopia in actuality was far from a constitutional monarchy in the Western sense. The Emperor hoped to prove to Europeans that the Ethiopian state was an equal in the growing international state system. How far this trend might have gone in the years that followed is uncertain, for the development was cut short in 1934–35, after the crisis with Italy at Walwal, which was followed by the Italian invasion of Ethiopia.

The story of European diplomacy with regard to Fascist aggression in Ethiopia need not be investigated here in detail.[17] Ethiopia had no effective allies. The Italians, with their military supremacy in airplanes and poison gas, overran the country; Adowa was avenged. By early May, 1936 the

[17] The most recent studies of this critical period are G. W. Baer, *The Coming of the Italian-Ethiopian War* (Cambridge: Harvard University Press, 1967); F. D. Laurens, *France and the Italo-Ethiopian Crisis, 1935–1936* (The Hague: Mouton, 1967); A. Del Boca, *La guerra d'Abissinia, 1935–1941* (Milan: Feltrinelli, 1965); L. Pignatelli, *La guerra dei sette mesi* (Milan: Longanesi, 1965); and Brice Harris, Jr., *The United States and the Italo-Ethiopian Crisis* (Stanford: Stanford University Press, 1964).

Emperor was forced to flee the country. But although the Italians occupied Ethiopia, the Emperor won a moral victory at one of his most famous appearances. On June 30, 1936, he gave a remarkable speech before the League of Nations and demanded to know why the principle of collective security did not protect or free Ethiopia. It was an eloquent plea, but it failed, and from 1936 to 1940 the Emperor lived in exile in England.

The Italian invasion, like the British punitive expedition of seventy years earlier, was aided by dissident Ethiopians who looked upon the departure of the Emperor as their golden opportunity to re-establish regional family interests. The outstanding example was Ras Hailu of Gojjam, whom the Emperor had refused to confirm as negus. Ras Hailu had been ordered to leave Ethiopia in the Emperor's entourage, but at the last moment he returned to Gojjam and by clever negotiations persuaded the Italians to confirm him as King of Gojjam.

Although there was some cooperation with the Italians, there was even greater resistance by guerrilla patriots.[18] The sons of Ras Kassa, a cousin of the Emperor, gave their lives in such resistance. Others attempted in 1937 to assassinate Rodolfo Graziani, the Italian military commander. Their failure unleashed a reign of terror on Addis Ababa, and in the weeks after the attempt on Graziani's life the Italians deliberately massacred hundreds of Ethiopians, especially many of those who had been educated abroad and others who had participated most devotedly in the modernizing process before 1934. After the outburst, however, the Italians imposed the milder administration of the Duke of Aosta. Nevertheless, the countryside was generally unsafe for Ital-

[18] The best account of the patriots' resistance is given by Greenfield, *Ethiopia,* pp. 224–256.

ians, and Addis Ababa remained a heavily fortified military garrison throughout the five-year period of the Italian occupation.

After relative peace and order were restored in late 1937, Fascist Italy embarked upon an extensive campaign to develop its new African empire. Millions upon millions of dollars were invested to create a basic infrastructure. At great cost the Italians built a network of superb roads across the rugged Ethiopian terrain, a tribute to their engineering talents. For the first time in Ethiopian history the main regions of the country were linked by motor roads. Unlike Haile Selassie, who had always been hampered by regional resistance and limited funds during his eighteen years as regent and emperor, the Italians, who poured virtually unlimited funds into a country where they maintained a large army, were able to accomplish much in the way of material modernization.[19]

Mussolini had great hopes of developing Ethiopia as a granary for Italy, a source of raw materials, and a colony of settlement, but in the years of occupation the Italians became increasingly disillusioned with their conquest of a land whose inhabitants they could not totally subdue. No profits were to be found in this new empire to justify the great expenditure in preparing naval bases, in underwriting the cost of the expensive military campaign, and in building bridges, tunnels, and thousands of miles of roads. The countryside was unpacified. Trade had been disrupted. It was impossible to

[19] Graphic descriptions and illustrations of this costly network of roads are presented by Giuseppe Cobolli Giglio, *Strade imperiali* (Milan: Mondadori, 1938). In addition to the Italian government's investment in 3,000 miles of roads, private investors invested 3.8 billion lire (approximately $760 million) in commercial and industrial enterprises, according to Del Boca, *La guerra in Abissinia*, pp. 213–214.

collect revenue from the peasants; even the Emperor had not been able to do this. Foreign capital was not attracted; minerals, especially petroleum, were not discovered in commercial quantities. Although the basis for long-term development was established, impatient Italy had little to show for it by 1940.

When Italy declared war on Great Britain in June, 1940, the British feared an Italian invasion of the Sudan from Ethiopia. Fascist propaganda concealed the true situation in Ethiopia from the Allies until reports finally leaked out that Ethiopia seemed ripe for rebellion.[20] Not only did internal insecurity prevent the Italians from invading the Sudan, but most important, despite Italian claims to the contrary, there was a great spirit of resistance in Ethiopia as well as great patriotism and loyalty to the exiled Emperor.

After consulting with Daniel Arthur Sandford, who had served as British consul in Addis Ababa during World War I and then from 1920 to 1936 as adviser to the Ethiopian government, the British planned an invasion of Ethiopia. They trained Ethiopian refugees at Khartoum, while Sandford made contact with Ethiopian patriots in Gojjam who, although divided among themselves, were still loyal to the Emperor. The plan envisaged a three-pronged attack on Ethiopia: British forces from Kenya would invade Somalia and then head toward Harar and Addis Ababa; British Sudanese troops would invade Eritrea; and a third force would invade from the Sudan into the area of Gojjam. A small group of English, Sudanese, and Ethiopian troops led by British officers entered Gojjam in January, 1941. The Italians, poorly informed of all developments in that isolated part of Ethiopia, assumed that the British and Ethiopians were in-

[20] Christopher Sykes, *Orde Wingate* (London: Collins, 1959), pp. 239–240.

vading in force and retreated. By the end of March, victories
were recorded on all three fronts. Early in May, Haile Selassie
re-entered Addis Ababa, and a new era began.[21]

Since the liberation of Ethiopia in 1941 the country has
continued to modernize. The British military occupation
permitted the extension of effective administration over large
areas of the empire previously only loosely controlled by
Addis Ababa.[22] The rough outlines of change suggested by
the policies of Haile Selassie in the years before the Italian
invasion have since been filled in. Thus, in the postwar era
the Ethiopian government has continued to modernize its
bureaucratic apparatus, to promote education, and to replace
those Western-educated men who perished during the Italian
occupation. Despite regional opposition (such as serious Tigrean and Gojjam revolts in the 1940's and Bale and Gojjam
revolts in the 1960's), continuing troubles with the Ogaden
Somali, Eritrean disaffection, and other local disturbances,
the process has been moderately effective. The central government has successfully displaced most regional rivals, although the historic centrifugal tendencies remain, complicated as always by the polyethnic nature of Ethiopia's
population and the conservative nature of Amhara society
which, as in Gojjam, has resisted so fundamental a government function as surveying of land for the purpose of deter-
mining ownership and, by implication, tax responsibilities.

[21] The invasion of Ethiopia is recounted by British, South African,
Italian, West African, Rhodesian, and Ethiopian participants in Ken-
neth Gandar Dower, *Abyssinian Patchwork, an Anthology* (London:
Frederick Muller, 1949).

[22] Lord Rennell of Rodd, *British Military Administration of Occupied Territories in Africa during the Years 1941–1947* (London: His
Majesty's Stationery Office, 1948), pp. 59–95.

The Emperor intended that modernization serve as a means to political stability. His policy has clearly produced a new generation of educated elite, but whereas the Emperor set the tone for modernization until the mid-1950's, since then the new elements of his own creation have been less easily controlled. University graduates have resented the authority of men of a previous generation who were recruited out of the old nobility to fill the Emperor's ministries. The Imperial Army, another of the Emperor's creations, disliked the favored treatment accorded the Imperial Body Guard, some of whose members harbored ambitions opposed to the goals of Haile Selassie.

In December, 1960 matters came to a head. While the Emperor was on a state visit to Brazil, the Imperial Body Guard staged an abortive coup. In the chaotic December days, as the leaders of the coup attempted to mobilize support, Addis Ababa reflected the stresses and strains of the changed Ethiopia. Some interpreted the slogans as revolutionary, but their actions reflected mainly the tensions between the old and the new. The coup, which was quickly put down by the army, marked a turning point in the relations between the Emperor and the elements of modernity. Since 1960 observers of the Ethiopian scene have speculated increasingly on the future of the state after the death of Haile Selassie, who, after all, first came to power more than fifty years ago.

During this postliberation period the Empire grew in size once again. But whereas Menelik and earlier emperors almost always expanded Ethiopian holdings through military conquest, Haile Selassie I has achieved his greatest successes through diplomacy. At the end of World War II, the Emperor proposed that Ethiopia annex the two former Italian colonies of Eritrea and Somalia, then occupied by the British. When Italy renounced all rights to its former colonies in 1947, the issue came to a head, and the hotly disputed matter was brought before the United Nations. In 1950, the Ethiopians suffered a diplomatic setback when the United Nations established a Trust Territory in Somalia under Italian administration for a ten-year period, after which Somalia was to become independent. In the following year, however, they won a major victory: after a great debate and some resistance by Eritrean Muslims, the United Nations approved the federation of Ethiopia and Eritrea.

The federation, established in 1952, was doomed from the beginning. The arrangement was complicated by the fact that the federation was between Ethiopia as a whole and little Eritrea.[23] Within the Ethiopian part of the federation all provinces were strictly subordinate to the central government, and in practice the Ethiopians treated Eritrea more as a new province than as a federated territory. Although the Eritreans had their own elected assembly, its members were influenced by the Ethiopian government and its prerogatives limited by Ethiopian practices. The federation came to an end in November, 1962, when Ethiopia annexed Eritrea as its thirteenth province.[24]

After 1941, Ethiopia also entered more fully into the realm of international politics. Until 1945 the British presence was strongly felt and resented in Ethiopia. The British, who had been slow in recognizing Haile Selassie as an independent sovereign in exile and at one time toyed with the idea of sponsoring a separate Galla state, had at first classified Ethiopia

[23] G. K. N. Trevaskis, *Eritrea, a Colony in Transition: 1941–52* (London: Oxford University Press, 1960), pp. 103–131.

[24] At that time Bale and Harar Provinces constituted one large province.

as Occupied Enemy Territory.[25] The proud Ethiopians, however, regarded themselves as a liberated allied country and sought to assert the Emperor's rule and to eliminate British influence as early as possible. By an agreement of January 31, 1942, Britain granted recognition to Ethiopia as a sovereign state, although the British military administration continued to control most of the government. By the end of 1944, a new agreement was negotiated, and the central government at Addis Ababa regained control, with certain limitations, over the administrative apparatus. In the following year Ethiopian sovereignty was completely restored. Since 1945 the Ethiopian government has curbed British influence in the country by turning first to the United States and then to a number of unaligned countries like Yugoslavia, India, and Israel.

Not only was the Emperor determined to be free from Italian and British influence, but he also sought to define an international role for Ethiopia. The experience of the Italian invasion reinforced the Emperor's belief in collective security, notwithstanding the failure of the League of Nations to give Ethiopia effective assistance when attacked. As evidence of this commitment to world politics, the Ethiopian government dispatched a force to serve in Korea in 1951 and in the Congo in 1960 and since then has expressed a willingness to extend this policy to other troubled areas.

Since 1950 the Emperor has made many important state visits: to the United States, the Soviet Union, India, Japan, Yugoslavia, France, and the Arab states. Increasingly, the Ethiopian government has taken an active part in the deliberations of the United Nations, especially at the 18 Nations

[25] Sykes, *Orde Wingate*, pp. 255–256; Philip Mitchell, *African Afterthoughts* (London: Hutchinson, 1954), pp. 195–196.

Disarmament Conference in Geneva and on the Committee of 24, which deals with problems of decolonization. But most striking of all changes has been Ethiopia's official commitment to Africa, originating in Ethiopia's participation at the first conference of independent African states in Accra in 1958, continuing through the support given African nationalist leaders in colonial territories, symbolized by Ethiopia's construction of Africa Hall in Addis Ababa as the headquarters for the United Nations Economic Commission for Africa, and culminating in 1963 in the selection of Addis Ababa as the seat of the permanent secretariat of the Organization of African Unity. Since then Ethiopia has played a leading role in all United Nations' matters dealing with Africa. Once one of the most isolated and essentially least involved of the sub-Saharan African states, Ethiopia has made its bid for leadership in the African solidarity movement. Few could have predicted such a startling development.

1. The steles at Axum

2. Crowns of the emperors and rases, the Treasury, Axum

3. The Castle of Emperor Fasilidas (1632-1667), Gondar

THE RELIGIOUS TRADITION

4. Priest of the Orthodox Church reading book in Geez, Lalibela

5. Falasha woman holding flour for unleavened bread for Passover, near Gondar

6. Ambara priest fasting on last day of Lent, Lalibela

7. Typical village dwelling, Lalibela

8. Seventeenth-century castle, Gondar

9. United Nations Economic Commission for Africa (Africa Hall), Addis Ababa

10. Falasha village near Gondar

11. The Saturday market, Lalibela

12. The Conquering Lion of Judah faces the Commercial Bank of Ethiopia, Addis Ababa

13. Two Amhara women act as hostesses at an international conference, Addis Ababa

14. Emperor Fasilidas leads his army against the Muslims, eighteenth-century Church of Debra Berhan Selassie, Gondar

15. Ethiopia leading Africa to its future; stained-glass window by Afework Tekle, Africa Hall, Addis Ababa

CHAPTER 4

The Veneer of
Modernization

> Can the Ethiopian change his skin,
> or the leopard his spots?
> —Jeremiah 13:23

The social and economic life of Ethiopia, heavily influenced by traditional values and institutions, has been undergoing modifications and a slow metamorphosis over the past decades. The major impetus for change has come from the Emperor, whose own position in Ethiopian politics greatly depends upon traditional values of political legitimacy. To modernize the Ethiopian state the Emperor created new social groups and new economic practices discussed in this chapter, and new theories of legality and new political institutions, dealt with in the next.

The traditional society of Amhara-dominated Ethiopia, like that of many culturally advanced premodern societies, was highly stratified. Until the coronation of Haile Selassie in 1930, Ethiopian society had remained largely unchanged. Since then new elements have emerged, some of them deliberately called into being by the Emperor to counter older elements, or, in some cases, to supplement those traditional elements adaptable to modernization.

At the apex of traditional society stood the emperor, not only ruler by the grace of God, but a monarch with quasi-divine attributes.[1] In theory the emperor reigned supreme. He was the commander-in-chief of the military, the chief executive, the supreme legislator and magistrate, the source of all land and confirmer of all titles, and the ultimate authority in matters of church administration and theological dogma. He had a mystic bond with the past, represented by his coronation at Axum and his claim of descent from Solomon and Sheba. There is no question but that the myths of legitimation were devoutly believed throughout Christian Ethiopia and were never challenged. In practice, however, the emperors had to fight for their rights against pretenders to the throne who relied upon similar claims of Solomonic descent. The emperor was also limited by the Church, whose head, the Abuna, consecrated his office. The Abuna alone could release the emperor's followers from their formal oath of loyalty, as happened in 1916 when the Church took an active role in deposing the Islamophile Lij Iasu.

The main control on the emperor's power was historically exercised by the nobility, who were of three types. The royal nobility, also descendants of Solomon and Sheba, were potential usurpers and regarded as dangerous. In earlier times royal princes were often exiled to remote mountain areas; the chronicles describe an amba inhabited by heavily guarded members of the royal family. In more recent times, when the power of the Emperor was threatened by a coup in December, 1960, the organizers of the coup apparently coerced the Crown Prince to accept a position as Head of State.

On the regional level there existed a powerful nobility

[1] D. N. Levine, *Wax and Gold: Tradition and Innovation in Ethiopian Culture* (Chicago: University of Chicago Press, 1965), pp. 150–155; M. Perham, *The Government of Ethiopia* (London: Faber and Faber, 1969), pp. 71–80.

with a history as ancient as that of the emperor.[2] This nobility, until the time of Menelik II, was of military origin, and their titles (*ras, dejazmatch, kenyazmatch, fitawrari,* and so forth) were originally military ranks appointed by the emperor. These nobles became a landed aristocracy, patterned themselves on a smaller scale after the imperial court, and eventually challenged the regional authority of the emperor. Such has been the case in Tigre and Gojjam in the past century, and such was the case in Shoa during the reign of Yohannes IV. From the late eighteenth century to the mid-nineteenth century, the regional nobility prevented the development of political unity in Ethiopia.

Over the past hundred years, Theodore II, Menelik II, and Haile Selassie I have pursued a policy of curbing and then breaking the power of the old nobility, who exercised almost sovereign rights in the once remote provinces. Theodore initiated the process by attempting to remove control of the armies from the regional chiefs and by appointing a new nobility loyal to him. Menelik appointed loyal Galla, as well as Amhara, to high positions; such was the case with Fitawrari Habte Giorgis. Despite their attempts, the basic structure did not undergo any major changes, but after Ras Tafari became regent, the decline of the old nobility was accelerated. Opposition flared up from time to time, but the process is now virtually complete. The old nobility has retained its prestige and social position, but its political power today is largely nonexistent outside the new framework of government. The old nobility can now act politically either as agents or as opponents of the Emperor, but it cannot regain its lost regional privileges without plunging Ethiopia into a

[2] Levine, *Wax and Gold,* pp. 155–167; Perham, *The Government of Ethiopia,* pp. 81–86.

disastrous civil war. On this level feudalism has died in Ethiopia and has been replaced by a national monarchy.

Although the higher nobility has suffered a diminution of power, the lesser nobility of rich landowners and district judges and chiefs has continued to enjoy its old powers and prestige on the local level. The political changes pressed forward by Haile Selassie have not yet filtered down to the village and district level, for the peasantry still consider land ownership and family connections the criteria for commanding respect and wielding power.

Side by side with the older traditional Ethiopia have developed the elements of a new Ethiopian society. The Emperor, though still claiming traditional prerogatives, has been one of the main forces that have reshaped parts of Ethiopian society. Intentionally or not, he has greatly influenced the nature of the monarchy. Some members of the old nobility have adapted to a redefined role in Ethiopian society. One means to this end has been marriage with members of the large royal family. More often, however, the old nobility has become a court nobility like that at Louis XIV's Versailles. Since 1960 there have been indications that members of old families may still have some power. The Senate, it will be shown, is no longer the safe home for old nobles envisaged by the Emperor. Indeed, it has occasionally shown strong signs of life and opposition to the Emperor.

The first element of the new society to emerge was the men raised to power by the emperors. When Menelik II created the first ministerial departments of the government in 1907, these men made their debut as a new force.[3] Although the development of this group was cut short by the death of Menelik, it was given fresh impetus after the accession of

[3] Perham, *The Government of Ethiopia*, pp. 87–92.

Haile Selassie. Since the end of the Italian occupation, the sixteen ministries of the government, the army, the judiciary, and the diplomatic corps have been staffed by men chosen for their loyalty to the Emperor and for their abilities. This new group of men rose rapidly after 1945, and as the bureaucracy, the military, and the economy expanded, they grew in numbers. Until 1950 most of them were recruited from the old nobility, whose ranks they abandoned for new offices and a new way of life. This new nobility, unchallenged until 1960, was exposed to Western education. At the same time the old values of family loyalty, of distaste for business, and of private gain through public office have continued within this new setting. Their position is difficult, for they have been identified by some as the Emperor's men, and a new generation of university students and graduates regards them as reactionary, self-seeking, corrupt, and harmful to the national development.[4]

In contrast to this transitional group, whose members have both traditional and forward-looking links, is the small but growing new elite. The expansion of the economy and bureaucracy has created new groups in Ethiopian society: military servicemen, workers, salaried employees, secondary-school and university students, and a group of Eritreans who acquired low-level administrative skills under the Italian colonial and the British military occupation regimes. These elements have only recently begun to show some signs of group solidarity. The most dynamic element is the students, whose secular education has alienated them from many, but not all, of the values of traditional Ethiopian society. These young men (comparatively few women have completed their education) have come from all levels and groups of the old

[4] Levine, *Wax and Gold,* pp. 190–194.

society, including Galla, Muslims, and Eritreans, but not
many Somali and Negroids. Upon graduation most have
been enlisted directly into government service at the middle
levels; since 1961 some have started their bureaucratic
careers at even higher levels. Others are teachers, including
over a hundred at the university level, journalists, and professional men. Only a few have pursued business careers,
although an increasing number (especially non-Amhara) are
now choosing this field. Most are concentrated in Addis
Ababa, the one urban center of any cultural or political
importance.[5]

At first a distinction could be made between those who
had been educated abroad and those who had remained in
Ethiopia, but this distinction seems to have broken down.
Modernization means much to this group, but it is doubtful
that they define it in the same terms as the Emperor. Like
the youth of many other countries, they speak of their impatience with the older generation, in this case the new
nobility, who do not appreciate their technical training. The
students have produced no leaders on the national level so
far, although they openly expressed their dissatisfaction with
contemporary Ethiopia as early as 1955. These young, educated Ethiopians vocally supported the attempted coup in
1960; since then their leaders have continually criticized the
Emperor for his policies, which they consider too conservative.

Until late 1962, it would have been meaningless to talk of
an Ethiopian labor movement. The first workers' association,
the Ethiopian Railroad Workers' Syndicate, was formed at
Dire Dawa in 1947 as an employee welfare organization, not

[5] R. Greenfield, *Ethiopia, A New Political History* (New York: Frederick A. Praeger, 1965), pp. 365–370.

a union proper. Its leadership was highly paternalistic and cooperated with the government in planning legislation governing unions. In 1956 the officers of the Syndicate were charged with embezzlement, and membership in the organization dropped to 2,500. In 1952, Woldeab Wolde Mariam, an opposition political leader, founded the Syndicate of the Union of Free Workers in Eritrea to represent workers' interests in the former Italian colony, then occupied by the British.[6] A few years later another workers' association was formed at the government-sponsored, Dutch-operated Wonji Sugar Estate.

The right to form unions did not exist before 1955. Government policy aimed at maintaining economic production and stability. Strikes were not a legal weapon of the worker, although a number did take place. A strike by the Railroad Workers' Syndicate in 1949 was so severe that the government sent in troops to subdue the workers. The Eritrean Syndicate also acted as a pressure group upon Arab merchants. More significantly, the strikes that the Syndicate organized often turned into political demonstrations against Ethiopian domination of Eritrean affairs. The leadership of the Eritrean group, it should be noted, consisted of anti-Amhara separatists who were both Christian Tigreans and Muslims.

Because it was feared that unions represented a modernizing force that could not be completely controlled by the government, and because they were a potential political force, the government long refused to grant Ethiopian unions the right of association. Although the revised Constitution of 1955 granted that right, not until 1962 was the formation

[6] G. Lipsky *et al.*, *Ethiopia, Its People, Its Society, Its Culture* (New Haven: HRAF Press, 1962), p. 280.

of legally recognized labor unions permitted for the first time in Ethiopian history, thereby opening the way for additional change.[7]

The Labor Relations Decree of September 5, 1962 recognized the principle of collective bargaining, prohibited unfair labor practices, and provided for the creation of a Labor Relations Board for the settlement of disputes. But the provisions of the decree did not apply to those in managerial positions or to public servants, domestic servants, and farm workers employed on farms having fewer than ten permanent workers. Moreover, unions could be organized only within industrial enterprises employing more than fifty workers.[8] At the time, it was estimated that only just over 200,000 Ethiopians were employed outside rural occupations.

Ethiopia's modern legislation uses the reform vocabulary of societies industrially far more advanced: freedom of vocation, vocational training, and action to prevent an exodus from rural areas into the city. It recognizes the need to reduce unemployment in Addis Ababa, where population growth has outstripped the rate of industrialization. Yet the government has been slow to define, much less implement, general minimum conditions of work, restrictions on child and female labor, overtime pay, and vacation pay. The government's main concern has been to control any labor movement in its incipient stages to prevent the growth of a rival agent of reform.

By mid-1963 forty-two labor unions had been formed, and a Confederation of Ethiopian Labor Unions was established. Claiming a membership of 70,000 industrial workers, the Confederation expanded rapidly, a development not fore-

[7] Georg Graf von Baudissin, "Labour Policy in Ethiopia," *International Labour Review*, LXXXIX (1964), 551–556.

[8] *Ibid.*, pp. 558–560.

seen by the government.[9] Since then there have been a significant number of strikes as the Ethiopian workers' movement has cautiously tested its strength. In 1963, for example, the Labor Relations Board considered 137 employee disputes; two years later, however, the number of cases had risen to 776, of which 80 were rejected, 182 were referred to court, and 382 were successfully conciliated.[10]

In December, 1965, 800 members of the Transport Workers Union held a one-day strike in Addis Ababa to force the local private bus company to observe a contract and to demand medical services and insurance. The bus strike visibly demonstrated to an otherwise uninterested public the potential organizing abilities of the union. In April, 1966 the 850 employees of the government-owned Berhanenna Selam Printing Press struck for better working conditions and overtime pay and closed down the five daily and four weekly newspapers in Addis Ababa. The strike, which lasted a week, was peacefully settled, but only after the workers had demonstrated their willingness and ability to challenge a government-owned operation.[11]

In July, 1963 the Confederation of Ethiopian Labor Unions began to publish both in Amharic and English a lively little semimonthly bulletin, *The Voice of Labour*. This publication did not limit itself to discussion of purely economic problems, but has sought to broaden the horizons of the small but growing working class beyond the narrow prospects of economic problems. In 1964, for example, the

[9] There were fewer than 50,000 dues-paying members as of 1968. In the early stages of the unions, not too much emphasis was placed on the dues. The idea was to claim as many members as possible.

[10] Ethiopia, Department of Labor, *Annual Report* (Addis Ababa, 1965).

[11] "La grève de la Berhanena Selam," *Addis-Soir,* April 6, 1966.

Confederation of Ethiopian Labor Unions embarked upon
a three-month literacy campaign among its members. Now
the literacy campaign is on a continuing basis; the Confederation is still one of the main agents of the movement.

In response to the growth of the trade union movement,
the Ethiopian delegation to the Forty-seventh Conference of
the International Labor Organization at Geneva in 1963 included a representative of the Confederation of Ethiopian
Labor Unions. Ethiopia had belonged to the International
Labor Organization since 1923 but had remained aloof from
its affairs for many years. That same year the Confederation
of Ethiopian Labor Unions joined the International Confederation of Free Trade Unions and sent delegates to the
Fourth African Regional Labor Conference and the Thirteenth Congress of Soviet Trade Unions in Moscow.[12]

The main organizers of trade unionism were at first not
government officials but university graduates, who not only
instructed labor leaders in their spare time, but also translated trade union materials from European languages into
Amharic. These university graduates played an important
role in organizing the unions and later in helping them to
negotiate and to cope with their internal problems. Now the
Confederation of Ethiopian Labor Unions has among its
permanent staff more than a half dozen men with a master's
degree in labor administration. Educated in the United
States under the auspices of the Agency for International
Development, they met with American union leaders of the
AFL-CIO and were introduced to a politically conscious
trade union leadership. In 1965/66 some of these men
lobbied in Parliament on behalf of a government-sponsored
bill that was in the interest of the Confederation; this is,
however, the only known example of trade union contact

[12] Von Baudissin, "Labour Policy in Ethiopia," pp. 567–568.

with the legislative branch of the government. The main contributors to *The Voice of Labour* seem also to have come from the ranks of the university graduates. At first this link had great potentialities.

Since 1966, however, the government has had firm control over the unions through the bureaucracy of the slow-moving Labor Board of the Ministry of National Community Development and through the staffing of the Confederation of Ethiopian Labor Unions, which upon settlement of the newspaper strike was widely publicized as "expressing wholehearted support for the recent steps taken by the Emperor by way of bringing about administrative reforms in the Government." [13] The young university graduates, who saw the movement's political potential have found that they have differing concepts from those of the older, more conservative bureaucrats, who see themselves as quasi-government employees. The government has observed a close scrutiny over the operations of the Confederation's administrators, while the Labor Board of the Ministry of National Development has been headed by Amde Mikael, an enlightened member of the nobility who is genuinely interested in the workers' welfare but is equally determined not to let the Confederation get out of hand politically. Nevertheless, as the monetized sector of the economy grows—the number of industrial plants in Ethiopia grew from 133 in 1958 to more than 275 in 1969—the number of workers will increase and the labor movement will develop a greater potential for political activity.

Statistics clearly reveal that Ethiopia is one of the most underdeveloped countries on the African continent. Ninety

[13] "Confederation of Trade Unions Supports Administrative Reforms," *Voice of Ethiopia,* April 7, 1966.

per cent of the population is engaged in subsistence agriculture unrelated to a money economy. Like many other agricultural lands, Ethiopia is mainly dependent on traditional
agriculture, which provides substantial harvests for its farmers, in some areas twice or three times a year. The rich soil
of the highland regions and the adequate rainfall ensure that
few go hungry, although in semiarid regions local areas can
suffer from drought-induced famine, as has been the case
historically in Tigre and Lasta. In arid regions what little
agriculture there is supplements a nomadic camel economy.

The great variations in soil, altitude, and land-formation
permit the cultivation of a wide range of tropical and temperate crops. Although half the land area of the country is
said to be arable, the Ethiopians have cultivated only 15 per
cent of it. Shifting patterns of cultivation in the past have
led to extensive deforestation. By Western standards the
Ethiopian farmer uses primitive methods; however, he does
use the plow, though a very shallow one.

By far the most popular crops are cereal grains, including
some varieties unknown outside Ethiopia. Barley, wheat,
sorghum, and teff are widely grown; in 1968 more than 5.3
million metric tons of cereals were produced.[14] Other important crops in the traditional agricultural sector include oil-
seeds, legumes, and vegetables. The production of fruit, for
which Ethiopia is well suited, is insignificant largely because
of a strong cultural food prejudice. Some subsistence farmers
also contribute to the production of coffee, sugar cane, and
chat (a mild narcotic highly prized by Muslims in Somalia,
Djibouti, Yemen, and elsewhere in southern Arabia) for the
money sector of the economy.

Agricultural experts believe that with improved technology
the Ethiopian farmer could make his country the granary of

[14] United States Department of Agriculture, *The Agricultural Situation in Africa and West Asia* (Washington, 1969), pp. 5–6.

Africa and the Middle East. A severe drought in 1965 and 1966 brought parts of the country to near famine conditions and necessitated the importation of food supplies under the United States Food for Peace plan, despite food surpluses in other regions of the country. By 1967, however, agricultural production was back to normal and in some areas surpassed production of predrought years. Unlike many other subsistence economies, the rate of growth in agricultural production has continued to exceed the rate of population growth. Total agricultural production has shown an impressive gain of almost 30 per cent in the 1959–1969 decennium, while per capita production for that same period shows an increase of 8 per cent.[15]

The traditional Ethiopian farmer also maintains large herds of livestock.[16] The traveler through the Ethiopian countryside has always been impressed by the huge numbers of domesticated animals, estimated at 75 million cattle, sheep, goats, donkeys, horses, mules, and camels. The pig, forbidden food for both Ethiopian Christians and Muslims, is virtually nonexistent. By far the most important animals are cattle, which number about 25.6 million, mostly of the short-horned zebu type, although occasionally one comes across cattle with lyre-shaped long horns reminiscent of the original cattle population of northeast Africa. In fact, Ethiopia has the ninth largest cattle population in the world. In the drier Muslim lowlands cattle give way to camels. Yet despite the abundance of domestic animals and the potential for exports, meat animals do not find their way into the export market. Although agriculture accounts for about 65 per cent of Ethiopia's gross domestic product, which in 1968 was about $1.3

[15] *Ibid.*, p. 45.

[16] Ethiopia, Ministry of Finance, *Statistical Abstract, 1965* (Addis Ababa, 1965), p. 53; United Nations, *Statistical Yearbook, 1968* (New York, 1969), Table 36.

billion, per capita gross domestic product is estimated to be about $55, the same figure given in United Nations' estimates for 1958.[17] Thus, despite the increase in agricultural production, there has been no appreciable change in the economic status of the Ethiopian farmer in the past decade.

In terms of a money economy, Ethiopia is poor. Industry is relatively new in Ethiopia. Until the mid-1930's the Ethiopian economy had grown at a much slower rate than the economies of colonial Africa. The first infusion of capital for the development of agricultural and mineral resources occurred during the brief Italian occupation of the country. Only in recent years has the nonsubsistence sector of the economy, which produces about 35 per cent of the gross national product, begun to grow. In 1958 there were 165 industrial establishments in Eritrea and only 55 in the rest of the empire. Three years later there were only 178 industrial establishments in all Ethiopia (excluding mining, construction, coffee- and grain-cleaning firms), of which only 83 were located in Eritrea. These establishments employed approximately 29,000 Ethiopians and 900 foreigners. In 1964, 111 industrial establishments employed 32,864 Ethiopians and 691 foreigners. The statistics clearly show the economic deemphasis of Eritrea as Italians gradually withdrew from that province, the disappearance of smaller uneconomic firms, and the importance, though declining, of foreigners in managerial posts. Today there are more than 55,000 salaried employees engaged in more than 275 establishments.[18]

[17] Groupe d'Assistance pour le Développement, *Annexe technique document numéro 5* (Tokyo: July, 1961); United States Department of Commerce, *Market Profiles for Africa* (Washington: July, 1969), p. 12.

[18] Ethiopia, Ministry of Finance, *Statistical Abstract, 1963* (Addis Ababa: Commercial Printing Press, 1963), pp. 11–12; *Statistical Abstract, 1965*, p. 59; United States Department of Labor, *Labor Law and Practice in the Empire of Ethiopia* (Washington, 1966), pp. 6, 52; United Nations, *Statistical Yearbook, 1968*, Table 82.

The most significant industries in Ethiopia are electric power, sugar cultivation and refining, salt, beer, cotton yarn and textiles, and cement. Between 1959 and 1969 the production of electricity, for the most part a government-owned industry, increased from 88.7 million kw-h. to more than 300 kw-h.[19] An increase of 22 per cent in 1960–1961 alone was due to the completion in 1960 of the Koka Dam project near the capital.

Because sugar and cotton imports were high, the government encouraged the growth of cotton and sugar cane in suitable areas of the country and the promotion of the appropriate manufacturing industries. In 1950 a Dutch firm received a concession to establish a sugar plantation at Wonji in the Awash River Valley not far from Addis Ababa, and after a refinery came into production in 1957, Ethiopia no longer needed to import great quantities of sugar.[20] Because the demand for sugar has greatly risen, Wonji's production since 1965 has occasionally been supplemented by importing sugar. So successful was this sugar venture that in July, 1967 the International Finance Corporation, an affiliate of the World Bank, agreed to invest $9 million in a $22.5 million sugar project co-sponsored by Dutch investors and the Ethiopian government. By 1970 the projected sugar plantation and refinery should provide 47,000 tons of white sugar annually, in addition to the more than 60,000 tons currently consumed.

A similar program has been followed in cotton and textiles. At Tendaho in the lower Awash Valley, Mitchell Cotts and Company, a British firm, has been given a plantation concession; company officials confidently predicted in 1963 that they would be able to supply Ethiopia's entire cotton

[19] *Statistical Abstract, 1965,* p. 76; *Statistical Yearbook, 1968,* Table 147.

[20] H. P. Huffnagel, *Agriculture in Ethiopia* (Rome: Food and Agricultural Organization of the United Nations, 1961), pp. 260–268.

needs within a few years. Indeed, Ethiopian cotton production expanded from 2,000 metric tons to 8,000 metric tons in the decade from 1959 to 1969. An unexpectedly large increase in domestic consumption of cotton goods took place, however, and despite this fourfold increase, Ethiopia's imports of cotton from the United States alone amounted to more than $1 million in 1967.[21]

Nevertheless, the government regards its cotton program as successful, and in 1969 the Ethiopian National Development Company concluded an agreement with Elda, an Israeli company, for the concession of a 5,000-acre cotton plantation 125 miles south of Addis Ababa. To meet the increased demand for textiles, the Awash Cotton Processing Company, an Ethiopian firm, announced plans in 1969 to construct two additional cotton-ginning plants in the middle Awash Valley and in Gondar. Thus, both domestic production and imports, with the aid of foreign technical assistance and capital, have contributed to the growth of textile manufacture, Ethiopia's largest industry.

The Emperor's government has sought to promote selective industrial development so that modernization will take place under its supervision. To accomplish its goals, the government has relied on investment from foreign sources, carefully balancing American, West European, East European, Japanese, and other investments to avoid becoming dependent on any one foreign power. In 1964, for example, the Ethiopian government concluded an oil exploration agreement with the American-owned Gulf Oil Company, an agreement with the Soviet government to construct an oil refinery at Assab, and an agreement with the Fuji Spinning Company and the Marubeni-Sida Trading Company of Japan to ex-

[21] *Statistical Abstract, 1965,* pp. 99–118; *The Agricultural Situation in Africa and West Asia,* p. 71.

pand the capital and double the production of the state-owned Cotton Company of Ethiopia. In subsequent years the Yugoslavs constructed a large cement plant at Addis Ababa, an American firm explored the possibilities of developing Ethiopian potash deposits in Dankalia, and a British firm was awarded a contract for a 10,000-ton silo and grain handling plant operated by the Ethiopian Grain Corporation. When the oil refinery came into production in 1967, the government announced that it was awarding exclusive rights for the Russian-built plant's annual output to four Western oil companies: Shell (British-Dutch), Mobil East Africa (American), Total Mer Rouge (French), and AGIP (Italian). In 1969 the Ethiopian Metal Tools Company, a joint project of the Ethiopian and Polish governments, began the manufacture of hammers, axes, pickaxes, shovels, and other tools previously imported, while the construction of a 65 per cent Czech-financed tire company was also announced. By 1971 the tire factory was to open with an initial production of 60,000 tires and 45,000 inner tubes, or an estimated 60 per cent of local demand. The Czechs have also financed a company that produces rubber and canvas shoewear; its output of more than 2,000 pairs daily will be more than sufficient to meet Ethiopia's present requirements of 250,000–300,000 pairs per year. In this same vein of autarchy, the Ethiopian Investment Corporation negotiated with NFC International, an American company, for the construction of a factory to manufacture bottles and other glass products.

Not all attempts at economic development have been successful. Mitchell Cotts and Brooke Bond formed an Ethiopian Tea Estate Share Company in 1964 and established a pilot scheme in Kaffa Province. At first they found Ethiopia admirably suited for the production of most of the best strains of tea, but a change in the world market negated their efforts.

In 1969, before it had even started production, the company announced its dissolution. An even greater fiasco was Mitchell Cotts' meat-canning factory at Shashamane, which went bankrupt in 1965/66.

Impressive as Ethiopia's solid accomplishments are, it must be remembered that the catalogue of large industrial establishments is still slight. Compared to other areas of Africa, the modernization of the Ethiopian economy has proceeded slowly. Indeed, the slowness of economic progress has provided critics of the regime with some strong arguments for political reform. The governmental bureaucracy, though now technically well equipped, has failed, in fact, to achieve spectacular breakthroughs or to arouse enthusiasm for economic change among tradition-minded peasants or confidence among the progress-minded new elites of university students, workers, military, and young government bureaucrats.

Ethiopia is still barely on the threshold of modern economic development. The total value of exports in 1929 was approximately $5.6 million, of which coffee, much of which grew wild, comprised 58 per cent and cattle hides 28 per cent. In 1945, the figure had risen to $15.2 million, coffee accounting for 45 per cent of this figure. In 1968, Ethiopia's trade totaled an estimated $246 million.[22] Coffee continues to be the major export, accounting for 50–60 per cent by value. Ethiopia, Africa's fourth largest producer of coffee, supplies about 11 per cent of Africa's total coffee production and about 3 per cent of the world's coffee trade and produc-

[22] Ethiopia, Ministry of Commerce and Industry, *Economic Progress of Ethiopia* (Addis Ababa: East African Standard, for the Ministry, 1955), pp. 88–90; *Statistical Abstract, 1963,* pp. 61–66; *Statistical Abstract, 1965,* pp. 99–118; United States Department of Commerce, *Foreign Economic Trends: Ethiopia* (Washington: March, 1969), p. 2.

tion.[23] The particular kind of coffee exported by Ethiopia, unwashed arabica, competes with Brazilian production, and is highly susceptible to fluctuations in the world market. Ethiopian trade is thus unhealthily based upon a single crop.

At the 1969 meetings of the International Coffee Council, which fixes export quotas for coffee-producing countries, Yilma Deressa, Minister of Commerce and Industry, pointed out Ethiopia's dilemma: between 1953 and 1968 the purchasing power of one pound of coffee dropped 50 per cent. Illegal quota evasions and large inventories held by Latin American producers work to the disadvantage of Ethiopia. Other kinds of coffee, like the Colombian milds grown in Kenya and Tanzania and other mild arabicas grown in Burundi and Rwanda, sell at higher prices per pound than the unwashed arabica exported by Ethiopia, which in turn commands a higher price than the African robustas grown in Congo-Brazzaville, Ghana, Guinea, Liberia, Nigeria, Portuguese Africa, Sierra Leone, and Uganda. But the Ethiopians are hardly in a good bargaining position, and regardless of their position, world demand for coffee has not increased significantly without threatening the pricing system. Consequently, the International Coffee Council fixed a global quota for 1969/70 of 46 million bags of coffee, or 1.8 million bags fewer than in 1968/69. Evidently the limit to the expansion of the world coffee market will also have an adverse effect on the growth potential of coffee in the Ethiopian economy.

Ethiopia's other major source of foreign exchange is the exportation of skins and hides, which bring in more than $8 million annually. Oilseeds and cereals comprise the bulk

[23] *Statistical Yearbook, 1968,* Table 30; United Nations Conference on Trade and Development, *Commodity Survey, 1968* (New York, 1968), pp. 18, 29.

of the other exports. An additional source of revenue has been the export of chat, which brings in more than $1.5 million each year.[24]

The principal importers of Ethiopian goods in 1968 were, in order of importance, the United States (which purchases most of Ethiopia's coffee and more than doubled the value of its imports between 1961 and 1969), West Germany, Saudi Arabia, Italy, Japan, and Great Britain. Only since 1960 has Japan surged ahead as a major customer of Ethiopia, while Lebanon, Israel, the United Arab Republic, and Yugoslavia have also been important trading partners.[25] The major suppliers, again in order of importance, were Italy, the United States, West Germany, Japan, and Great Britain. For a while Japan occupied second place as Ethiopia's chief source of imports, displacing many imports from India (which also suffered from the expansion of the Ethiopian cotton industry), and forcing the United States temporarily into third place.

The pattern of Ethiopia's imports has undergone change as a result of the government's policy of selective industrialization, not only in sugar and cotton, but also in petroleum products. Since the end of 1967 the Assab refinery has met most of the country's national needs, although Ethiopia must import increasing quantities of crude oil, as well as lubricating oils and some specialty items. Ethiopia is also dependent on the developed countries for motor vehicles, machinery, and metals and metal goods. Since 1957 machinery imports have virtually trebled. This dependence on imported machine goods and the susceptibility of Ethiopian exports to world market conditions (and, since 1967, to the

[24] *Statistical Abstract, 1965,* p. 117.
[25] L. Wohlgemuth, *Etiopiens Ekonomi* (Uppsala: Nordiska Afrikainstitutet, 1967), p. 24.

closure of the Suez Canal) has given Ethiopia a trade deficit in recent years. In 1967, for example, exports were valued at $101 million and imports about $143 million, while in 1968 the figures were $105 million and $130 million respectively.[26]

Other African nations have held only a minute share of the total value of imports and exports. It is worth noting, however, that despite poor transportation facilities and a disputed border, Ethiopian trade with the neighboring countries of Kenya and the Somali Republic tripled between 1957 and 1961 and has shown relatively vigorous growth since then.

The road system of Ethiopia requires much development if the wealth of rural Ethiopia is to aid national economic growth. The once extensive Italian colonial road system deteriorated after the Italian occupation ended, and extensive repairs were required to make the existing roads passable for motor vehicles. Additions to the network were built by the Imperial Highway Authority, and today roads connect most provincial capitals with Addis Ababa. Few of these roads are paved, however; many of them are gravel, and others are passable only in the dry season.

The main highway axis runs from Addis Ababa to Asmara and has branches leading from Kombolcha near Dessie to Assab, from Asmara to Massawa, and from Adigrat to Gondar and Lake Tana. An all-weather road has been opened from Addis Ababa to Gondar via Debra Markos and Bahr Dar. There are also important routes leading from Addis Ababa southwest to the coffee regions of Kaffa Province and south to those of Sidamo Province. An all-weather highway system is slowly penetrating beyond Jimma into the remote southwest, and a planned Addis Ababa–Nairobi highway will pro-

26 *Statistical Abstract, 1963,* pp. 42–44; *Statistical Abstract, 1965,* pp. 99–118; *Market Profiles for Africa,* p. 12.

vide a link with Kenya. In 1968 the highway program was bolstered by a $27 million loan from the World Bank, the International Development Association, and the Swedish government for a four-year highway program costing $38.4 million. This would include construction of a highway into the middle Awash Valley, where cotton and sugar plantations have been so successfully developed. The following year a loan of $35 million from West Germany permitted the government to begin construction of a 240-mile road from Dilla in Sidamo to Moyale on the Kenya border, the Ethiopian segment of the Addis Ababa–Nairobi highway.

According to the Imperial Highway Authority there are approximately 4,100 miles of all-weather roads in Ethiopia (of which less than 1,000 miles are asphalted) and 10,700 miles of other roads. But even today less than 20 per cent of the country lies within twenty miles of all-weather roads. In fact, more than half the country lies more than twenty miles from roads of any kind. Not surprisingly, fewer than 38,000 motor vehicles are registered in Ethiopia, including about 9,000 commercial vehicles, and of this total about two-thirds are to be found in Addis Ababa.[27]

The main railway line, extremely important for the transportation of export goods, runs from Addis Ababa to the port of Djibouti in the French Territory of the Afar and Issa, a total of some 476 miles. A shorter line runs from the port of Massawa to Asmara and on to Adigrat, a total of 184 miles. In 1965 the French government agreed to underwrite 70 per cent of the cost of a $20 million rail spur, 180 miles long, linking the main rail line with the coffee-producing areas of Sidamo Province. Construction has not begun on this spur. It is doubtful whether the project will be implemented, for

[27] *Statistical Abstract, 1965,* pp. 78, 81; *Statistical Yearbook, 1968,* Table 155.

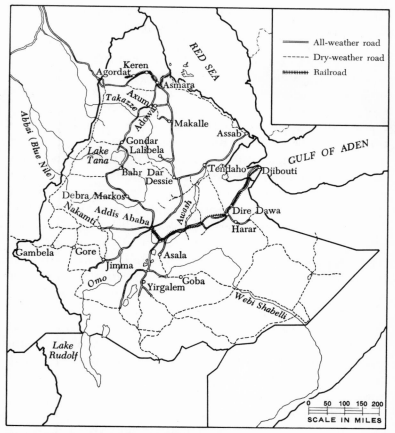

Legend:
- All-weather road
- Dry-weather road
- Railroad

RED SEA

Keren
Agordat
Takazze
Axum
Asmara
Adowa
Makalle
Assab
GULF OF ADEN
Gondar
Lalibela
Lake
Tana
Abbai (Blue Nile)
Bahr Dar
Tendaho
Djibouti
Dessie
Debra Markos
Awash
Dire Dawa
Nakamti
Addis Ababa
Harar
Gambela
Gore
Asala
Jimma
Omo
Yirgalem
Goba
Webi Shabelli
Lake
Rudolf

0 50 100 150 200
SCALE IN MILES

Map 5. Transportation in Ethiopia

it would be a costly duplication of an all-weather road that already exists.

In recent years Ethiopian Air Lines has played a major role in connecting distant parts of the country, and air transport, which is highly developed, is of unusual importance in this otherwise highly underdeveloped country.[28] The airplane links 39 points within Ethiopia and offers service between Ethiopia and sixteen other countries. Air cargo transportation has grown at the rate of from 20 to 33 per cent annually since 1963. Today an airplane flight of a few hours can accomplish what formerly took as much as thirty days of travel by mule or foot. But in so mountainous a country topography, climate, and costs limit what air travel and transport can contribute. The economic development of Ethiopia, as well as its political unity, is greatly dependent on the expansion of its communications and transportation system.

As the Ethiopian government expanded its activities in the years after World War II the state budget increased steadily. The total government revenue of $11.1 million in fiscal 1943 increased to $24.7 million in 1949, $79.8 million in 1962, and an estimated $185 million in fiscal 1969. Significantly, this income represents ordinary revenues, exclusive of foreign loans and credits, which have ranged from $20 million in 1961 to an estimated $62 million in 1969. In the same period, government expenditures rose from $10.7 million in fiscal 1943 to $27.6 million in 1949, $101.2 million in 1962, and an estimated $268 million in fiscal 1969 (an ordinary budget of approximately $200 million and a capital expenditures budget virtually entirely underwritten by foreign aid). Thus, government revenues and expenditures have

[28] The genesis of air transport in Ethiopia is detailed in T. Geiger, *TWA's Services to Ethiopia* (Washington: National Planning Association, 1959).

been increasing at an average rate of about 15 per cent per year, an index both of government commitment to economic development and of increasing government marshaling of Ethiopia's internal fiscal resources.[29]

Until 1965/66 the Ethiopian government did not practice deficit financing to any great extent and maintained a balanced budget. In fiscal 1965, expenditures exceeded revenue by only $2.5 million. Given the underdeveloped economy of the country, it is possible that the government's conservative fiscal policy, so attractive to private investors from abroad, actually limited the expansion of the economy. Only in 1963 did the government issue its first bonds, a first step toward increasing public financing of development projects. Then, in 1969, the government established a Treasury Bill Tender Board of officials from the Ministry of Finance and the National Bank to supervise the award of Ethiopia's first treasury bills. A limit of $15 million was placed on the amount issued in fiscal 1969 and $20 million in fiscal 1970; thereafter the government would issue 93-day bills in amounts up to 25 per cent of the ordinary revenues for the preceding fiscal year. The breakdown of *published* major budgetary expenditures for 1967/68 was: Defense, 17 per cent; Interior, 10 per cent; Education, 9 per cent; Public Debt, 7 per cent; Public Health, 4 per cent; Public Works, 4 per cent; Mining and Agriculture, 3.5 per cent; Finance Ministry, 2.5 per cent; Palace, 1.3 per cent; and Church, .05 per cent. Impressively enough, 20 per cent of the budget, or $46.4 million, was

[29] *Economic Progress of Ethiopia,* pp. 103–107; *Statistical Abstract, 1963,* pp. 90–93; *Statistical Abstract, 1965,* p. 141; "The Ethiopian Budget for the Year 1965–66," *Ethiopia Observer,* X, no. 3 (1966), pp. 192–198; Eli Ginzberg and Herbert A. Smith, *Manpower Strategy for Developing Countries: Lessons from Ethiopia* (New York: Columbia University Press, 1967), pp. 25–29, 86; *Market Profiles for Africa,* p. 12.

destined for capital expenditures in economic development.[30] "Capital expenditures," however, is partly a contingency budget for deficits in the operating budget.

Since 1950, Ethiopia has received more than $584 million in foreign loans and credits. As of 1969, Ethiopia's creditors were the United States ($211.9 million, of which $14.5 million had been repaid), the Soviet Union ($100 million), the International Bank for Rehabilitation and Development and its affiliates ($120.7 million), Yugoslavia ($15.4 million), France ($14.3 million), Czechoslovakia ($11.6 million), West Germany ($46.1 million), the United Kingdom ($6.4 million), Sweden ($5.8 million), Italy ($662,000), Belgium ($400,000), and Israel ($114,000). For the most part, the government has used foreign loans and credits to develop a modern army and for specific projects, like roads, telecommunications, a development bank, technical surveys, port facilities, the Assab oil refinery, hydroelectric installations, mining equipment, a cement factory, a shoe factory, agricultural machinery, and woolen mills. Italian war reparations amounting to $16 million underwrote the cost of the Koka Dam hydroelectric project and textile plants. Ethiopian dependence on foreign capital is striking, but so too is its policy of avoiding excessive dependence on any single foreign creditor.[31]

In Addis Ababa four daily newspapers are published, two in Amharic, and one each in English and French. The Ethio-

[30] *Statistical Yearbook, 1968,* Table 199.

[31] Lipsky, *Ethiopia,* pp. 318–319; *Statistical Abstract, 1963,* pp. 90–91; "U.S. Aid to Africa through 1967," *Africa Report,* June, 1967, pp. 12–13; Krishna Ahooja, "Development and Legislation in Ethiopia," *Ethiopia Observer,* X, no. 4 (1966), p. 317; House of Representatives, *Foreign Assistance Act of 1969: Hearings* (Washington, 1969), pp. 826–828.

pian Patriotic Association, an organization of veterans of the war against the Italians, publishes *Ya-Ityopya Dems*; an English version, the *Voice of Ethiopia,* has been discontinued. A tabloid, *Dems* depends on foreign news agencies and official government releases for most of its news. The Ministry of Information publishes the *Ethiopian Herald, Addis Zemen* ("New Times," in Amharic), and *Addis-Soir.* The first three usually consist of eight pages of general reporting of world news and feature articles; *Addis-Soir* generally has four pages. The number of readers of *Ya-Ityopya Dems* is about 50,000 (based on a circulation of 10,000), while *Addis Zemen* (circulation, 20,000) has about 100,000 readers, the *Ethiopian Herald* (circulation, 8,000) about 25,000, and *Addis-Soir* (circulation, 3,000) about 9,000. In Addis Ababa there are also four weekly publications, *Ya-Zareitu Ityopya* and *Sendek Alematchin* in Amharic, *Addis Reporter* in English, and *al-Alam* in Arabic, with circulations of 18,000, 10,000, 6,000, and 5,000 respectively. Periodical literature includes *Menen,* a bimonthly Amharic magazine published by the Patriotic Association with a circulation of 5,000; *Sports Fana,* an Amharic-English sports magazine with a circulation of 15,000; *Wotadernia Gizew,* the Imperial Body Guard's Amharic bimonthly aimed at an estimated 9,000 readers in the military; and *Policena Ermjaw,* an Amharic bimonthly with a circulation of 40,000, a publication covering news of crime and features of interest to the police force.

In Asmara, where there is a greater Italian influence, there are three daily newspapers and two weekly publications: *Quotidiano Eritreo* (4,500), *Zemen* (Tigrinya and Arabic, 2,800), *Giornale dell'Eritrea* (1,000), *Mattino del Lunedì* (2,500), and *Lunedì* (2,200).[32] For the foreigner resident in

[32] *Statesman's Yearbook, 1968.*

Ethiopia it is difficult to keep abreast of current affairs because of the superficiality of much of the reporting. The reporting of domestic news is also inadequate, although the Ethiopian news agency, ENA, now has a staff of about fifty stationed throughout the country. In recent years the newspapers have printed strong editorials, though never critical of government administration of internal affairs.

At the time of the Third International Conference of Ethiopian Studies in 1966, the English-language edition of *Ya-Ityopya Dems* urged Ethiopian scholars to work in the cause of national unity and suggested,

There is a great urgency for future Ethiopian Ethiopicists not to repeat the same mistakes made by the European scholars. . . . Let us leave the writing of the histories of separate ethnic groups and divisions in the hands of foreign scholars and strengthen the foundation of modern Ethiopia by dealing with the history of the Ethiopian people taken as a whole. What must interest the Ethiopian more is the study of the Ethiopian—and one comes across the Ethiopian everywhere no matter whether one be in Axum, Gondar, Yirgalem, or Jimma.[33]

A more succinct statement of the government's policy of promoting national unity over ethnic and regional differences would be hard to find.

The monopoly of newspapers by governmental and paragovernmental offices extends to periodicals. In addition to publishing English and Amharic editions of *Menen*, the Patriotic Association has occasionally presented plays at its clubroom. Comparable to medieval morality plays in their simplicity, the Ethiopian plays try to instill a love of country and Emperor; they meet with a fair degree of success among

[33] *Voice of Ethiopia,* April 7, 1966.

the older patriots. The musical productions of the Patriotic Association are universally popular. The Ministry of Education also publishes several official periodicals, while the Ministry of Information sponsors *Addis Reporter* and an Italian-language magazine, *Sestante,* both of which document an official version of Ethiopia's political, economic, cultural, and social life. Apart from the official publications is the *Ethiopia Observer,* a monthly issued through the Institute of Ethiopian Studies, which deals with nonpolitical matters.

The government censors all materials printed in Ethiopia; since there are fewer than a dozen printing presses in the country, some of them government-owned, control is facilitated. Official laws and appointments are printed in the *Negarit Gazeta,* an official journal established in 1942. Although there is no official index of forbidden books, books critical of the country are rarely sold publicly. Occasionally the government has also banned foreign periodicals.

Bookshops are few. In Addis Ababa there is only one large bookstore. Significantly, it displays only a few dozen titles dealing with Ethiopia. A National Library was founded in 1944, but its facilities are too limited for a city the size of Addis Ababa. As the University College of Addis Ababa and the Haile Sellassie I University both grow, presumably their library facilities will augment the limited facilities available to the public at present. At the University the Institute of Ethiopian Studies has gathered an excellent collection of materials dealing with all aspects of Ethiopian culture and history.

Publications in Amharic have increased in the past two decades, but few works of quality have been produced. Ethiopian intellectuals have been critical of a government policy that tends to stifle creativity. But the Amharic language, with its ambiguities and opportunities for double and triple meanings, has permitted some writers to circumvent government restrictions. Particularly popular is the *qene,* a traditional form of Geez poetry adapted to the modern Amharic for purposes of political satire.[34] Here traditionalist scholars and university students who are beginning to learn the richness of expression in the national language have found an effective way to evade government censorship. But because the *qene* is so difficult for many of the younger writers to master, they are turning increasingly to the novel, short story, and play to voice their criticism of social and, less often, political matters. In smaller towns the literate element of the population is completely isolated from any contact with intellectual life other than the traditional Church-inspired paintings, poetry, and folk arts.

Radio Addis Ababa does not yet reach the whole country, which has approximately 100,000 radios. Most villages still do not have the proper receiving equipment. Programs are broadcast in Amharic, English, Swahili, and occasionally Somali, but the schedule of radio programming is not published in the daily newspapers. Like the press, the radio is a useful means of disseminating official information, and one can easily foresee the same kind of transistor-inspired revolution in communications in Ethiopia that has taken place in other once remote parts of Africa. In 1966 the government instituted television programming, which is still limited to the capital.

In communications, as in other areas, Ethiopia has been gradually introduced to one element after another of modern technologically oriented societies. It remains to be seen at

[34] Alemayyehu Moges, "Geez and Amharic Study without Qene is Incomplete," paper prepared for the Third International Conference of Ethiopian Studies, Addis Ababa, April, 1966. See also Levine, *Wax and Gold,* pp. 5–9, with which Alemayyehu Moges takes sharp issue.

what point the cumulative effect of government-sponsored change will cause basic irreversible changes in the structure of society and in the balance between the traditional and the modern sectors of the economy. When that happens, change will not be limited to society and economy, but will also manifest itself on the political scene.

CHAPTER 5

The Politics
of Stability

> You must remember that Ethiopia is like Sleeping
> Beauty, that time has stood still here for 2,000 years.
> We must take great care, therefore, not to overwhelm
> her with changes now that she is beginning to awaken
> from her long sleep.   —Haile Selassie [1]

Ethiopian political life today is an often confusing mixture
of traditional and nontraditional elements. It is full of contradictions and contrasts, and a great gap exists between
theory and practice. Diagnosis is difficult; there is still so
much that we do not know about Ethiopian politics. Accurate prognosis is problematic, for Ethiopia has been undergoing a period of transition in the past decade, entering
what may be called a political pre-take-off period.

If a slow modernization has taken place in Ethiopian society and in the country's economic life in accordance with
plans and policies formulated by the Emperor, the same
cannot be said about political life. Here is the one area where
the Emperor has tried hardest to maintain his own unchallenged authority. In introducing social and economic
reforms, he has done so with the idea of increasing the authority and power of the central government. If there was
to be disruption, it was to be at the expense of the regional
lords and the older aristocracy. For the central government,

[1] Henry de Monfreid, *Vers les terres hostiles de l'Ethiopie* (Paris:
Bernard Grasset, 1933), pp. 229–230.

however, social and economic change was envisioned as promoting political stability, a task in which this long-lived monarchy has not always been entirely successful.

The government of Ethiopia is essentially that of the Emperor Haile Selassie I, King of Kings, Elect of God, and, in the words of the Constitution of 1955, descendant "without interruption from the dynasty of Menelik I, son of the Queen of Ethiopia, the Queen of Sheba, and King Solomon of Jerusalem." Here traces of divine kingship still survive: "By virtue of His Imperial Blood, as well as by the anointing he has received, the person of the Emperor is sacred, His dignity is inviolable and His power indisputable." [2]

Haile Selassie has held power longer than any other political figure in the contemporary world. After coming to power in 1916 as regent at the age of twenty-four, he successfully prepared the way for his coronation as emperor in 1930. During his fourteen years as regent he demonstrated his political shrewdness by undercutting the power of all potential rivals to the throne and his political astuteness by pursuing a policy of modernization that saw Ethiopia join the League of Nations, abolish the slave trade, and lay the basis for increased effectiveness of his authority. In his years as regent and emperor he steadily undermined the power of traditional forces within Ethiopia and promoted the authority and bureaucratic apparatus of the central government. His enemies accuse the Emperor of extending the authority of the State in order to expand his own personal power, and certainly Haile Selassie enjoys more power than any previous emperor of Ethiopia. Until December, 1960, it could be pointed out that modernization was intended to increase the

[2] Articles 2 and 4, "Proclamation No. 149 of 1955: Proclamation Promulgating the Revised Constitution of the Empire of Ethiopia," *Negarit Gazeta*, XV, no. 2 (November 4, 1955).

stability of the regime, but other factors make the imperial power-state authority argument irrelevant.

Haile Selassie still depends to a great extent, however, on traditional politics.[3] In his early years his power was based on regional strength; he had assumed his father's place as governor of Harar in 1909. Like Menelik II and earlier monarchs, he has strengthened his position through matrimonial alliances. He has been more successful than any other ruler of Ethiopia in balancing the political elements that too easily could turn into palace intriguing. He has maintained himself in power through extraordinary powers of memory and attention to detail, a strong sense of timing, and use of ambitious and talented men of humble origins; he has appealed to the awe of the peasant for the sacred person of the king. Indeed, there is strong evidence that the quasi-divine kingship is the one institution that can successfully bind Ethiopia together.

Yet in his pronouncements and actions Haile Selassie has demonstrated that he has been less deeply attached than most Ethiopians to the *status quo*. This is borne out by an examination of his behavior as regent in the early years of his reign; after World War II he gave further evidence of a willingness to innovate. Although he came to power when the Christian Amhara and Tigreans had rallied against Lij Iasu, he has continually demonstrated his intention to act outside the historically narrow framework of a purely Christian "Abyssinian" Ethiopia.

In the four decades after the coronation of Haile Selassie the role of the emperor expanded immensely. To give Ethiopia stability, Haile Selassie had to curb the powers of the three traditional conservative elements which in the past had

[3] C. Clapham, "Imperial Leadership in Ethiopia," *African Affairs,* LXVIII, no. 271 (1968), pp. 110–120.

driven the country to the verge of civil war or had even destroyed the political entity, as in the early nineteenth century. Church, regional nobility, and military all have yielded to the inexorable political pressure from the center. In the process, the Emperor has done more than any other Ethiopian ruler to prepare the way for modernization and national unity.

Through a series of measures the Emperor has controlled the power of the conservative clergy for state purposes. As regent in 1929 he took the first step in securing the independence of the Ethiopian Orthodox Church from Alexandria by obtaining the right to invest four Ethiopian bishops who, like the Egyptian-born Abuna, had the power to ordain priests. In 1950 the Emperor successfully arranged for the installation of the first native Ethiopian Abuna, a move opposed by some members of the Ethiopian clergy. Finally, in 1958, the Ethiopian Church became completely independent of Alexandria. Fourteen bishops, one for each province, were appointed, with an Abuna elected from their own number but confirmed in office by the Emperor, and the hierarchy of the Church was reorganized.[4]

Independence from the Coptic Church of Egypt, however, has meant greater dependence on the State. The new organization of the Church corresponds to the political administration of the State. Moreover, the Constitution of 1955 defined the clergy as subordinate to the power of the Emperor, who is not only Head of State but also Defender of the Faith, Head of the Ethiopian Orthodox Church, and the only reigning Oriental Christian (Monophysite) monarch.[5]

During his reign the Emperor has completed the task of

[4] Articles 21, 126, and 127 of the Constitution of 1955.
[5] Nicholas, Archbishop of Axum, *Church's Revival: Emancipation from 1600 Years Guardianship* (Cairo: Costa Tsouma, 1955), pp. 21–22.

weakening the Church's hold over his subjects as a rival political force. In this he was aided by the events of the Italian occupation. Although the Abuna went into exile with the Emperor and two bishops were martyred by the Fascists, the other two Ethiopian bishops collaborated with the Italians.[6] Upon returning from exile the Emperor dealt strongly with those members of the Church hierarchy whose loyalty was suspect. Furthermore, in 1942 the Church was theoretically deprived of its exemption from land taxes and all temporal jurisdiction over Ethiopians. In practice, however, the Church continued to levy fines, conscript labor, and collect rents on lands it owned. All revenue from Church lands was supposed to go to a central treasury administered for the Church by the government.[7] Lastly, the Church's monopoly of education has ended, and the prestige of church schools has fallen. To modernize the Church along lines of his own choosing, the Emperor has encouraged the use of Amharic in place of Geez, and sponsored a new translation of the Bible from the ancient liturgical language into the Amharic vernacular. The founding of a Theological College in Addis Ababa was also intended to produce a loyal but more progressive group of leaders for the Church, although the Church indicated that it would not ordain graduates of the Theological College.

A devout man who believes in the revitalization of the Ethiopian Orthodox Church, the Emperor does not view the Church as the sole binding force for national unity. The Church may once have served as a political cement, but in late twentieth-century Ethiopia its conservatism has operated

[6] A. Del Boca, *La guerra d'Abissinia 1935–1941* (Milan: Feltrinelli, 1965), pp. 196, 203–204.

[7] George Lipsky *et al., Ethiopia, Its People, Its Society, Its Culture* (New Haven: HRAF Press, 1962), pp. 106, 188.

against modernization and its particularism has been a divisive force. The more than 170,000 clergymen in Ethiopia have been untouched by the stirrings for reform in other areas of Ethiopian life. Attempts to modernize the structure of the Church have failed, except for substitution of subservience to the state for dependency on the Coptic Church of Alexandria.[8] The modern Theological College graduated several dozen seminarians, not one of whom has entered the Orthodox priesthood. The Emperor even encouraged the university students to take the lead in pressing for the modernization of the Church through the *Haimanote Abew* (Faith of the Fathers), a student movement founded in 1958 for the purpose of changing the forms of congregational worship. At present this movement is nearly dormant at the University but has some adherents at the secondary-school level. In a flanking move, as head of the Church, Haile Selassie has called international conferences of the Monophysite churches of Alexandria, Syria, Armenia, and India to discuss their common problems and ways to update their religious institutions, but all this has been in vain to date.[9] Ethiopia's Church, divested of much of its influence in national affairs and unable to cope with the demands of modernizing elements, instead distrusts change and the unknown. Moreover, although the Emperor has partially tamed the Church, it is confident that its influence is still great on the

[8] H. J. Schultz, "Reform and Reaction in the Ethiopian Orthodox Church," *Christian Century*, LXXXV, no. 5 (January 31, 1968), pp. 142–143.

[9] The proceedings of the conference have been published by Oriental Orthodox Conference, Interim Secretariat, *The Oriental Orthodox Churches Addis Ababa Conference, January 1965* (Addis Ababa: Artistic Printers, 1965).

local level because of its large landholdings and the religious
devotion of the peasant.[10]

The abandonment of the Church as a pillar of political
unity marks a major change in the operation of the Ethiopian
state. In his words and deeds the Emperor has striven to
achieve political unity in the midst of religious pluralism.
The age-old struggle between Christianity and Islam in
Ethiopia has *officially* come to a halt. Few Muslims hold high
positions in the government today, although the door in
theory has been opened to them. In the name of national
unity, the Emperor has declared that Christian or Muslim,
all are Ethiopians. Whether all Muslims want to be Ethiopians, however, is doubtful. The continual resistance of
Muslims in Eritrea, Harar, Sidamo, Arussi, and Bale Provinces to the policy of national unity indicates that the end
of the religious struggle is only official. The road to religious
coexistence may prove to be as rough as Ethiopia's terrain.
Indeed, beginning in 1968 the government began to move
away in a practical vein from this policy. The government
has good reason to believe that its Muslim citizens have
divided loyalties and that it would be a safer policy to play
up to the Christians and against the Muslims.

The Emperor has also broken the power of the old nobility
as an independent political force, although to do so took almost forty years. As regent, Haile Selassie built up his own
local forces and revenues in Harar Province until he was in
a position to take command of the imperial army and bring

[10] D. N. Levine, *Wax and Gold: Tradition and Innovation in Ethio-
pian Culture* (Chicago: University of Chicago Press, 1965), pp. 181–183;
Richard Greenfield, *Ethiopia, A New Political History* (New York:
Frederick A. Praeger, 1965), pp. 36–39.

his own forces into Addis Ababa in 1926. In that same year he angered the provincial rulers of Gojjam, Amhara (Begemder), Tigre, and Shoa by suggesting that the provinces be administered by paid officials appointed by the Imperial Government. After his accession to the throne he faced a series of revolts by the nobility of Tigre and Gojjam, some of whom threw in their lot with the Italians in 1935 in order to preserve their traditional privileges.

Only after his restoration in 1941 did the Emperor find himself in an opportune position to check the nobility. In the aftermath of reconquest, the imperial forces directly under the control of the Emperor became stronger than the regional armies, which had been weakened by their opposition to or collaboration with the Italians. Since then the army has become an instrument of the State, and the nobility has lost its original character as a military aristocracy. To train a new group of military elite, Haile Selassie instituted the Imperial Body Guard.

After the loss of military power, the second blow to the nobility came in 1942 with the beginning of centralization of tax collection. The Ministry of Finance by law, if not completely in practice, became the sole collector of taxes. Shortly thereafter the Ministry of the Interior redrew provincial boundaries and assigned new governors to the new provinces. Thus the nobility lost a major source of wealth and has since been limited to the rents and income in kind from its own estates. These reforms deprived the nobility of its role as independent local agents for the central government. Because of the Emperor's new position of power, greatly augmented by the presence of British occupation forces, the old nobility had to yield. In some cases it was bought off by titles or assignments to diplomatic posts. In other cases nobles were raised to the powerless rank of senator and compelled to remain in Addis Ababa under the watchful vigilance of the government and far from their regional backers; sometimes they were made governor-generals of provinces far from their home base. In still other cases the Emperor has won the cooperation of nobles who have made the best of a bad situation.

The men who hold the highest offices and titles in the empire today are either members of the old nobility, relatives of the Emperor, or men who have risen on the basis of talent and loyalty. The old nobility, stripped of much of its power, still survives in significant ways on the local level. To control them the Emperor has given them offices, titles, and wives in the royal family.

Some of the members of the old nobility were themselves in the royal line; many of them are tied to the royal family by bonds of matrimony and have also forged marriage links among themselves. The late Ras Seyum of Tigre, for example, was a grandson of Emperor Yohannes IV; Ras Imru and Ras Kassa, as cousins of the Emperor, both had valid claims to the throne. Although some of their relatives who might have served as nuclei for political activity in Ethiopia prefer to live outside Ethiopia in self-imposed exile, others have found a place in the imperial system. Asrate Kassa, a fourth cousin of the Emperor and sole surviving son of Ras Kassa, has held the high office of president of the Senate and the important governorship of Eritrea; his extensive land-holdings give him a large income and local influence. He is married to a granddaughter of the late Empress Menen. A nephew, Amaha Aberra Kassa, has served as ambassador to Yugoslavia and governor-general of the important province of Begemder. Mangasha Seyum, son of Ras Seyum, is popular among those northern elements hostile to the regime. He was active in the Tigrean revolt of 1943, but because of his position in that key province and his noble origins, he was appointed Minister of Public Works in 1958 and now is governor-general of Tigre Province, where he has won an enviable reputation for his energetic policies. His mother was a daughter of Ras Darge, an uncle of Emperor Menelik. He is married to a granddaughter of the Emperor, Princess Aida, while his sister was once married to the Crown Prince, Asfa Wossen. Zawde Gabre Selassie, a grandson of Ras Seyum, has served as mayor of Addis Ababa, ambassador to the Somali Republic, and Minister of Justice. Ras Imru served as governor-general of Gojjam and of Begemder and then, in turn, as ambassador to Washington, New Delhi, and Moscow. It should not be overlooked that in the 1960 attempted coup the rebels nominated him as their apparently unwilling choice for Prime Minister.

A personal friend of the Emperor, Makonnen Endal-katchew, who died in 1963, served as mayor of Addis Ababa, governor-general of Illubabor Province, Minister of the Interior, Prime Minister from 1945 to 1957, and Senate president from 1957 to 1961. He was the holder of the title of Ras-Bitwoded, the highest honorific ever awarded outside the royal family. His son, Endalkatchew Makonnen, also served as Senate president, at one time was representative to the Bandung Conference and later ambassador to Great Britain; he also has been Minister of Commerce, Industry, and Development, and until recently headed the Ethiopian delegation to the United Nations. Endalkatchew Makonnen is a brother-in-law of Amaha Aberra Kassa. Still another noble family is represented by Andargatchew Massai, Ethiopia's representative to the League of Nations in 1923, one-time governor-general of Begemder, former viceroy in Eritrea, Minister of the Interior, and governor-general of Sidamo.

Andargatchew Massai is married to the Emperor's eldest daughter, Princess Tenagne Worq. All these men were loyal during the 1960 coup.

The Emperor has also raised men of humble and often non-Amhara origins to high positions. These men, dependent on the Emperor for their positions, have exhibited a strong loyalty and have been rewarded by office, rank, wealth, and marriage. General Merid Mangasha, largely responsible for the suppression of the 1960 coup, was discovered by the Emperor in exile in the Sudan shortly before Haile Selassie re-entered Ethiopia; by 1959 Merid had risen from aide-de-camp to Chief of Staff of the Army. He faithfully served as Defense Minister from 1961 until his death in 1966. Lieutenant-General Abeye Abeba, of fairly modest background, has served as governor-general of Wollega, Minister of War, ambassador to Paris, Minister of Justice, governor-general of Eritrea, and Minister of Interior, and became president of the Senate in 1964. In 1942 he married the Emperor's youngest daughter, Tsahai, shortly before her death. Aklilou Habte Wold also belongs to this aristocracy of loyal talent; through his competence he rose to become Minister of Commerce, Foreign Minister in 1943, Minister of Pen (i.e., Keeper of the Privy Seal, who coordinates all administration) in 1960, and Prime Minister in 1961. Similarly, Ketema Yifru, the Foreign Minister, was discovered by General Merid Mangasha and brought to the Emperor's attention. Lastly, there is Yilma Deressa, a British-educated Galla who has served as Minister of Finance, Minister of Commerce, ambassador to Washington, and Minister of Foreign Affairs. These are some of the men of the new nobility who have been disliked by the other new elements of Ethiopian society.

There has been much speculation about the nature of the newer elements in Ethiopian society. The products of postwar attempts at modernization, these include the younger, middle-level civil servants and university students and recent graduates who comprise a small but growing intellectual class, labor leaders, and members of the military, as well as a few Eritrean separatists.

Little evidence exists to indicate the positive aspirations of the first group. In informal discussions they exhibit a general distaste for the *status quo* and often sharply criticize the distribution of political power in the hands of the Emperor, the old families, and the aristocracy of privilege and loyal talent. Occasionally the landholding system has been the object of their complaints. From time to time they have also attacked the judicial and administrative systems for inefficiency and corruption. For them too much of Ethiopia is too far from modernization.

These impatient young men talk of having a greater share in national policy-making. Whether their impatience reflects their youth or indicates real disaffection, they regard Ethiopia as behind the times. Those who studied abroad are painfully aware of Ethiopian backwardness. For the most part, however, these young men cannot be labeled ardent nationalists or pan-Africanists. They are the generation caught between the dream of the future and the reality of the present. For them talk has been an adequate substitute for action. Significantly, they played no part in planning the 1960 coup, although many of them voiced sympathy for the aspirations of the rebels. Moreover, many of these young men are still tied to Ethiopia's past by family connections. In government service they rise with initial rapidity. Many of them have been recruited into the ranks of the new aristocracy. At present they seem to offer no political threat, but it remains to be seen how they would behave in a future crisis.

The second potentially active group is the military. Estimates of the size of the Ethiopian army range from 30,000 to 40,000 men.[11] The army has proved itself in Korea and the Congo, as well as in the continual fights against the Eritreans, Somali, and Arussi. Moreover, there is an important cadre of army and air force officers who have received the equivalent of a university education in officer-training school. Several thousand men have been exposed to American influence through training in Ethiopia and in the United States. Many of these men were the pick of secondary-school graduates who were arbitrarily assigned by the government to the military.

Originally the army was developed by the Emperor as a counterweight to the regional armies of the rases. Between 1947 and 1951, British officers trained the army; after that, Britain was supplanted by the United States, whose financial assistance has been a major factor in the expansion, equipment, and training of the Ethiopian army and in the creation of an air force and a navy. The Ethiopian government employs a few Swedish advisers and Israeli and Indian instructors, but United States influence predominates.

Today the army includes such services requiring highly sophisticated military training as tank and artillery battalions, antiaircraft batteries, a corps of combat engineers, and an airborne infantry. The American military mission, first established in 1954, has worked with the Ethiopian military down to the battalion level. Israeli training teams have given particularly valuable assistance at the company and battalion levels and in training the commando police in antiguerrilla tactics. Officers are prepared for modern military requirements at the Military Training College at Holetta near Addis Ababa and at the Haile Sellassie Military Academy in Harar.

In addition to American personnel, Swedish missions in

[11] *Africa Report,* January, 1964, pp. 8–9.

the past have trained the Ethiopian Air Force. Air force headquarters at Debra Zeit, also near Addis Ababa, include a training school and a central workshop. In the event of a political upheaval, the air force, with its more than 300 officers and approximately 1,800 men, will be a force to be reckoned with. Here everything is modern: Ethiopia's ground-attack, fighter, and reconnaissance squadrons are equipped with Swedish Saabs and American F-86 and F-5 jet aircraft—an impressive offensive-defensive force with considerable striking power that can be readily mobilized.

In contrast, the least developed of the military forces is the navy, with its one training ship (formerly a United States seaplane tender), two torpedo boats of Yugoslav origin, five patrol boats obtained from the United States, and two small landing craft. The navy has been assisted by a small staff of Norwegian, French, Indian, British, and American advisers and training officers. Many of the 210 officers and approximately 1,000 men who safeguard the Red Sea coast of a once-landlocked empire were trained at the Naval School at Massawa.

Augmenting the military in preserving internal security is a police force of an estimated 28,000. Germans have equipped and trained the police, a task once assigned to Americans. Israeli-trained commando police units have operated against Eritrean *shifta* (brigands) and presumably also against the elusive guerrillas of the Eritrean separatist movement that has continued to plague the military in northern Ethiopia.

After the liberation of Ethiopia from the Italians the Emperor promoted an Imperial Body Guard as an elite corps. The events of December, 1960 reveal that the Emperor had misplaced his faith in that military unit. At that time the army remained loyal and was the principal instrument for the suppression of the attempted coup. It is worth noting, however, that after the coup the army, asserting itself for the first time, demanded and received an increase in pay. Since 1960 the Emperor has encouraged the organization of the militia-like territorial army as a balance to the army.

These events have led some observers to infer some restlessness in the army. Certainly army officers have family connections, regional ties, and common school experiences with the civilian intelligentsia. The army is still an unknown factor, however, and appears less politically conscious than in other underdeveloped countries where a pattern of military coups has established itself. The American training of army officers has been technical and largely devoid of political content. If a political interest has developed in the officer corps, it has been through contact with other elements of Ethiopian society. Older officers, as loyal to the Emperor as members of the new aristocracy, still have considerable power. It may be that restlessness will first become apparent among the younger officer group. The air force, the elite branch of the military, may very well bear watching as a future political nucleus. Whatever happens, it would be politically naive to ignore the fact that the army, the air force, and the police are the only groups in Ethiopia today with organized strength sufficient to determine the outcome of a future crisis.

The third new element in the political process is in many respects a latter-day version of the traditional problem of regional separatism. The federation of Ethiopia and Eritrea in 1952 added to the empire a group of people politically more sophisticated, with a history of activity by more than a half-dozen political parties dating from 1947. Historically, the peoples of Eritrea—both Muslim and Christian—have had strong links with the rest of Ethiopia; Eritreans *are* Ethiopians. But in 1962, after the Assembly of Eritrea, which some observers regarded as packed by the Addis Ababa government, went through the necessary parliamentary motions, Ethiopia willingly annexed the province. Since annexation Eritrea has been less prosperous, and there has been general dissatisfaction. Political parties no longer exist, and political groupings have not been permitted to develop. Muslim and Christian Eritreans, often Tigrinya-speaking (Christian Eritreans are really Tigreans), resent the forced spread of the Amharic language and Amhara influence.

Ethiopia is determined to maintain firm control over Eritrea; Massawa and Assab are valued by the government. Eritrean dissatisfaction, however, is symptomatic of the tendencies toward regionalism in the empire and is symbolic of the constant threat to political stability from this quarter. It is ironic that just when the older problems of regionalism were being controlled by the central government, the annexation of Eritrea revived them. Eritrean separatism, especially in times of trouble, could easily encourage separatist feelings elsewhere in the empire, in Tigre or Gojjam Provinces, if left unchecked. This new element in Ethiopian politics also complicates relations with Arab states, inasmuch as Christian Ethiopians of all educational levels suspect the motives of the Arabs in the Red Sea and in the Horn of Africa, overestimate their capabilities toward Ethiopia, and consequently speak of the threat of Muslim encirclement.

Since the suppression of Eritrean political parties, Ethiopia has maintained its peculiar identity as a state without political parties. In a continent that has seen a proliferation of political movements, the absence of modern political organizations is striking. No provision is made in the Constitution for political parties, though there is no outright ban. Imperial appointment has prevented the Senate from becoming a nucleus of party activity. Similarly, in the elections of 1957 —the first in Ethiopian history—candidates for the Chamber of Deputies were carefully screened and generally were not interested in running on party tickets.

The lack of modern political sophistication on the part of the peasant masses means that the proper environment for a mass party is yet to be created. Both traditional and new elements of Ethiopian society show remarkable political astuteness in everyday situations, and traditional Ethiopian politics was highly developed; these two groups have not cared (or dared) to depart from the traditional bases of operations: personalism and factionalism. Not only the Emperor but also the aristocracy have strong tendencies toward personal rule. This is true on the local level as well as on the regional and national levels. The tendency toward factionalism, which has precluded the development of a political party, has splintered political groupings to the point of petty intrigue or impotence. In such an environment Haile Selassie has proved a master of political manipulation. He has outmaneuvered rivals by their own methods. To this he has added a generous amount of paternalism and personal interest in the few thousands who comprise the Ethiopian elites. An extensive information-gathering service for both palace and government enables him to remain closely informed about the activities of potential political activists.

The Ethiopian political scene is singularly devoid of political slogans. No external threat exists to unite the country. The colonial experience was too brief to produce the kind of nationalism found elsewhere in Africa. Thus, one observes a great deal of political intriguing but little of the political activity characteristic of other African states. The sole rallying point of the state has become the person of the Emperor. The army, although it hesitantly took a position in the 1960 coup and later flexed its muscles by demanding a raise in pay, has remained apolitical, and the Emperor is the only basis for unified political action on a national scale.

Through elections to the Parliament the rural masses may slowly be brought into the modern political arena. For the first parliamentary elections in 1957, 2.6 million of 3.7 million registered voters went to the polls. There was no significant change in the 1961 elections, but in 1965, when the third parliamentary elections were held, the official number of registered voters swelled to 5.1 million, of whom 3.2 million actually voted. Curiously enough, the turnout was lightest in Addis Ababa, where one should have expected the greatest political awareness; educated Ethiopians tend to dismiss the Parliament out of hand without knowledge of how Parliament actually behaves. The highest participation was in Kaffa, Eritrea, Gamu-Gofa, Wollo, and Arussi, while the least interest in the elections was generated in Sidamo, Wollega, and Bale. In 1969 there were 5,249,000 registered voters; more than 3,600,000 cast their ballots. The parliamentary election of 1969 apparently followed the same pattern. Al-

Table 1. Percentage of registered voters participating in the parliamentary election of 1965.[12]

Arussi	70	Gamu-Gofa	72	Kaffa	81	Tigre	64
Bale	54	Gojjam	62	Shoa	66	Wollega	51
Begemder	68	Harar	60	Addis Ababa*	25	Wollo	72
Eritrea	76	Illubabor	62	Sidamo	42		

* Addis Ababa comprises a separate electoral district.

[12] Ethiopia, Ministry of Finance, *Statistical Abstract, 1965* (Addis Ababa: Commercial Printing Press, 1965), p. 35.

though Parliament has been powerless to initiate large-scale political or administrative reform, voter dissatisfaction may be seen in the great turnover of parliamentary representatives after each election. Each parliament's lower house has had a carry-over of less than 40 per cent of the previous session. This is partly due to government pressure on certain candidates potentially hostile to the regime, usually the provincial authorities or the Church acting independently, less often by the direct intervention of the central government's Ministry of the Interior. It is also indicative, however, of an awareness by voters of the ineffectiveness of Parliament in meeting the demands of both the electorate and its representatives. Naturally, the great number of new representatives after each election only perpetuate the situation and make for lack of continuity. In such circumstances it is virtually impossible for an *esprit de corps* to develop in the legislature.

In maintaining Ethiopia as a no-party state, the Emperor has walked a tightrope between traditionalism and modernism, stability and change, direct and indirect controls. We have seen how he has undermined much of Ethiopian traditionalism. At the same time he has often declared that change must be firmly rooted in the traditional values of Ethiopian culture—as he defines it. Undeniably, the modernization that has taken place in Ethiopia has strengthened the ancient institution of the monarchy. In modernizing, however, new elements making for change have been created. How well they can continue to be controlled remains to be seen. Whether Ethiopia will continue to have the outward appearance of political stability is dependent on the present regime's ability to institute change sufficient to placate its critics without yielding real power to them.

Lastly, the *status quo* within Ethiopia received to some

degree the official approval of the Heads of the African States in assembly at Addis Ababa in May, 1963, when Ethiopia emerged as a possible leader on the African continent. Had an important African state chosen to criticize Ethiopia for the absence of those institutions considered characteristic of most African countries, then the authority of the Emperor at home would have been shaken. The Emperor has been welcomed into the fold of African unity perhaps because his position in Ethiopia, though without benefit of a mass movement, nevertheless has some analogies to that of leaders of one-party states where the government is clearly dominant over any political movement.

Realities of political life in Ethiopia contrast sharply with the formal structure of Ethiopian politics, the Constitution of 1955. This basic law gives Ethiopia the appearance of a constitutional monarchy guaranteeing the fundamental human rights so often mentioned in Western liberal constitutions. Like its predecessor, the Constitution of 1931, the first in the history of Ethiopia, the Constitution of 1955 establishes a constitutional monarchy, but not in the Western sense of the phrase. Article 26, for example, states "the Sovereignty of the Empire is vested in the Emperor and the supreme authority over all the affairs of the Empire is exercised by Him as Head of State." In reality, then, the Constitution provides for a monarchy that would have existed otherwise. Described by some as medieval or Byzantine, by others as an autocracy or a benevolent despotism, in practice it amounts to a constitutionalized absolutism.

When one remembers that Ethiopia is one of the few surviving absolute monarchies in this world, it comes as no surprise that the Constitution assigns to the Emperor his traditional privileges, that is, the right to determine the organization, powers, and duties of all executive and administrative offices. He has full powers over the armed forces, including the right to declare martial law or a national emergency. "Supreme direction of the foreign relations of the Empire" also belongs to the Emperor, who alone can ratify international treaties. Only the Emperor can confer and withdraw titles and honors. He can initiate legislation; his is the sole right to maintain justice. Thus, constitutional limitations on the powers of the Emperor are few and vague. The role of the Emperor may be defined in modern terms, but his real power is no different from that of former emperors who never heard of the concept of limited monarchy.

The Constitution borrows freely from European and American models. Within the limits of the law, never clearly defined, the Constitution provides for freedom of religion, speech, assembly, and the press, and speaks of the due process of law and the basic rights of life, liberty, and property. In accordance with ancient tradition, Article 63 states that all have the right to petition the Emperor in person. It would be difficult to find a more liberal statement of the rights and duties of the people. It would be more difficult to demonstrate that the peasant or nomadic population is even aware of the existence of the Constitution, let alone of the meaning of these rights. It is less difficult to discover that the government itself has not always respected the paper rights set forth in the Constitution.

A Cabinet, whose members are chosen and dismissed at the Emperor's will, is also mentioned in the basic law. Until 1966 Cabinet ministers were individually responsible to the Emperor, rather than to Parliament. In practice this arrangement tended to stifle individual initiative, yet the Emperor, who always had the final word, repeatedly encouraged his ministers to take the initiative. Even after the Emperor made the Cabinet responsible to the prime minister and gave him the right to select his own cabinet ministers, subject, of course, to the imperial veto, there was no appreciable change in the composition of the Cabinet. Since 1966, Haile Selassie's main interest has been foreign affairs, and he has apparently intervened less in the internal operations of his government. Like the Constitution, however, the Cabinet is still the Emperor's creation. Through it he has governed; through it he has introduced those reforms that he chose to introduce; and through it he has given Ethiopia a government whose stability is envied by some and deplored as inertia by others.

The administration of government business, always carefully supervised by the Emperor, is conducted by seventeen ministries: Pen, Foreign Affairs, Defense, Interior, Education, Justice, Finance, Public Health, Mines and State Domains, Agriculture, Public Works, Communications, Telegraphs and Posts, Commerce and Industry, Information and Tourism, National Community Development and Social Affairs, Land Reform and Administration, and the Imperial Court. The Emperor formerly held several ministries personally. Until the Cabinet reform of 1966, dealt with in the next chapter, he always held the portfolio of Education, his special interest.

According to the Constitution, the Cabinet can present legislative proposals to Parliament only with the approval of the Emperor. Ministers are required to answer before Parliament questions concerning their particular offices, and they are forbidden to have a conflict of interest between public and private affairs; critics of the government have said that this is a farce. In addition to the ministerial Cabinet, the Constitution provides for a Crown Council consisting of the Abuna, princes, ministers, the president of the Senate, and dignitaries selected by the Emperor. In the final analysis, the whole decision-making process is directed and controlled by the Emperor.

Article 76 of the Constitution calls for the annual convening of a salaried bicameral Parliament consisting of a Chamber of Deputies and a Senate. Legislative initiative, however, comes only from the Emperor or from a group of ten or more members of either chamber. In budgetary matters, all proposals must first be presented to the Chamber of Deputies. Deputies, elected for a four-year term by universal suffrage, must be Ethiopian, at least twenty-five years old, and own property in their home constituency. Senators, appointed by the Emperor for a six-year term, must be at least thirty-five years old, and a prince or other dignitary or a former high government official. The senators are to number no more than half the total number of deputies.

At present the Chamber of Deputies numbers 250, and there are approximately 125 senators. For a bill to become law, both chambers must approve it. In the event that the two chambers disagree, a joint session takes place. The senators, appointed by the Emperor, can then tip the balance in favor of the regime. Moreover, the president and two vice-presidents of the Senate are appointed by the Emperor, although the same officers in the Chamber of Deputies are elected by members of the Chamber from among their own number.

Elections, which were last held in 1969, were characterized then, as in the elections of 1957, 1961, and 1965, by the absence of political parties, little campaigning, nomination of "government" candidates, and the election of men who had strong local influence based on traditional regional interests. In the 1969 elections 70 per cent of the 5,249,000 registered voters voted for 250 deputies in a field of 2,000 candidates. More than two-thirds of the previous parliament's deputies were not returned to office. To date the Parliament has not functioned as an element in a Western-style system of checks and balances. More often than not, opposition to the Emperor within Parliament reflects petty regional cleavages and family rivalries rather than the nucleus of a true political opposition. It appears to be a clear example of the Emperor's policy of *divide et impera*. Since 1963, however, Parliament too has begun to awaken from Ethiopia's political lethargy, and the first signs of stirrings incompatible with the Emperor's politics of stability have become visible. Such was not the intent of the Constitution, which describes Parliament more as a body rubber-stamping legislation emanating from Haile Selassie.

The Constitution also provides for a Supreme Court and other courts as authorized or established by law. All judges are appointed and can be removed by the Emperor. Except in cases endangering public order or affecting public morals, courts must hold public sessions. Occasionally public executions take place for such crimes as murder and treason. The courts established by the government find themselves in a peculiar position vis-à-vis the traditional legal system. In theory, the laws of Ethiopia derived from such Geez books as the *Fetha Nagast* (Legislation of the Kings, based on Mosaic, Roman, and canonical law) and the *Serata Mangest* (Laws of the State) and from legislative enactments in religious books, like Zara Yaqob's Book of the Nativity, and royal chronicles. In practice, however, there has grown up a huge body of customary law which, like the Anglo-Saxon common law for many centuries, has not been written down. The criminal and civil codes promulgated in 1957 and 1960 are based on Western models, but to be effective in the eyes of Ethiopian litigants, the central courts must also take into account local precedent. Consequently, one of the main tasks of the Law School of Haile Sellassie I University is the compilation of cases tried in local courts, whether in matters of family law, land litigation, or other cases. On the lowest local level, justice is actually in the hands of traditional leaders: landowners in Amhara regions, religious judges in Muslim areas, and tribal elders or village chiefs elsewhere in the empire.

In addition to articles establishing Addis Ababa as the capital of the empire and Amharic as the official language, there are articles defining the Ethiopian Orthodox Church as the Established Church of the empire, supported by the State. Not unexpectedly, the Emperor, who must always be an adherent of that confession, has the right to legislate in all Church matters except monastic regulations and "other spiritual administrations." Envisaging the future development of Ethiopia, the Constitution declares all subsoil natural resources to be State Domain, as is—significantly—"all property not held and possessed in the name of any person, natural or juridical, including all land in escheat, and all abandoned property, whether real or personal, as well as all products of the subsoil, all forests and all grazing lands, watercourses, lakes and territorial waters."

The Constitution carefully states the powers and prerogatives of the Emperor and even goes so far as to detail the oaths of office for Emperor, Crown Prince, members of the Crown Council, and members of Parliament. Twenty-nine articles are devoted to the rights and duties of the people, ten to the ministers of the empire, and thirty-two to the legislative chambers, yet virtually nothing is said about the administration of the empire outside the central government in Addis Ababa. Article 27 briefly states: "The Emperor determines the organization, powers and duties of all Ministries, executive departments and the administrations of the Government and appoints, promotes, transfers, suspends and dismisses the officials of the same." Oddly enough, the Constitution has nothing else to say about the provinces and their administration. As the Emperor's greatest accomplishment has been the consolidation of the government and its extension into the provinces on a scale unprecedented in Ethiopian history, this brevity is all the more surprising.

The main task of provincial administration to the present has been to ensure that the centralization of authority continues and that the provinces remain loyal to the Emperor. Ethiopia is divided into fourteen provinces, some of them roughly corresponding to older regional divisions. Gojjam, for example, is clearly delimited by the gorge of the Blue Nile, while Eritrea has the boundaries of the former Italian colony. The other provinces are Arussi, once the seat of a powerful sultanate; Bale, once a part of the province of Harar; Begemder, an Amhara region of which Gondar is the capital; Gamu-Gofa; Harar, the largest province in the empire; Illubabor, with its Negroid population; Kaffa, a province thought to have given its name to coffee; Shoa, the center of political activity; Sidamo, rich in coffee lands; Tigre, the northern political rival of Shoa; Wollega, inhabited mostly by Galla; and Wollo, once an influential Galla area, but now with its redrawn borders a deliberate mixture of Amhara, Galla, and Danakil peoples.

All provinces are ruled in the Emperor's name by governor-generals, some of whom spend their time in Addis Ababa and not in the provincial capitals. The affairs of the provinces are usually managed by younger men assigned to the provincial administration by the Ministry of the Interior. The borders of the provinces have been shifted about from time to time in the past sixty years in a conscious attempt to destroy the cohesion of older political units. Thus, the region of Amhara, which loomed large in Ethiopian history, has been divided between Begemder and Wollo Provinces. In making such changes, the Emperor has pursued a policy of undermining the power of regional leaders and replacing them with bureaucrats loyal to the State.

As a consequence of this policy, two forms of government, the modern state and the traditional local government, co-exist in Ethiopia. The regional governments have yielded to governmental pressure from the center, but modernization of the state apparatus has yet to percolate down to the local level. The governors at these lower levels are often appointed by the Emperor from among the ranks of a traditional ruling family or tribal chieftainship of the given area.

The farther removed from the central government, the more the local political pattern asserts itself. On the village level men still hold office by virtue of local tradition. Where this older pattern prevails, the government frequently finds difficulty in collecting its full share of taxes or land dues. In the past fifteen years the government has made some effort to use the traditional local headmen to enforce government policies, but the degree of success is debatable. Among the Somali, the Danakil, and the Negroid tribes, the Ethiopian government deals with the people only indirectly through their traditional tribal representatives. It remains to be seen whether in time of crisis the central government will exert effective authority down to the village level.

Will the "Sleeping Beauty," to use Haile Selassie's phrase for Ethiopia, then awaken?

CHAPTER 6

"Trees That Are Planted Do Not Always Bear the Desired Fruit"

The one serious challenge to the Emperor's authority and to Ethiopia's stability since World War II occurred in December, 1960, while he was on a state visit to Brazil.

On the evening of December 13, 1960, numerous ministers and other important people received telephone calls urging them to come to the royal palace as quickly as possible. The appeal was made in the name of the Emperor's eldest son, Crown Prince Asfa Wossen. Those who went to the palace found themselves prisoners of a group of conspirators. Others, especially high-ranking army officers, were suspicious about the whole affair, and soon the army was alerted, as were tank and air units outside the capital. The following morning key army positions in Addis Ababa were surrounded by units of the Imperial Body Guard. In the confusion that followed there took place the first attempt in Ethiopian history at what might have developed into a real revolution. Hitherto there had been a number of court intrigues, palace coups reminiscent of fifteenth- or sixteenth-century Italy, and regional disturbances as in the Tigrean uprisings of 1943 and 1952 and the defection of Ras Hailu of Gojjam to the Italians in 1936. At first it seemed that the purpose of the leaders of the attempted coup was different, however, and the feeling that revolution was in the air marks a major turning point in modern Ethiopian history.

In the early hours of December 14, it was uncertain whether the army or the Imperial Body Guard had initiated the coup. Officers of the Body Guard claimed that the army had revolted, while the army stated that the Body Guard had begun the disturbances. On that day the Crown Prince read a speech over Radio Addis Ababa in which he declared that the old regime had come to an end; no more would it oppress the people of Ethiopia, who, he said, "have lived by words and promises which have never been fulfilled." The radio speech referred to Ethiopia's lag behind the former African colonies in economic, social, and political development and attributed it to "repeated corruption in the government" and "selfish people with unquenchable thirsts." Furthermore, the broadcast stated that the army, the police force, and the young educated class all supported the new regime. It was unknown at the time whether the Crown Prince was reading his own words or those of a speech prepared for him.

On the morning of December 15 the Imperial Body Guard Headquarters issued the following statement to the students for publication in their newspaper, *News and Views*:

This movement occurred because of the excessive oppression of the Ethiopian people. This oppression by a few persons caused poor farm production, poor health and a general backwardness in every respect among the people of Ethiopia. This has been realized by all the people.

The oppression of the people by a few persons was not limited to physical conditions. Those few persons had also restricted freedom of speech and freedom of press among the people.

This movement, and the overthrow of the old government, which started at 8.30 on the night of 13 December, were undertaken to prevent these few persons and their kind from continuing their oppressive actions. It is the duty of everyone of the Ethiopian people to join this movement and see it through to its goal.

On that same morning, a series of announcements was made on the rebel-controlled radio station. All air service was suspended, supposedly by order of the army. Yet the Crown Prince a half hour later declared the army leaders enemies of the people. In the same declaration the Prince announced an immediate raise of $20 per month for all soldiers. By midmorning Radio Addis Ababa announced the appointment of Haile Selassie's cousin, the elderly Ras Imru, as prime minister. Then, to rally the populace behind the new leadership, the local radio station broadcasted a statement by students of the University College of Addis Ababa: "The new government is doing all in its power to free you from all oppression, giving you freedom of speech, press, and political parties."

That afternoon, after thirty-six hours of mounting tension, fighting broke out between the army and the Body Guard. Meanwhile, the Emperor had received news of the challenge to his authority and was en route back to Ethiopia; he arrived in Asmara on December 16. After several days of sharp fighting, the back of the revolt was broken by December 19, although mopping-up operations continued for several days. In one last act of desperation the rebels shot their hostages, killing fifteen of the twenty-one important Ethiopians whom they had held as hostages throughout the coup.

In the aftermath of the coup the government sought to identify the main conspirators. What they discovered must have been disturbing. The two chief leaders, without a doubt, were the brothers Mengistu and Girmame Neway. Mengistu had served as deputy commander of the Imperial Body Guard for ten years and then for five years as commander; Girmame had been governor of the Wollamo subprovince in Sidamo and the Jijiga subprovince east of Harar. With them was a cousin, Girmame Wondefrash, governor of Ulat Awlalo in Tigre. All three were members of the powerful Moja clan of Shoa. Brigadier-General Tsigue Dibou, Commissioner of Police, and Lieutenant-Colonel Workeneh Gebeyehu, Chief of Security, also figured in the organization of the conspiracy. Involved in the events were various second-rank officials, some of whom were also of the Moja clan.

Although family ties were significant, as in traditional Ethiopian politics, additional motives came into play, some of them personal, others symptomatic of the changes that had taken place in Ethiopia. Mengistu Neway was known as an able man of apparently unquestioned loyalty; he had first come to the attention of the Emperor at Khartoum in 1940. In 1951 he was active in the suppression of a plot against the Emperor. Afterwards he served with distinction as commander of the Kagnew Battalion sent by Ethiopia to join the United Nations forces in Korea. In 1955, Mengistu was made commander of the Imperial Body Guard and welded it into a real force again after a period of deterioration. In Addis Ababa it was rumored that Mengistu had ambitions to marry one of the Emperor's granddaughters; his rejection as a suitor in mid-1960 allegedly was the cause of his disaffection. He was known as a man without ideas, other than the basic distrust of all foreigners that he shared with many Ethiopians of the same background. Mengistu's home was the scene of a weekly luncheon for a group of frustrated men who soon came under the influence not of Mengistu, but of his brother Girmame. It would seem that as late as the first week of December Mengistu still knew little of the projected coup d'état.

Girmame Neway was admired by many for his education, which included several years of training in the United States, where he had an outstanding record. At Columbia University he wrote a thesis on colonialism in Kenya for his master's degree in political science. In Ethiopia as governor of Wollamo (Sidamo) he won a reputation for progressiveness and antagonism toward the old landed nobility and the foreign missionaries. Girmame was responsible for the establishment of several schools financed by "voluntary" contributions from the landed aristocracy, and he attempted to increase government services in his area. Foreign missionaries in Sidamo distrusted Girmame for his Marxist bookshelf. There is little evidence that he was an ideological Marxist, however; those who knew him claim that he enjoyed distressing the missionaries and that he may have been little more than a clever young man trying to shock his conservative elders. Yet he was determined to ameliorate the conditions of the people whom he governed. Among his several remarkable achievements was winning the affection of local Somali by digging wells and storing grain for them.

Outraged by his disrespect, the local aristocracy arranged to have Girmame appointed titular governor of Jijiga. Transferred to Addis Ababa, where he was free of administrative duties, he was able to develop his ideas of revolution and come into contact with others who sympathized with his goals. Girmame soon assumed leadership of his brother's luncheons and gave the gathering a political direction. Known for his forcefulness, within the first twenty-four hours of the coup Girmame was directing everything. Some of the ruthlessness of the rebels during those eventful days is attributable to Girmame's singlemindedness.

In November, 1960, Workeneh Gebeyehu, Chief of Security, discovered the plot. Rather than report their activities, he joined the plotters, possibly because of his admiration for Mengistu Neway, under whom he had once trained for the Imperial Body Guard. Tsigue Dibou, the Commissioner of

Police, was a close friend of Workeneh, but he did not join the conspirators until the coup was well under way. Curiously, neither man brought with him any of his followers in the security police or the general police force. Later events revealed that the police, apparently neutralized by army action, were not an effective fighting unit during the coup.

For several months before the coup the Body Guard had been building up a number of grievances against the Emperor. Some of the officers of that elite corps, as well as Girmame Neway, had taken extension courses at the University College of Addis Ababa, where they had had some contact with the students and faculty. These men took courses in constitutional history, European history, and economics, in which there was discussion of political and economic matters. From the students the officers developed a keen awareness of Ethiopia's backwardness. They placed the blame for this partly on the Emperor, who, it was thought, had not proceeded with modernization at a fast enough pace, but mostly on members of the old and new aristocracies who opposed change. Clearly, some of the conspirators were young idealists; a few of them were even reinstated by the Emperor after a two- or three-year period of probation.

It is also apparent that a large number of men in the Imperial Body Guard did not understand the nature of the coup. Cooperation with the army was rendered difficult by the Body Guards' tendency to look down on the army, which was in turn jealous of that elite group. It would also seem that the Body Guard feared the air force and navy as rivals for the Emperor's favor. In this confused welter of events and attitudes, certain rebels joined the coup to protect their privileges or to pursue selfish interests. Others, however, were idealistic, if inexperienced, and Girmame Neway's proposed People's Government of Ethiopia appealed to them in a vague sort of way; this accounts for the students' reaction and inaction.

The elements of idealism and revolution for progress are also seen in several documents discovered in the possession of Girmame Neway. According to official government sources, Girmame advocated the nationalization of all land, especially that of the Church, and the disestablishment of the Ethiopian Orthodox Church. To achieve his goal of a new Ethiopia, there is evidence that he was willing to assassinate ruthlessly all government officials from the level of governor-general to the subdistrict governors, ministers, judges, notables, and tribal leaders; in other words, the whole of the traditional and new aristocracies. If the government's allegations can be believed, Girmame Neway would have ordered the execution of all commissioned army officers, all higher officers in the police force, and all private soldiers within the armed forces and the police force above the age of forty. This ruthless Terror, which is not out of keeping with Girmame's character, would have irrevocably destroyed the old regime.

As their final desperate and perhaps irrational act, the rebels ordered the execution of the hostages held in the imperial palace. Their victims had in common only the fact that they were important men; they were executed regardless of their attitude toward the regime. Some of the victims went unmourned: Ras Abebe Aragaye, pretentious Minister of National Defense, who had a bad reputation with the educated group; Makonnen Habte Wold, Ras Abebe's hated colleague, brother of the Prime Minister and, as Minister of Commerce, Industry, and Planning, one of the men most distasteful to the young progressive element; Tadesse Negash, Minister of State in the Ministry of Justice, member of a prominent Tigrean family, who had personal enemies among the rebels; Abba Hanna Jimma, a priest and chaplain to the royal family, despised for his venality; and Lemma Wolde Gabriel, Vice-Minister of Mines and the State Domain, a protégé of Makonnen Habte Wold.

Others had been seized only because of the office they held; this was true of Ayale Gabre and Letibelou Gabre, senators of little consequence; Ishete Geda, who occupied the office of Afa Negus (Chief Justice); Dawit Ogbagzy, a Minister of State in the Foreign Ministry, who had no known enemies; Amde Mikael Dessalegne, who, although he had once collaborated with the Italians, held the important position of Acting Minister of Information; Gabrewold Ingedaworq, a minister in the Ministry of the Pen; Abdullahi Mumie, a vice-minister of Finance; and Kebrete Astakkie, an assistant minister in the Ministry of the Interior. But what was most shocking to many educated and politically experienced Ethiopians was the death of the well-known Ras Seyum, governor of Tigre, who could by no stretch of the imagination be considered a supporter of the Emperor, and Major-General Mulugeta Bulli, Minister of National Community Development, a national hero for his role in the liberation of Ethiopia and one of the most popular men in the country.

There were other elements of confusion about the events. For reasons unknown—perhaps only by a fortuitous accident —six other men escaped the rebels' bullets, including the Crown Prince, the universally respected Ras Imru, and the Emperor's son-in-law, Ras Andargatchew Massai, who was high on the list of those whom the rebels disliked. During the early hours of the coup Major-General Mulugeta Bulli was appointed rebel chief of staff of the armed forces without his knowledge, and Ras Imru, who never agreed to an appointment, was nominated prime minister. Similarly, the evidence indicates that Crown Prince Asfa Wossen was coerced into acting as the rebels' choice for Head of State. These actions were apparently an attempt by the rebels to win badly needed popular support, for outside Addis Ababa the provinces remained loyal to the Emperor. Abroad only the Ethiopian ambassador to Sweden, Tafari Sharew, and his chargé d'affaires, Lij Abate Getachew, declared for the rebels. Both had been sent abroad by the Emperor as a form of political exile. The ambassador to the Congo, Kinshasa, suspected of sympathizing with the rebel cause, later denied any such sentiment. All this points to poor planning on the part of the rebels, who acted inconsistently throughout. When casualty lists were compiled, it was found that 174 Body Guards, 29 soldiers, and 120 civilians had been killed, and 300 Body Guards, 43 soldiers, and 442 civilians wounded. Official sources also indicated that approximately two thousand members of the Imperial Body Guard had been captured, of whom one thousand were subsequently released. The government claimed that no more than twenty University College students had supported the coup, although there is evidence that as many as one hundred had.

In a press conference for foreign journalists shortly after his return to Ethiopia from Brazil, the Emperor avowed that "the force which motivated these men was clearly personal ambition and lust for power." The Emperor made a point of referring to the rebel program as "only a copy of existing programs." Since their program was the program of the Imperial Ethiopian Government, the Emperor reasoned, it was obvious that these men had acted only to improve their own personal positions. But the Emperor also recognized the difficulties of his own program; in a special editorial of the *Ethiopian Herald* on December 9, 1960, Haile Selassie I with sad insight stated, "Trees that are planted do not always bear the desired fruit."

In the aftermath of the coup, the Neway brothers fled southward. Early in January, 1961, the army cornered the two men at Mojo, some fifty miles from the capital. Girmame was shot while resisting capture. Seriously wounded, Mengistu was taken to Addis Ababa to stand trial in a special court. Although the trial was supposedly open to the public, the spectators consisted mostly of the families of the victims of the coup. At the end of the trial Mengistu gave a stirring speech to the court and predicted ultimate success for the forces that sponsored the coup. The sentence of death by hanging was carried out at the end of March.

On the day of Mengistu's execution, the Emperor announced several appointments that were interpreted as the beginning of liberalization of the regime. It was thought that great changes were in the offing. In April the army successfully demonstrated for a raise in pay, which was granted at the expense of civil servants, who received an equivalent cut. Because the army, the mainstay of the regime, acted in such a disrespectful way and because younger men were appointed to the Cabinet, it was popularly believed that the Emperor was trying to forestall a second coup.

By August, 1961, however, the government had consolidated its position. Only one of the new appointments remained in office after August. At that time Aklilou Habte Wold, brother of the dead Makonnen Habte Wold and more or less an enlightened conservative, became Foreign Minister, marking a return to the earlier practice of appointing loyalist men of talent. The Emperor also took steps to lessen his dependence on the army; a territorial army, or militia, was formed to redress the older imbalance between army and Imperial Body Guard.

What went on during the trials of the lesser leaders of the coup is unknown. Many of them had been killed in the fighting. Ethiopia is short of educated and talented men, and the execution or imprisonment of many of the men involved in the coup would have supplied more fuel for the fires of criticism. Moreover, the Emperor had frequently demonstrated a willingness to restore to office men who had purged themselves of disloyalty. Such was the case with the regional leaders, many of whom have been more useful alive than dead, and such was the case with some of the rebels. Thus, Getachew Bekele, Acting Minister of Marine, was made governor of Bahr Dar in November, 1961, barely eleven months after the coup. In February, 1963 he was placed in foreign exile as Ethiopian ambassador to Haiti. Ras Imru, who not only was publicly cleared by the Emperor of complicity in the coup, but also was frequently seen in the Emperor's company in the days immediately following the coup, was appointed ambassador to India. Lastly, Lemma Frewehot, former executive secretary of the National Coffee Board, whose name appeared in the published list of conspirators in the *Ethiopian Herald* in December, 1960, was quietly reinstated in his former position after a suitable period of "exile" in Asmara.

Although the threat of a new coup subsided, evidence of unrest among the young men of talent, and particularly among the students, has persisted. By the time of the African Heads of State Conference in Addis Ababa in May, 1963, the Emperor had regained full control of the situation. His achievements in the field of African diplomacy have been most useful in demonstrating the vitality of Ethiopian leadership in Africa, effectively blunting much of the criticism of the regime from abroad. But the coup has had its impact, and the Emperor has in some respects been compelled to move faster than he cared. Since the coup he has followed rather than directed the tide of modernization. He is still

respected for his power, but that power is no longer surrounded with a near religious awe in the eyes of students,
army officers, labor leaders, and young officials.

The coup suggested for the first time in Ethiopian history
that great change might be possible; this further aggravated
the impatience of youth with government inactivity. Since
1960, however, the government has successfully maintained
a close surveillance over the army in order to forestall further
challenges. Thus, in November, 1966 nine conspirators were
arrested for plotting against the government. When their
trial ended in August, 1968, the two chief leaders, Brigadier
Tadesse Biru and army lieutenant Mammo Mezemir, were
sentenced to death; the others were given three-to-ten years
at hard labor. Biru, interestingly enough, had served as deputy chief of staff of the territorial army formed after the 1960
coup as a counterbalance to the army and the Imperial Body
Guard.

Until 1960 "reform" in Ethiopia meant those changes
instituted by the Emperor as he saw fit. Thus, the Constitutions of 1931 and 1955 did change the theoretical structure
of Ethiopian government and, in the long run, will probably
have contributed to changes in the practical operation of the
government. Similar reforms were the Penal Code of 1957
and the Civil Code of 1960, both of which attempted to
rationalize the legal system by imitating advanced European
models. Since 1960, however, the impetus for reform has
come from other sources than the Emperor, who, somewhat
bitter about the coup, said, "I am reaping the crop I have
sown." [1] Yet even if he wished to halt the process, he cannot,

[1] Quoted by Drew Pearson in *The Washington Post,* June 14, 1965,
p. B11. In this sense, too, the 1960 coup affected the direction of Ethiopian history and must be taken into consideration by those who feel
that the impact of the coup is to be found in the legends it engendered

and the Emperor must now make reforms as concessions to those who might otherwise challenge his regime.

Pressures for reform have come from student groups and the young intellectuals in the government, from occasional defectors, and from local groups within the empire whose self-help associations cannot help but have political overtones. The Emperor has resisted pressures for immediate reform, but he cannot do so indefinitely, for he does not wish to range himself with the conservative opposition of the old aristocracy to *all* reforms. The loudest demands for reform have been for revision of the landholding system and the tax structure, delegation of political authority to Parliament and the Cabinet, and decentralizing the government through provincial autonomy. Haile Selassie, who planted the seeds of all earlier reform measures, is thus called upon to nurture reforms far more extensive than he envisaged for Ethiopia at its present stage of development.

In Ethiopia for the past decade land reform has been bruited about by foreign advisers, foreign visitors, Western-educated Ethiopians, and from time to time the government. Too often it is urged as a panacea for Ethiopia's social, economic, and political problems. Both critics and advocates of the government's economic policies recognize that Ethiopia will remain an agricultural country, and that if its economic position is to improve, agricultural production must be increased and diversified. The danger of a coffee monoculture is obvious, and the government has experimented with the introduction of various export crops. But the greatest drawback to increased production, it has been argued, is the own-

rather than in its political repercussions. See also C. Clapham, "The December 1960 Ethiopian Coup d'Etat," *Journal of Modern African Studies,* VI (1968), 495–507.

ership of land by absentee landlords and the consequent lack of incentive for farmers to increase their productivity.

There is no single system of land tenure in Ethiopia, nor is there a simple means to determine ownership.[2] A complete land ownership survey is in progress, but it will be years until its results will be known. Some lands are the hereditary property of individuals or of villages where the individual shares in the inalienable collective land. Local surveys are being conducted on a selective basis, but it is unknown what proportion of the land in Ethiopia falls under the category of individual or collective hereditary ownership. Because of the lack of clear title to the land, Ethiopians often find themselves in litigation over rival claims.

A second type of landholding was granted by the Emperor to his civil servants or military leaders before the advent of a salaried bureaucracy. This system, like that of early medieval Europe, gave the official the right to collect taxes from his benefice and promoted tenant farming. Here the line between rent and taxes was blurred. In general, the official did not have the right to dispose of such land; at his death full title reverted to the emperor, who often invested this right in another member of the same family. In this manner Menelik secured the loyalty of his nobility. Similarly, after the conquest of Galla lands in the south in the last century, land was distributed to soldiers, who were obligated to quarter horses or donkeys of the imperial army on such land. In

[2] For a study of landholding, see H. S. Mann, *Land Tenure in Chore (Shoa), A Pilot Study* (Addis Ababa: Institute of Ethiopian Studies and Faculty of Law, Haile Sellassie I University in association with Oxford University Press, 1965), and Allan Hoben, "Land Tenure and Social Mobility Among the Damot Amhara," paper presented for the Third International Conference of Ethiopian Studies, Addis Ababa, April, 1966.

certain areas local officials were given the right to collect taxes in lieu of pay from the central government. Still another form of land tenure, often given to churches and monasteries, was a permanent right to collect and use taxes on certain landed properties. Upon the death of the landlord, his heir could be confirmed in this right after payment of a fee, usually a mule. In Muslim areas, variants of Muslim and pre-Islamic customary law determined land tenure. These are but the most important types of land tenure and indicate the complexity of the problem.

Because of the many varying systems of land tenure and the complicated history of local tenure rights, there has been much property litigation in local courts. In Ethiopia, it has been said, land is wealth and an indication of status. Yet less than a tenth of the land is owned by small farmers. Church holdings, in some provinces as much as 40 per cent of the land, account for approximately 28 per cent of the arable land of the nation.[3] Most of the rest of the land is the property of the imperial family and the nobility. In Menelik's time whole conquered provinces became the property of individual officials. Further complicating the matter is the lack of a clear distinction between state property and that of the imperial family, a situation reminiscent of premodern Europe.

It has been argued that land reform would increase agricultural production, but with present Ethiopian agricultural techniques, there is no guarantee that the farmer would have adequate incentive to use increased landholdings for productive purposes. Moreover, cash crop agriculture is develop-

[3] P. Schwab, "An Analysis of Decision-Making in the Political System of Ethiopia" (Ph.D. dissertation, New School for Social Research, 1969), p. 27; Ministry of Land Reform and Administration, *Report on Land Tenure Surveys* (Addis Ababa, 1967 and 1968).

ing on large private estates and only to a much lesser extent on small holdings, which all too often are far removed from the transportation network. Ethiopia is relatively sparsely populated in some places, and there is little pressure on the land in many areas, as in other parts of the world. The farmer still has little political consciousness at the national level, and it is difficult to determine what the political consequence of land reform might be. Lastly, there has been no demand for land reform from those whom it might benefit most directly; on the contrary, in Gojjam the peasant has resisted any attempts by the government to conduct the land surveys fundamental to any program of land reform. Except for his deep-seated conservatism, the Ethiopian peasant has remained politically an unknown factor.

A first small step in the direction of land reform was taken in 1964, but when major reforms were proposed in 1966 the Senate balked. To give the peasant incentive to produce more agricultural goods for export, the Chamber of Deputies passed a bill reducing the landowner's share of crops from 75 to 50 per cent of a sharecropper's production. Moreover, tenant farmers were to be freed from *corvée* obligations to the landowners. If the bill had not been killed in the Senate, tenant farmers would also have been protected from arbitrary eviction, for the law would have provided for a delay of four harvests before eviction.[4] At the same time an attempt to revamp the tax structure was also blocked. Both measures would have weakened the local power basis of the old aristocracy, shifting the burden of taxation from the peasant to the landowner. Curiously enough, such a land reform would at one and the same time have increased the power and prestige of the central government and aided the peasant

[4] *The Economist*, CCXVII (December 18, 1965), p. 1306.

both economically and politically along lines favored by the intelligentsia. When an Agricultural Income Tax law was finally passed in November, 1967, the Orthodox Church, which had received 11.5 per cent of the total revenue from land taxes, was excluded from payment of the new taxes.[5] Moreover, even though the landlords lost the legal right to tithe their tenants, they have continued to do so throughout Ethiopia. Even more serious opposition came from the petty landholders throughout the provinces as they resisted all attempts to have their lands surveyed.

Although Parliament prevented the passage of a major land reform bill, in other matters it has proved an agent for government revision. For years Parliament, as the Emperor's creation, merely ratified the Emperor's program. As one government official candidly admitted, "We did not want a person who could work well in the Parliament and legislate good and modern laws. We wanted people to accept those laws which were to be legislated, and these laws could only get acceptance if they were discussed by the nobility and accepted by them first. . . . We used them as instruments for the achievement of our plans and goals."[6] In 1964, Haile Selassie told the members of Parliament, "Laws proposed to you have been prepared by experts, reviewed by the responsible Minister and the Council of Ministers as a whole and approved by Us. Only when they have been found to serve the interest of the nation are they submitted to you."[7]

[5] Schwab, "Analysis of Decision-Making," p. 29.

[6] Statement by Fitawrari Tekla Hawaryat, cited by J. Markakis and Asmelash Beyene, "Representative Institutions in Ethiopia," *Journal of Modern African Studies*, V, no. 2 (1967), p. 203.

[7] "The Emperor Haile Sellassie I's Speech on the Opening of Parliament delivered on November 2nd, 1964," *Ethiopia Observer*, VIII, no. 4 (1965), pp. 274–276.

When the Chamber of Deputies became an elected body in 1957, the nature of Parliament began to change.[8] Although there were no political parties, and a candidate for office could not openly discuss all political issues, 597 candidates ran for 210 seats in 1957, and the number of candidates increased to 940 in 1961, 1,308 for 240 seats in 1965, and about 2,000 candidates for 250 seats in 1969. An important incentive to run for office was the extraordinarily high salary of $300 per month paid to members of Parliament. Most candidates for the Chamber of Deputies have been civil servants and teachers. As such they are subject to the government's influence. The government also maintains indirect control over admission to the Chamber by rigorously checking the qualifications of candidates as required by law: nomination to candidacy through a petition signed by at least fifty voters, payment of a deposit of $500, adherence to a strict registration schedule, and a literacy test. These qualifications effectively limit candidacy to Parliament to relatively wealthy and educated Amharic-speakers who are already in a position to influence a group of voters to back them. Hence, candidates tend to be drawn from among those who already had traditional political influence and from the products of the Emperor's educational and bureaucratic system. In the 1969 election, according to Legesse Bezu, general manager of the Election Board, 653 of the 2,000 who sought candidacy were disqualified for failure to meet one or another of the qualifications.

Although the main task of the carefully screened members of the Chamber of Deputies and of the selectively appointed senators is the approval of laws, Parliament has managed to

[8] C. Clapham, "The Functions and Development of Parliament in Ethiopia," paper prepared for the Third International Conference of Ethiopian Studies, Addis Ababa, April, 1966.

expand its activities beyond mere rubber-stamping of government-sponsored legislation, as was seen in the Senate's
rejection of the sharecropping reform bill in 1966. In 1964
the Senate rejected a proposed loan from the Italian government; apparently the senators were less forgiving to the
former colonial power than was the Emperor. A proposed
loan from the World Bank was also voted down in 1966 as
a show of independence. Both loans were in the economic
interest of the country, and eventually the Senate did as the
government wanted, but not until it had plainly flexed its
newly found legislative muscles. Parliament seemed to de-
light in asserting itself, and foreign observers felt compelled
to speculate upon the meaning of the opposition of aristo-
cratic landholders in the Senate for the future functioning of
Parliament, even though it was abundantly clear that Senate
opposition to the bills was based on self-interest. Parliament
has raised the hopes of students, although it has always failed
to fulfill those hopes. There is considerable speculation also
whether Parliament's challenge to the government in legislative matters might not develop to the point that Parliament
could emerge as a rival to the all-powerful executive branch.
It is doubtful that the Emperor foresaw this possibility when
he promulgated the Constitutions.

Recent studies indicate that Parliament does not hesitate
to assert itself whenever it can avoid direct conflict with the
Emperor. Thus, when a proposal for new legislation is introduced by one of the Emperor's ministers, it is not uncommon
for some members of Parliament to launch into a lengthy
criticism not of the proposed legislation but of the minister's
conduct. Often this is done in the guise of raising questions
on behalf of their constituents. Similarly, after a legislative
bill has been proposed, Parliament has the right to interro-
gate the appropriate cabinet minister about the significance

of the measure. When a high administrative official is called to testify on such occasions, Parliament suddenly comes to life and aggressively challenges those members of the executive branch to whom the Emperor has delegated some authority. In the small political world of Addis Ababa, such assaults on the members of the executive are quickly publicized and serve to enhance Parliament's small prestige. Naturally this process of questioning has not always been welcome to the administrators, who consequently have begun to take parliamentary reaction into consideration when they draft new legislation. If Parliament can become a forum for criticism of laws as well as officials, then a new concept, a *loyal* opposition, may be introduced into a country where open discussion of political issues has been politically unwise.

Rumors of parliamentary opposition to executive proposals have always electrified the politically alert in Addis Ababa, but no news excited the modernizing elements of Ethiopian society more than the talk of impending cabinet reforms in the spring of 1966. It was hoped that the long-awaited liberalization of the country's political life was about to take place. Parliament, the press, and the labor movement hailed the announcement when it finally came on March 22 that the Emperor was yielding some of his political prerogatives. From then on the prime minister was to nominate his own ministers, whose names would be submitted for the Emperor's approval; those ministers would be responsible to the prime minister; and lastly, the Cabinet would be collectively responsible to the Emperor but not to Parliament. Until then the Emperor had personally chosen and controlled each of his ministers, the prime minister had had no control over the Cabinet, and the idea of ministerial responsibility was alien to Ethiopia. The significance of the reform was that in practice and not just in theory a constitutional monarchy might emerge. All depended on the spirit of the reform.

For almost three weeks rumors were rife about how extensive the changes would be. The more cynical observers reminded others that the prime minister designate was Aklilou Habte Wold, who had served as prime minister and was thoroughly subservient to the Emperor. They could also point out that Aklilou's brother was one of the victims of the 1960 coup. When Aklilou finally named his cabinet in mid-April, there was enthusiasm for the appointment of men like Haddis Alemayehou, the American-educated former envoy to Britain and representative in the United Nations, who was to head the Ministry of Planning and Development, Seyum Harogot, a graduate of Harvard Law School, at thirty-three the youngest of the ministers, and the able and versatile French-educated Mammo Taddessa. Many young assistant ministers were at the same time promoted to vice-ministers, thereby securing the coveted title of "Excellency." Thus, for the first time the young modernizers appeared to be in positions of political significance. Soon, however, most of the other positions in the Cabinet were filled by men who had served time and again in former cabinets, and the new blood was diluted by older bureaucrats.

At the same time, this new government examined measures to grant "local self-administration" to some of the provinces. For the first time regional interests in Ethiopia would be recognized as a positive force for progress. Such concessions would have been unheard of ten years earlier; twenty years ago they would have been regarded as an indication of Haile Selassie's weakness and an invitation to regional uprisings against the central government. In a major concession to those who demand democracy in Ethiopia, the Emperor has given his tacit approval to a policy that may eventuate in

the creation of popularly elected provincial assemblies em-
powered to collect taxes for general and developmental purposes, and given the authority to administer educational and
public health services on the provincial level. In Ethiopia
such reforms often meet with great delays between proposal
and implementation. Inevitably the reform will create appe-
tites for further reforms. The immediate effect is to give hope
that reform is still possible, thus forestalling the formation
of a united opposition dedicated to immediate radical change.
The tree of change has been fertilized with concessionary
reforms; the alternative would have been to prune offending
shoots which would doubtless grow back with increasing
foliage.

One last area of change bears watching. Since 1960 there
has been a great increase in the number of self-help groups,
or "brotherhoods." [9] Originally of Gurage inspiration, these
voluntary associations served as credit unions, burial societies, and agencies for achieving a common social or economic
goal. In the case of the Gurage in Addis Ababa, the voluntary
association also served as a pressure group lobbying to get the
government to extend roads into the Gurage country south
of the capital.[10] In this case the Gurage raised money for the
construction of the road, donated the money to the government, and requested that the government then build more
schools and health centers in their home region. As Levine
has shown, the Amhara and other ethnic groups have quickly
followed the Gurage example, and voluntary associations
have become the focal point for all sorts of activities, includ-

[9] D. N. Levine, *Wax and Gold: Tradition and Innovation in Ethiopian Culture* (Chicago: University of Chicago Press, 1965), pp. 277–279.

[10] Fecadu Gadamu, "The Social and Cultural Foundation of Gurage
Association," paper prepared for the Third International Conference of
Ethiopian Studies, Addis Ababa, April, 1966.

ing those with political ramifications. A government concerned with developing the nation's resources can only laud these efforts at self-help and community development. In a state without political parties, the voluntary associations may provide an excellent alternative to political organizations for progressive purposes. At what point these parapolitical groupings will give the government cause to feel threatened is unknown. After all, trees that are planted do not always bear the desired fruit.

CHAPTER 7

The Tree
of Knowledge

Of Man's first disobedience, and the fruit
Of that forbidden tree. . . .
—Milton, *Paradise Lost*

Knowledge is more than equivalent to force.
—Johnson, *History of Rasselas,*
Prince of Abyssinia

World literature is filled with references to the dangers
of education. The tree of knowledge from which Eve plucked
the apple was the tree of knowledge of good *and* evil. The
moral for modernizing states is a simple one: education for
purely technical purposes may ultimately be used for political purposes.

Education and the creation of a national awareness super-
seding strong regional, ethnic, and religious loyalties have
received particular emphasis in Ethiopia. Both may be
viewed as solutions of the central problem of modernizing
and strengthening the State. Education as a means to achieving national goals has been given special recognition by the
Emperor, who until 1966 had always held the portfolio of
Minister of Education. Ever since his early years as regent,
Haile Selassie has been deeply concerned with the development of an educational system that would serve state purposes.

Paradoxically, although Ethiopia is the one sub-Saharan
land where a literate culture has thrived for some two thou-

sand years, today it has one of the lowest literacy rates in the whole continent. A United Nations survey of African education in 1963 revealed that the continent as a whole had a literacy rate of approximately 15 per cent. The highest rate, that of Malagasy, was between 30 and 35 per cent; southern and central Africa had rates above 20 per cent; that of northern Africa was slightly above the continental average; while eastern Africa's rate of 9 to 14 per cent was still considerably higher than that of Ethiopia, where not more than 5 or 6 per cent of the population was then literate.[1] The Ethiopian government now claims that only 9 to 10 per cent of the population is literate. There has been some progress, but no spectacular development has occurred. As the third most populous country in Africa, Ethiopia still faces the tremendous task of eradicating illiteracy among its millions.

There are great variations within Ethiopia. In urban areas 57 per cent of the male population is literate compared to 6.5 per cent of rural males, while the corresponding figures for females are 16 and 0.5 per cent. The level of literacy across the country varies from 56 per cent in Addis Ababa and 27 per cent in Eritrea to 4.3 per cent in Gamu-Gofa, 3.5 per cent in Harar, and 3 per cent in Wollo.[2]

In the traditional society of premodern Ethiopia education in reading and writing was the province of the religious schools. In the Muslim eastern half of the country Koranic schools gave a minimum education in liturgical Arabic. Only in the city of Harar did there develop a creative literature, written in the Arabic script, but in the Harari language. But no more than a few thousand Harari can have been literate. In the Christian Amhara and Tigrean areas the schools of the

[1] Personal communication from Richard Jolly, United Nations Economic Commission for Africa, Addis Ababa, August 1, 1963.

[2] *Ethiopian Herald,* January 23, 1969.

Ethiopian Orthodox Church were the mainstay of the literate culture. There the children of the clergy and the aristocracy were taught to read and write. The church schools had their limitations in terms of modern pedagogy and utility, for not Amharic but ancient Ethiopic was the main language of rote study. Nevertheless, since Amharic is written in an expanded form of the Geez syllabary, some were able to make the transition from sight-reading of Geez to literacy in the vernacular Amharic. Thus, the religious school also indirectly promoted secular studies.

In recent years the administrative organization of the Church has come increasingly under the control of the Imperial Government, but the resources of the Church as an educational institution have not been fully employed because of the resistance of many of the conservative clergy to the secularizing reforms that have accompanied modernization. Many clergymen bitterly resented the early educational reforms of the 1920's as a threat to their monopoly of education. Only in the past decade have some of the church schools accepted the curriculum established by the Ministry of Education. The number of church schools in Ethiopia is unknown. Traditionally, every church is supposed to instruct the young in the fundamentals of the Geez liturgy. Estimates of the number of students enrolled in all church schools have run from 100,000 to 600,000.[3]

Today government schools are the main means of effective education. The first modern school was established by Menelik II in Addis Ababa in 1908. In 1929, shortly before he became Emperor, Haile Selassie founded the Tafari Makonnen School, but Ethiopia's embryonic educational system did not grow rapidly. The Italian invasion was a major setback,

---

[3] George Lipsky *et al.*, *Ethiopia, Its People, Its Society, Its Culture* (New Haven: HRAF Press, 1962), p. 89.

and no serious attempt to improve education could be made until after World War II. Only slowly did a system of elementary education develop. By 1955 not more than 70,000 students were enrolled. Since then in relative terms the system has greatly expanded. In 1961/62 the system embraced more than 180,000 students; three years later primary-school enrollment rose to 327,000, while estimates of enrollment for 1968/69 amount to approximately 514,000.[4] There is much to be done, however, for even after this expansion less than 10 per cent of the seven-through-twelve-year old age group attend school. Moreover, the enrollment in the thirteen- and fourteen-year old age group is only 2.5 per cent, while that in the age group fifteen to nineteen is only 1.5 per cent.[5] Long-range plans by the Ministry of Education call for the enrollment of 82 per cent of the primary-school age population by 1980.

Since 1953 the government has increased its budgetary expenditures on education from $4.9 million to $8.2 million in 1961/62 and an estimated $26 million in 1969/70. The rate of expansion of the school system has been stepped up, and currently the enrollment in elementary schools has been increasing at the rate of 12 per cent per year. In 1961/62 there were only 635 government schools, with a faculty of 4,642 Ethiopian and 355 foreign teachers; in 1968/69 an estimated 514,000 students were enrolled in more than 1,000 govern-

[4] Ethiopia, Ministry of Finance, *Statistical Abstract, 1963* (Addis Ababa: Commercial Printing Press, 1963), p. 63; Assefa Bequele, "The Educational Framework of Economic Development in Ethiopia," *Ethiopia Observer*, XI, no. 1 (1967), p. 51; E. Ginzberg and H. A. Smith, *Manpower Strategy for Developing Countries: Lessons from Ethiopia* (New York: Columbia University Press, 1967), p. 50.

[5] Ginzberg and Smith, *Manpower Strategy*, pp. 49–54; *Ethiopian Herald*, January 23, 1969.

ment schools, with a faculty of more than 9,000 teachers.[6] In 1969 the Ethiopian and Swedish governments signed a five-year agreement for a $50 million program of construction for 7,000 elementary-school classrooms, half of which would be paid by the Swedish government. When the program is completed in 1974, the number of pupils in the first six years of elementary education will double.

In addition to the public school system, there are now more than 260 mission schools, whereas in 1961/62, 185 mission schools taught 27,096 students. Mission schools are limited to those areas where they are not in competition with the Ethiopian Orthodox Church. Private schools, originally established for the children of the aristocracy and of foreigners, but now ostensibly open to all, number 325, compared to 138 in 1961. More than 100 church schools following the government curriculum have an enrollment of over 20,000 and a faculty of 375 Ethiopians.[7]

The drop-out rate in Ethiopian primary schools is discouragingly high. To provide an alternate form of education, the United Nations Development Program, the International Labor Organization, and the Ethiopian government established a national industrial vocational training program in 1969. Initially a vocational training development center is to be set up in Addis Ababa and will enroll 300 students in day and evening courses. At the same time the Department of Labor's vocational training section will also develop additional training programs with international assistance.

[6] Ginzberg and Smith, *Manpower Strategy,* pp. 23–24; Assefa Bequele, "Educational Framework of Economic Development," pp. 52–53; *Statistical Abstract, 1963,* pp. 103–106; *Statistical Abstract, 1965,* pp. 141–144; Ministry of Education and Fine Arts, *School Census for Ethiopia, 1966–1967* (Addis Ababa, 1967).

[7] *Ibid.*

Although the number of elementary-school children has increased annually, the percentage of primary-school students who complete eight years of education is still small. While the Ministry of Education plans for the secondary education of 19.2 per cent of the school-age population in 1980, only 9 per cent of primary students have been continuing their education. Whereas the United Nations Economic Commission for Africa reports that about 5.5 per cent of those of secondary-school age are in school in all Africa, for Ethiopia the figure is about 1 per cent. But although the last figure is tiny, more than 30 per cent of those completing secondary school continue their education on the university or technical college level, and Ethiopia has been training at home and abroad more than 2,800 advanced students annually in recent years.[8] Ethiopian students have gone abroad to study in the United States, Italy, Germany, Austria, the United Arab Republic, Lebanon, the United Kingdom, Israel, France, Czechoslovakia, Yugoslavia, the Soviet Union, and at least eighteen other countries. Since the opening of the Haile Sellassie I University in 1959 the number of those studying abroad has declined slightly.

Ethiopia still has only about fifty trained physicians, most of whom are in Addis Ababa, while the modern medical installations of the country are still handled by approximately three hundred foreign physicians. Progress has been made in the training of public health officers and community nurses, and in 1969 approximately three hundred Ethiopians were studying abroad in one or another of the medical sciences. The university medical school, founded in 1965, still

[8] Ethiopia, Ministry of Education and Fine Arts, *A Proposed Plan for the Development of Education in Ethiopia* (Addis Ababa, 1961); Assefa Bequele, "Educational Framework of Economic Development," p. 56.

has a small enrollment. Other technicians are also in great demand to meet the developing manpower needs of the modernizing economy and to replace foreign technicians upon whom Ethiopia is heavily dependent. More than fifteen hundred foreigners have been teaching in schools in Ethiopia; they still comprise more than half of the teaching staff of secondary schools. The secondary-school system benefited greatly from the presence of American Peace Corps volunteers, who still number over four hundred. This influx of foreign teachers permitted an increase in the number of secondary-school students from 6,200 in 1959/60 to an estimated 34,050 in 1968/69.[9] In addition to American teachers, Frenchmen, British, Indians, and various Europeans have been employed by the government and private schools.

Besides the University College of Addis Ababa, founded in 1950, and the Haile Sellassie I University, advanced training is given at the Public Health College in Gondar, the Agricultural College at Alemaya near Harar, the Ethio-Swedish Building College in Addis Ababa, the Law School of the University (opened in 1963), the Medical College, and the Theological College. It is estimated that by 1972 these institutions will have produced 3,044 graduates, and an additional 1,528 Ethiopians will have received training abroad. But by then Ethiopia will need 3,655 secondary-school teachers, 2,453 government administrators, 1,352 engineers, 628 physicians and surgeons, 516 jurists and lawyers, 400 agronomists, 377 accountants and auditors, 367 biologists, 289 university teachers, 187 economists and statisticians, 125 pharmacists, 120 veterinarians, 120 social workers, and lesser numbers of architects, scientists, dentists, pilots, and other trained manpower, or a total of 11,866 highly trained personnel. A report on high-level manpower needs prepared by

[9] Ginzberg and Smith, *Manpower Strategy,* pp. 61–66.

the Haile Sellassie I University and the Ministry of National Community Development indicates that only 60 per cent of technical occupations projected for 1972 could possibly be staffed by Ethiopians; the deficit of 4,872 trained men represents places that must be filled, if at all, by foreigners. For a long time to come, as in all Africa, there will continue to be a serious shortage of trained personnel.[10]

Thus, Ethiopia has a long and difficult road to travel, for an infinitesimally small portion of the population has completed a primary education, and all told not more than 10,000 to 15,000 Ethiopians have completed their secondary or higher education. Yet the Emperor regards education not only as the means to economic development but also as one of the keys to greater political unity through a common school curriculum and through a more highly educated cadre of administrators in the central government. There has been, therefore, a policy of promoting the teaching of Amharic in all schools as an instrument of national unity. In 1963 the government required that all schools in all areas henceforth employ Amharic, not the local vernacular, as the means of instruction at the primary level. No doubt in non-Amhara areas the rate of school-leaving will initially increase; throughout their school career native Amharic-speakers will probably maintain an advantage over students from other ethnic groups. Ultimately, those who do survive the educational process will become assimilated to the Amhara and enter into the service of the government. The government's language policy may therefore serve a dual purpose: Amharization of the country as the school system expands, and

[10] Duri Mohammed and Arnold Zack, *High Level Manpower in Ethiopia* (Addis Ababa: Ministry of National Community Development, 1966), pp. 28–38; Assefa Bequele, "Educational Framework of Economic Development," p. 55.

siphoning away from ethnic and religious minorities educated youth who might otherwise serve as modernizing leaders for dissident regional groupings.

The educated classes thus are a product of a policy deliberately decided upon by the Emperor. They are his creation,
conceived with the purpose of staffing an expanding and
centralizing modern government. Until 1960 they appeared
far more loyal to the modernizing Emperor than the old nobility who had a regional basis of power that had to be
subordinated to the government of Addis Ababa. Haile
Selassie succeeded in breaking the power of the regional
lords only to discover that the educated classes, created to
further the modernization of the state and to introduce
Western ideas of progress, harbor some of his sharpest critics.
They repeatedly criticize his political conservatism and prefer to ignore his solid accomplishments.

At home and abroad university students have challenged
the government's policies, yet the Emperor has no choice but
to view the students as a manpower reserve for the staffing
of government offices and for the implementation of his policies. He intends to use them as a force for modernization to
introduce new ideas and techniques into the rural area. The
students, however, have a different understanding of modernization and have been unhappy at the slow rate of change.

Although the students played no part in organizing the
abortive coup in December, 1960, they greatly sympathized
with the aims of the conspirators. An account of student reaction to the coup was contained in a suppressed edition of
the University College of Addis Ababa student publication,
News and Views, on December 16. After listening to their
leaders and to representatives of the Imperial Body Guard
on December 14, the students declared their support of the
new regime, "provided that it is not a military coup d'état,"

and marched in Addis Ababa, bearing placards supporting the aims of the rebels. However, they apparently were not involved as a group in the fighting that took place on the streets of Addis Ababa. Nevertheless, this marked the debut of the students as a potential political force and an indication of the disillusion of the students with the government that had made their education possible.

To contain the students' enthusiasm for reform, the Ministry of National Community Development drafted a plan for national service by all university students.[11] Inasmuch as Ethiopia lacked teachers in rural areas, the Ministry decided to increase the secondary-school enrollment by expanding the number of seventh- and eighth-grade classrooms through use of university students as teachers. At first some 134 students were sent out on national service, of whom all but twenty were teachers. All soon became involved in the national literacy campaign. The following year 194 students served. Here, it seemed, was a way in which students could directly and immediately become involved in the problems of modernizing Ethiopia. As the government sought to channel student exuberance for its own purposes rather than chastise the students for having supported the coup, the program took on a different aspect. What was initially regarded by the students as a program of voluntary service became compulsory for all degree candidates. Moreover, once in the field, the student was largely on his own, far removed from contact with other students. His responsibility, however, was not to the university, but to a government ministry.

The attitude of the students soon became negative in opposition to still another extension of governmental authority.

[11] D. C. Korten and F. K. Korten, "Ethiopia's Use of National University Students in a Year of Rural Service," *Comparative Education Review*, X (1966), pp. 482–492.

They resented the fact that teaching service was rarely related to the career interests of most students and criticized the government for lack of student participation in the planning and development of the national service program. Gradually student resentment abated. It still remains to be seen how effective the program will be and whether or not for the first time a modernizing agency will succeed in reaching out to the rural masses. Here too the results may have political implications differing from those anticipated by the government. Already a number of university service teachers have been arrested or chastised for preaching subversive doctrines to their students.

Although the threat of a new coup subsided, evidence of unrest among the young persisted. In the year following the coup the students finally organized a student government, which the government refused to recognize. At Student Day ceremonies in May, 1962 a group of students read poems containing ambiguous references to politics, and the government took steps to restrain the students, who were warned by college authorities to steer clear of politics. Boarding privileges were withdrawn from Ethiopian students at University College, and some students were suspended. Nevertheless, a National Union of Ethiopian Students was reconstituted, and those interested in contemporary politics closely watched the students as a force making for change.

Because the students were a diffuse group, their demands took specific form only gradually. They continually exerted pressure for reform, but their leadership was weak and uncertain. With great difficulty they attempted to convert the organs of student government into political sounding boards, but the government severely circumscribed their tactics. They could not with impunity attack the government as autocratic or repressive. They had no access to the public forum. They had to find an issue, and the one area of reform where they could hope to embarrass the government was land ownership. Here the old nobility and the new were divided, and the Emperor could not count on regional support for any reapportionment of landholdings that would undercut the power of local landlords.

In February, 1965, while Parliament was deliberating over a land reform bill, students in Addis Ababa demonstrated against the inequities of the land system. At first the students were allowed to gather outside Parliament, but the government feared that the demonstration might turn into a broader political protest movement. To weaken the student movement, university officials found a pretext to ban student government on the campus of Haile Sellassie I University. The situation was tense. Nine students were summarily suspended when they flouted the ban and tried to hold student meetings. In May fighting broke out between the police and students demonstrating on behalf of the suspended students. It appeared that the government was prepared to meet force with force, but a confrontation was postponed by the closing of the academic year.

The one group in Ethiopia most keenly aware of the glaring contradictions between the rights granted to the people by the Constitution of 1955 and the limitations the government placed on those rights is the students. In April, 1967 the students tested Article 45 of the Constitution: "Ethiopian subjects shall have the right, in accordance with the conditions prescribed by law, to assemble peaceably and without arms." Angry with the government's continual harassment of the student union, student leaders planned a march in the streets of Addis Ababa. When the Ministry of the Interior refused to sanction the march, a small group of students decided to march anyway. As soon as the students left the university campus, they were set upon by army units. General chaos ensued, and a number of innocent students were beaten and arrested when the army occupied the campus. The students, who had not anticipated this turn of events, were helpless. Later they were perturbed to learn that the Emperor threatened to suspend all financial aid to students contesting the government; few students could afford to attend the university without such assistance. The government, however, limited itself to suspending some of the student leaders.

Force could not dissolve the student movement, no doubt to the government's subsequent dismay. Each spring since 1967 the student movement has challenged the government; each year student demonstrations have increased in their outspoken criticism of the government. In late March, 1968 the students acted again. Their main concern that year was the agricultural income tax, which they regarded as unfair to the peasantry. At campus meetings and discussions articulate students, seeking a way in which they could safely give vent to their discontent with the regime, claimed that the students had the right to speak for the peasants; the rural background of many of the students made them sensitive to the burden imposed upon the peasant by the new tax. Because many students were reluctant to oppose the Emperor's law, especially in the light of government action against the students the previous year, they chose to demonstrate over an otherwise trivial matter: they attacked a miniskirt fashion show organized by a young American teacher as un-Ethiopian. When the university officials, unswayed by their arguments in favor of the *shamma* (the national costume), refused to deny the use of a university hall for the fashion show, the students used this relatively unimportant issue to force the administration and the government into an untenable position. Picketing students boycotted classes, and the demonstration gained momentum. Soon hundreds of students were marching from the university to the very center of Addis Ababa. When student leaders lost control of this greatly enlarged demonstration, the police and the army moved in. Cars were overturned, shop windows were broken, and about three hundred students smashed the windows of the United States Information Office in the ensuing riots. As the violence mounted, the Emperor closed the university and stationed troops around the campus. Student leaders were arrested, but the disorders continued for an entire week. The situation calmed down only after Haile Selassie pleaded with the students on radio and television to end their demonstration and agreed to discuss their grievances. Three weeks later the university reopened and the capital city returned to normal. The fashion show crisis itself served to indicate that politically motivated students, whose counterparts in Europe, Asia, and the Americas are miniskirt-minded, had developed the sophistication to turn an insignificant issue into a catalyst for the politics of confrontation typical of student dissent movements throughout the world. They had bearded the Lion of Judah in his den.

As in Europe and America, dissenting university students in Ethiopia became the model for protest by secondary-school students. Ironically, the government itself established the link between the two groups of students through the Ministry of National Community Development's program of national service. Between December, 1968 and February, 1969 high-school students voiced their grievances in a number of unrelated cases. Eighty miles north of Addis Ababa, in Debra Berhan students went on strike after their headmaster dismissed two popular Ethiopian teachers, ostensibly at the instigation of non-Ethiopian teachers. After stoning government buildings and persuading students at other schools to join them, the students faced the police of that provincial town. The police fired into the crowd and killed one of the students, a son of a member of Parliament.

At Nazareth, sixty miles east of Addis Ababa, students protested against a new four-dollar school-leaving examination fee. They stoned the provincial governor, the local military commander, and the town elders who tried to persuade them to pay the fee. At Soddo, 230 miles south of the capital, a romantic triangle involving the president of the student body, a primary-school physical education instructor, and an attractive young lady led to abuse of political connections and the expulsion of the student leader. The students went on strike on his behalf.

Secondary-school unrest quickly spread to Addis Ababa, where high-school and university students struck and demanded compensation for the parents of the dead student in Debra Berhan, the trial of the Debra Berhan police chief, elimination of the new fee, automatic entrance into the university for all secondary-school graduates, a more just allotment of the three thousand scholarships for advanced study, an increase in the budget for education, dismissal of the Minister of Education, faster economic growth, an end to unemployment, curtailment of government expenditures on "embassies, banquets and Ministers' salaries, and travel," and expulsion of "immoral Indian and American Peace Corps professors."

On March 3, 1969, the government closed the university and all secondary schools in Addis Ababa for an indefinite time. In the wake of renewed incidents, the police and army patrolled the streets of the capital but were unable to prevent the throwing of several Molotov cocktails at the headquarters of the Peace Corps, the most visible symbol of American support of Haile Selassie's regime. Student-circulated pamphlets attacked the government as "corrupt and senile" and urged peasants, workers, and soldiers to revolt. More than two hundred students were arrested after police used tear gas to break up a demonstration that was a blanket condemnation of the government's educational policies.

At first the government placed the blame for student agitation on a handful of students allegedly duped by foreign agents and declared several Czechs and Russians *persona non grata*. Nevertheless, the Emperor publicly acknowledged the threat posed by the students in a radio broadcast on March 7. "It is clear," he said, "that the agitation and attempts to agitate the majority of peaceful students were intended to disrupt public security and to shake the firm foundation of the country's unity." A month later the university was still closed. Ethiopia's educational system, once the Emperor's pride, was paralyzed.

On April 1 five hundred university students were arrested after staging a sit-down strike protesting the resumption of classes in secondary schools. As the police drove off the arrested students, one of them fell to his death from a police truck. Two days later, police and military arrested another five hundred students in a funeral procession for the unfortunate student. Then, the next day the government released its prisoners and promulgated a series of strict security measures permitting the government to detain persons without trial for up to six months. As the imperial decree proclaimed, "Public order, security, and people's welfare were threatened in several parts of the empire by certain evilly disposed persons." Thus, the government's police force was given a free hand to arrest any individual suspected of threatening order and public security. There could be no stronger evidence that Haile Selassie regarded the student unrest as one of the most ominous threats to his regime's stability since the abortive coup d'état of 1960.

Unexpectedly, in September, 1969, Haile Selassie made two gestures of conciliation toward the students. In keeping with his procedures in the past, he pardoned those who had challenged his rule; all the students jailed or penalized in the spring demonstrations were forgiven. More significantly, he removed the Minister of Education, Akale Work Habte Wold, the target of much of the student agitation for reform; Akale Work remained in the government, however, as Minister of Justice. His replacement, Seifu Mahtema Selassie, appeared to be conciliatory toward the students.

Student unrest came to a head again on December 28, 1969, when Tillahun Gizaw, president of the student union, was found shot to death near the university campus. Official news releases suggested that his murder was the result of bitter divisions between militant and moderate students over the tactics the students should pursue in making their demands for educational and political reform. Tillahun, a militant leftist, had strangely enough been left alone by the police authorities. Speculation followed whether he had been removed from the political scene by student opponents, other militants who sought to embarrass the government, or the government itself. No mention appeared in print of the significant fact that he was the younger brother of Princess Sarah Gizaw, widow of the Emperor's favorite son, Makonnen. In the clashes between students and riot police that ensued when the students refused to turn over Tillahun's body to his family, three students were killed and five wounded. The government then shut down the university for most of January, 1970.

Abroad Ethiopian students have been even more outspoken, despite the potential for government reprisal upon their return to Ethiopia. At the Fifth Annual Conference of the Ethiopian Students Union in Europe, held in Vienna in August, 1965, some three hundred Ethiopian students, echoing events among the students in Addis Ababa that year, raised the cry for reform. As was customary, a member of the Ethiopian diplomatic corps in Europe greeted the students, thus indicating that the Ethiopian government granted the Union semiofficial recognition. Word of what took place at the conference must have been disconcerting when it reached Addis Ababa. In a broad salvo fired against the absolute monarchy, the students declared their opposition to Ethiopian "feudalism" and condemned the Church, the royal family, the aristocracy, and the landed gentry for preventing Ethiopia from making progress. Significantly, the students did not berate the army.[12]

Land reform, the role of intellectuals in bringing about change, and the need for an independent trade union movement were also discussed. The students denounced their government as an agent of imperialism and aimed their barbs at the United States, its program of military aid and advisers, its base at Kagnew, and the Peace Corps. While advocating a peaceful solution to Ethiopia's border dispute with Somalia, the students nevertheless went on record as opposing Somali expansionism.

The militancy of the European Union was echoed by the Ethiopian Students Association in North America. At its Thirteenth Annual Congress held in Cambridge, Massachusetts in September, 1965, the association took an even stronger stand as it dedicated itself to voicing the needs and demands

---

[12] The resolutions passed by the Fifth Congress of the Union of Ethiopian Students in Europe are found in *Challenge: Journal of the Ethiopian Students Association in North America,* VI, no. 1 (August, 1966), pp. 17–41.

of Ethiopia's oppressed people. The students damned their government for its inability to realize Ethiopia's full social and economic potential. Mincing no words, the students called the government of their homeland a "festering dictatorship . . . characterized by a total absence of all civil rights and liberties." The Constitution, Parliament, the Church—all were termed governmental instruments of oppression. Land reform and greater education were again looked upon as the means to progress. Like its European-based counterpart, the Ethiopian Students Association in North America condemned colonialism, neocolonialism, *apartheid* and racial discrimination, and the United States' war in Vietnam. The over-all impression of these resolutions was that the students were organizing themselves into the spearhead of a socialist revolution.[13]

Individuals and small groups of Ethiopian students abroad have been even more outspokenly radical in criticizing the government of their homeland. Exemplifying extremist criticism are the ephemeral mimeographed publications that have appeared from time to time. *The Patriot,* a monthly edited in Brussels and published in Amsterdam, is a good example. Calling itself the "organ of the Ethiopian Revolutionary Organization and the Ethiopian People's Movement Council," a shadowy opposition group of students in western Europe, *The Patriot* peppered its articles with such slogans as:

Young people and Revolutionary Intellectuals of Ethiopia, Unite against Feudalism!

Youth and People of Ethiopia, united against the enemies of our progress: Feudalism, Imperialism, Forces of Reaction and Backwardness.

[13] The resolutions passed by the Thirteenth Congress of the Ethiopian Students Association in North America are found in *ibid.* pp. 3–17.

Support the Ethiopian and African Revolution TODAY; To-MORROW will be too late!

Do you know? Kuwait has one of the highest living standards, Ethiopia one of the lowest in THE WORLD.

Its bitterest gibes were reserved for those Ethiopian opportunists who had once supported the aims of the 1960 coup but later returned to imperial favor. But what was distinctive about this publication was not its condemnation of Ethiopian backwardness or its sarcasm toward "the so-called government of 'the beloved Emperor.'" Unlike most Ethiopians abroad, the members of the Ethiopian People's Movement Council have been outspokenly sympathetic to both Eritrean separatists and Somali irredentists, and they nettled their government by saluting "the valiant brotherly peoples of Somalia and the Sudan for the diplomatic risks they have taken while defending the just cause of freedom in Ethiopia."[14]

During the serious student manifestations in Addis Ababa in 1969, Ethiopian students in the United States, the Soviet Union, France, and Sweden dramatized their cause by occupying their country's embassies in Washington, Moscow, Paris, and Stockholm. On March 28, more than thirty students occupied part of the Ethiopian embassy in Washington to protest the "systematic persecution of all students" by their Emperor's "reactionary, oppressive, and neo-colonialist" government. When police threatened to evict them from the building, they left peacefully and shouted, "Freedom for the Ethiopian people." The next day, twenty-five Ethiopian students occupied the Ethiopian embassy in Moscow for three hours. Their slogans were "Down with feudal monarchy" and "Down with oppression" as they demanded educational

[14] *The Patriot,* August, 1965, p. 7.

reforms and the removal of Peace Corps volunteers. Both groups achieved their purpose: they received worldwide newspaper coverage of student dissatisfaction with a regime otherwise regarded as one of the most stable in Africa.

When Haile Selassie arrived in Washington for a state visit in July, he was met by a group of protesting students outside the White House, shortly after a number of students had assaulted the virtually empty Ethiopian embassy. Fourteen students were arrested, and a chagrined Department of State apologized to the Emperor for not having provided better protection for the embassy of a friendly foreign power.

Thus, Ethiopian students abroad speak in terms of revolutionary change in Ethiopia. The students who dare to speak so harshly of their government know that they are indispensable for the country's progress, regardless of regime. The government must therefore tolerate this criticism abroad, although individual student leaders have been recalled to Ethiopia. Even in Ethiopia not all student opposition is repressed. The Ethiopian government is aware that just as it is dependent upon the students for manpower reserve, so the student has only one alternative for employment, the government. In the past the political idealism of the student rapidly gave way to the material yearnings of the new bureaucrat. It is no wonder then that the students abroad also felt it necessary to censure themselves for "their abysmal failure to live up to the duties and responsibilities expected of them." They knew that they too could become "opportunists bent on amassing wealth and engaged in the pursuit of their selfish personal interest."

Both the Emperor and the students know that the political future of Ethiopia may well hinge upon the students, who more than any other segment of the population urge ever greater control of Ethiopian life by the central government in order to change Ethiopia at a faster rate than that ordained by the Emperor. If the students can influence labor, the army, and the peasantry, then their political promise as radicals may be realized. Meanwhile, the Emperor has walked a tight-rope, swayed by stirrings for change among the students but determined to pursue the goals he has established for himself. Education will still be the means to achieve economic and social goals in Ethiopia, no matter what the regime, but it remains to be seen what influence students will have in rede-fining those goals. The tree of knowledge has grown mightily.

CHAPTER 8

Challenge to
National Unity

Like other traditional states that pursue a policy of deliberate modernization, Ethiopia must face the central problem of strengthening national unity at the expense of regionalism: promoting centralizing ideas and institutions at the expense of the decentralizing tendencies represented by religious, ethnic, or regional interests so deeply rooted in the history of the country.

In certain areas the government has made great strides in centralization. Because the apparatus of the modern state cannot grow beyond the limits imposed by the economy, the Emperor, whose wealth traditionally consisted of land and service, has had to promote a money economy in order to give Ethiopia the economic viability that must underlie political unity. Thus, economic development may be regarded as one means to further the development of Ethiopia as a centralized nation-state, rather than a dynastic state or a loose federation of diverse regions. We have already seen how the Church—a unifying force in Christian Abyssinia, but a divisive force in religiously pluralistic Ethiopia—has been subjected to the control of the Emperor. Similar steps have been taken in the field of education, as well as in the administrative unification of the State. On the other hand, there have been serious problems in coping with the centrifugal tendencies of regions like Eritrea and Gojjam. Lastly, there are the omnipresent traditions of a conservative society that in the past on more than one occasion caused the dissolution of the central state apparatus. In the second half of the twentieth century these local traditions have often taken the form of usually passive, but occasionally very active resistance to legislation emanating from Addis Ababa.

If the creation of a new class of educated Ethiopians has stimulated a demand for greater development at the national level, on the regional level there has been great resistance to the centralization policies of Haile Selassie's government. Here the old centrifugal tendencies all too easily come into full play. In questions of regional traditions and prerogatives, as in matters of religion, the government has pursued a policy of promoting a national unity that is meant to supersede all older loyalties. In this area, however, the government has met with less than full success. Muslim Eritreans, Christian Tigreans and Gojjami, and Somali have all displayed separatist tendencies, while on occasion the Galla have given cause for suspecting their loyalty. Shoan Amhara are still greatly resented throughout the empire for their favored position. Yet officially the government makes no mention of Gojjami, or Shoans, or Eritreans, but deliberately refers only to Ethiopians.

Although the traditional role of Amhara culture has been played down by the government, in the area of language the Amhara may always maintain their dominance. In describing the linguistic complexities of Ethiopia, some authors have been discouraged by the implications of such diversity for national unity. It is true that the languages of the empire present an appalling array of tongues, yet the fact remains that Amharic has become the language of almost half of Ethiopia; it has been learned through trade, through the army, through the schools, and through government. Even in remote Dankalia a bit of Amharic is spoken. In other words, in the twentieth century Amharic has made tremendous strides as the language of national unity. It may be only a matter of time before all Ethiopians acquire a working knowledge of Amharic. As with many of the Agaw, one can almost foresee the day when Amharic will displace the other Semitic languages and many of the Cushitic languages of Ethiopia. It is open to conjecture whether the Somali or the Tigreans will yield to this pressure, but numerous Galla have been willing to accept elements of Amhara culture and have readily learned Amharic. Here an interesting process takes place: in the western plateau Christian converts who have learned Amharic have taken Christian Amharic names. They have come to consider themselves, and to be considered, Amhara. Thus, as the Galla and other peoples are assimilated to the Amhara, there will probably develop an Amhara people very different from the historical Amhara. All this may facilitate unification.

Ethiopian emperors historically have sought various solutions for the problems of ruling a heterogeneous empire. The imposition of Christian Amhara culture worked in some areas but failed in dealings with the Muslims. Zara Yaqob in the fifteenth century, Menelik in the nineteenth, and Haile Selassie in the twentieth have each cultivated among the diverse ethnic elements a personal loyalty to the monarch. Yet at the same time that Haile Selassie has continued in this tradition and has enjoyed being a living myth, a modern incarnation of the traditional African divine king, he has deliberately cultivated the idea of an Ethiopian identity. In this age of growing nationalism it remains to be seen whether or not an Ethiopian nationalism can be forged out of the various elements that constitute the empire. The new government emphasis on Ethiopians as Africans may also be an attempt to foster the idea of an overriding unity. For Ethiopia, whose diverse elements are held together by the slender threads of history and the sinewy will of the Emperor, the future may well depend on the success with which new bonds of unity are forged.

Although Ethiopian unity has at one time or another been threatened by the centrifugal tendencies of the provinces of Tigre and Gojjam, and although some responsible Ethiopian officials fear the possibility of Galla separatism more than that of any other group simply because the Galla comprise the largest single ethnic group in the country, the strongest continuing challenge to the imperial authority has come from Eritrea. Somali political activity, which will be dealt with in the next chapter, is for the most part inspired from the Somali Republic, but Eritrean discontent, though encouraged by Muslims in the Arab world, feeds from within the province.

Anciently Eritrea had been an Ethiopian province, but after the fifteenth century Ethiopian control of the coastal strip diminished to the vanishing point as first the Turks and then the Egyptians won control over the Red Sea. They were supplanted on the coast by the Italians, who occupied Massawa in 1885. Although the coast had been subject to Muslim influence for more than a thousand years, Ethiopian merchants, mercenaries, and Jerusalem-bound pilgrims were always to be found there. Some of the lesser officials along the coast, such as the naib of Arkiko, were at times equally subject to the authority of the Ottomans on the coast and the Ethiopians in the interior. Barely fifteen miles inland, still in the coastal tract, the frontier outposts of the Ethiopian monarchy maintained a vigilant guard over the neighboring Muslim enclave and the potential threat of attack.

Inland, the population was clearly Ethiopian. As soon as one climbed the escarpment to the plateau, Tigrinya-speaking people were encountered. Not a separate ethnic group, they represented the northernmost Tigreans. Their main settlement was at Asmara, which until 1890 served as the headquarters of a provincial governor appointed by the Ethiopian emperor. In the lowlands to the east, subject to neither the Ottomans nor the Ethiopians, were the nomadic Danakil and the related sedentary Saho. These two Muslim groups had close trading relationships with the Tigreans and the Shoans; because of these commercial connections the Danakil sultans occasionally became political vassals of the Ethiopians. To the west of the Tigreans were peoples whom they had conquered in the eighteenth and nineteenth century. The Baria and the Kunama, whom the Ethiopians had raided for slaves for centuries, had abandoned their traditional religion for Islam before they were incorporated into the empire. Along the coast to the north and inland, in the area now referred to as western Eritrea, could be found the Beni Amer, a Muslim group that resisted all attempts at government by Turk, Egyptian, and Ethiopian, and the Tigrai, or lowland Tigreans, who some centuries ago abandoned Christianity for Islam.

Between 1885 and 1890 the Italians penetrated inland from their beachhead at torrid Massawa and occupied part of the cooler plateau to create their colony of Eritrea, whose name they adapted from the Greek *Erythraea,* literally "Red Sea." Never secure in their colony, which was but a tiny fragment of the Ethiopian empire, the Italians feared an Ethiopian invasion that would drive them into the sea, and at the same time they plotted to use Eritrea as a springboard for the invasion of Ethiopia proper. The Italian government was aware of the ethnic and religious divisions of their colony and of Ethiopia and turned this to their advantage; the fact that Christian Eritreans were Tigrean and not Amhara worked to the Italians' benefit as they encouraged the separate development of Eritrea apart from Ethiopia. Indeed, for thirty years before the Fascist invasion of Ethiopia in 1935 they assiduously wooed Tigrean leaders in the Ethiopian province of Tigre. During their brief occupation of Ethiopia they redrew administrative boundaries so that the Tigreans of Eritrea and the Tigreans of Tigre Province were governed together in one greater Tigrean administrative province.

The Italian presence in Eritrea ended in 1941 when the British invaded and conquered the colony. There they remained for eleven years until the fate of the colony was decided. Beginning September 15, 1952, under terms of a United Nations resolution passed in 1950, Eritrea and Ethiopia were federated under the Ethiopian monarchy. Thus the separate identity of Eritrea (restored to its colonial borders) was preserved, as was the foreign name of the area, which in its Amharic form, *Ertra,* has completely supplanted the traditional Ethiopian name for the coastal province, Bahr Nagash.

During the British occupation, when the future of the territory was uncertain, Eritrean political movements flourished. One group of Christian Tigreans proposed union with Ethiopia; a second Christian group, more conscious of its Tigrean culture and of the heritage of Italian colonialism and schooling, desired a separate Eritrean identity and resisted unification with Ethiopia for fear of Amhara domination. Some even favored the creation of a separate and independent state composed of Eritrea and Tigre Province. A Muslim group, sometime advocating a separate Muslim Eritrea, sometime toying with the idea of partition of the territory and the annexation of western (Muslim) Eritrea by the Sudan, also emerged. The war also produced a brief economic boom, and an Eritrean labor movement took shape. During the British administration political life developed rapidly, and Eritrean politics was characterized by the growth of a vigorous party system.[1] This did not bode well for the future, however, for the ethnic and religious divisions of the country manifested themselves in the political parties; the population of the territory, which numbered about 1,000,000 in 1952, was almost evenly divided between Christians and Muslims.[2] Since then a higher birth rate among the Muslims probably has tilted the balance in their favor.

For Christian separatists and leaders of the Muslim movement alike, the federation of Eritrea and Ethiopia in 1952 was a political disaster. The Eritrean parliament, noted for its political liveliness, was a stark contrast to its quiescent Ethiopian counterpart. The lack of free political institutions in the Ethiopian no-party state was apparent. With federation, their political alternatives disappeared, and some left Eritrea for exile abroad. In Cairo, Ibrahim Sultan Ali, onetime leader of the Eritrean Muslim League, and Woldeab Wolde Mariam, leader of the anti-Ethiopian Christian separatists and of the labor movement, formed a coalition Eritrean Democratic Front. At first they bombarded the United Nations and the governments of Britain, the United States, France, Italy, and the Soviet Union with letters and petitions protesting Ethiopian violations of the federal charter and of the Eritrean constitution. Their fears of progressive Ethiopianization of the territory through Amhara dominance were not baseless; Eritrean political parties, under constant pressure from the Ethiopian government, diminished in strength,

[1] G. K. N. Trevaskis, *Eritrea, A Colony in Transition, 1941–52* (London: Oxford University Press, 1960), pp. 46–80.

[2] *Ibid.,* pp. 132–133.

while the Eritrean parliament, apparently packed by order of Addis Ababa to insure a pro-Ethiopian majority, provided no effective opposition to Ethiopian policy. When Ethiopia informed the United Nations in 1962 of its intention to end the federal arrangement and annex Eritrea, with the endorsement of the supposedly representative Eritrean parliament, the leaders of the Eritrean opposition urged the United Nations to protest the action as a flagrant violation of the Eritreans' right of self-determination and as a unilateral act in contravention of the United Nations resolution of 1950. Helplessly they watched the annexation of Eritrea by what they called "the rotten Empire of Ethiopia." [3]

When the Conference of African Heads of State met in Addis Ababa in 1963, they again attempted to present to an international forum "the calamity of the people of Eritrea who are giving their last breath under the feet of the barbaric conquerors, the Ethiopians." [4] With sadness they accused the United Nations of having exposed them to genocide and homicide under the pretext of federating with Ethiopia. In vain they sought open support from Muslim leaders. Their cause seemed dead; at the moment independent Africa was bent on consolidation, not change. The Organization of African Unity was interested only in those liberation movements aimed at European colonial powers; convened as the African states were in Addis Ababa at the Emperor's request,

[3] Letter from Ibrahim Sultan, Idris Mohamed Adum, and Woldeab Wolde Mariam to United Nations Secretary Dag Hammerskjold, Cairo, June 30, 1959; mimeographed copies of the letter were distributed to the major embassies in Cairo.

[4] Ibrahim Sultan Ali on behalf of the United Parts of the Eritrean Democratic Front, "A Call from the People of Eritrea," Cairo, March 20, 1963, 23 pp.; mimeographed copies of the letter were sent to all African delegations and to the United Nations.

it was highly unlikely that the Eritreans could receive a sympathetic hearing.

Although the exiled leaders exerted little influence on international opinion as they lost contact with events in Ethiopia, tribal dissatisfaction, religious antipathy, and international complications worked to keep the Eritrean question alive. The Ethiopian government gave little publicity to its difficulties in Eritrea after annexation. The first task, bringing law and order to the territory, was far from easy. The border tribes of western Eritrea, always a problem to the Italian colonial administration and never completely subdued by the British, preferred to ignore the new government and its demands for taxation. The government officially referred to Beni Amer and other dissident tribesmen in that area as *shifta,* or bandits, drawing no distinction between them and the brigands who occasionally interrupted highway traffic between Asmara and Massawa at night. In June, 1965, however, government newspapers publicly condemned Syria for shipping arms to dissident Eritreans. Eritrean dissatisfaction thus had international ramifications. Since most of the arms were smuggled in overland from the Sudan, Ethiopian policy toward the Sudan had as one of its goals isolation of the Eritrean Muslims from contact with their Sudanese neighbors, a task that was never fully achieved.[5]

Throughout 1965 the situation in western Eritrea worsened. An Eritrean Liberation Front with Cairo connections issued communiqués from Mogadishu and claimed that the Ethiopians were combating not shifta but nationalist guerrillas. For the Somali Republic, embroiled as it then was in a border war with Ethiopia, the Eritreans were a valuable distraction. The skirmishes soon developed into small-scale

[5] "Ethiopian Agreement with Sudan," *The New York Times,* August 11, 1965, p. 9.

battles. The Eritrean Liberation Front claimed the death of hundreds of Ethiopian troops, while the Ethiopian government claimed the capture of thousands of rifles of Russian, Czech, British, and even Spanish origin. The "shifta" no longer seemed to be mere bandits; word leaked out that they acknowledged one leader, Idris Awate, who had served in the Italian colonial troops. Moreover, the Beni Amer, an important tribal group strategically located on both sides of the Sudanese-Eritrean border, gave its tacit support to the rebels, although it did not join with any sizable number of men.

The Eritrean Liberation Front, which drew its membership from several waves of exiles (after federation in 1952 and annexation in 1962), claimed that its hand was behind every shifta raid. In December, 1965 its secretary, Osman Saleh Sabbe, called upon all Arab and Muslim states to help Eritrea in its fight for freedom.[6] The rebels continued to wage their small war of terror against the six thousand Ethiopian troops garrisoned in Eritrea. Early in 1967 it was rumored that both Cuba and Communist China had agreed to train Eritrean guerrillas, some of whom allegedly were in Zanzibar and Pemba. Again the Ethiopian army met force with force.[7] To control the border region more easily, they drove as many as nine thousand Eritrean tribesmen of doubtful political loyalty across the frontier into the Sudan, creating a major refugee problem for the Sudanese government. Tension flared between Khartoum and Addis Ababa as the Eritrean Liberation Front desperately tried to draw world attention to its efforts. Because the Front was largely Muslim, it experienced difficulty in attracting the support of Eritrean

[6] "News in Brief," *Africa Report,* February, 1966, p. 28.

[7] Eric Pace, "Cuba and China Train Guerrillas for Eritrea," *The New York Times,* March 3, 1967, p. 3.

Christians or of Ethiopian political exiles like Tafari Sharew, the former Ethiopian ambassador to Sweden. Not until relatively recently did Ethiopian students abroad regard the Eritrean separatists' struggle as having anything in common with their protest against the Emperor's authoritarian rule.

In the spring of 1967 the movement took on new life when Tedla Bairu, a Christian Tigrean who had once led the movement for union with Ethiopia, defected to the Front. The major hope of the Front, however, was to obtain significant support from the Arab states. Whatever hopes they nurtured soon disappeared; one of the results of the Israel-Arab War of June, 1967 was the virtual disappearance of Arab involvement in Ethiopian Muslim affairs. Within a matter of months the Ethiopian army increased its campaign to pacify western Eritrea, and the Emperor obtained from Khartoum an agreement to resettle Eritrean refugees more than fifty miles from the Sudanese-Ethiopian border.

Yet the movement did not die. When Haile Selassie visited Lebanon in 1967 he was greeted by a published demand for Eritrean independence; it is also probable that he cancelled a planned visit to Iraq because of its support of the Front. In September, 1968, Radio Damascus beamed its Voice of the Eritrean Revolution southward to mark the eighth anniversary of the regional uprising and to vaunt its extravagant claims that the Eritreans were responsible for the death of five thousand of the Ethiopian troops sent in to pacify the rebellious province. At the same time, however, Ethiopian officials in Asmara confidently claimed that they had "broken the back" of the Eritrean rebellion. In no small degree this was attributable to the sharp decrease in supplies of weapons and ammunition from the Arab world.

In 1969 the Eritrean Liberation Front finally captured world newspaper headlines. With offices in Damascus, Khartoum, Baghdad, Aden, and Algiers, it was perhaps almost inevitable that the Front would sooner or later adopt Arab guerrilla tactics. On March 11, the Front bombed and heavily damaged an Ethiopian Air Lines jet plane at Frankfurt Airport. It appeared that the Front, weakened in Eritrea, in its desperation to strike back at its enemy was taking a page out of the book of Palestinian extremists also based in Damascus; or as the Ethiopian government claimed, "Failure breeds frustration."

This act gave the Eritrean Liberation Front the publicity it desired. Encouraged by its success at hitting vulnerable Ethiopian targets abroad, the Front attacked and badly damaged a second Ethiopian jet airliner at Karachi Airport two months later, while other Front agents in the French Territory of the Afar and Issa attacked the Ethiopian embassy in Djibouti, blew up a section of the Addis Ababa-Djibouti railway, and destroyed several locomotives. In August the guerrillas staged their first hijacking and forced a DC-3 Bahr Dar-Addis Ababa domestic flight to detour to Khartoum; the following month they hijacked a Djibouti-bound DC-6 shortly after taking off from Addis Ababa and ordered the captain to take them to Aden. Other Front activities in Eritrea itself included disruption of the Asmara water supply, raids on police outposts, and the destruction of petroleum tank-trucks.

Not all Front activities were successful, however: in Rome a student, Hagos Tesfai, blew himself to bits in his hotel room in mid-June as he clumsily assembled a bomb meant for the Ethiopian embassy in the Italian capital. In the young terrorist's possession were found leaflets denouncing "ferocious Ethiopian imperialism." The Eritrean Liberation Front, nevertheless, exulted over its accomplishments. In August a Front spokesman in Damascus stated that in the first two weeks of that month Eritrean fighters had killed 113 Ethiopian officers and soldiers in two ambushes between Massawa and Keren despite heavy shelling and bombing of their bases by Ethiopian artillery and bomber aircraft.

In reaction to the revival of the Eritrean insurgency and to Syrian sponsorship of the Eritrean Liberation Front, crowds surged through the streets of Asmara and Addis Ababa denouncing Arab interference in what they believed to be Ethiopian internal affairs. Ethiopian troops in Eritrea were increased to eight thousand. Thus, one-fourth of the army has been deployed to Eritrea for the purpose of controlling Ethiopia's sole coastal province. Given this strong force with its helicopters and fighter jets, the guerrillas stand little chance of overrunning Eritrea at present. They still number not more than eight hundred men in uniform, but can call upon an additional force of five thousand drawn from dissident Muslim tribesmen and from the ranks of shiftas. The government has warned the vulnerable Arabs living in Ethiopia about the consequences of supporting this movement. As for the university students who hijacked the Bahr Dar-Addis Ababa flight and then declared their support of the goals of the Eritrean separatists, the government has called attention to their own claims to be Maoists and has dismissed them as "foreign dupes." Nevertheless, to the chagrin of the army, the government has been unable to pacify western Eritrea, which is as much of a political no-man's land as it was a century ago.

Most recently the Eritrean Liberation Front has identified itself with the cause of Pan-Arabism, and Muslim Eritreans occasionally speak of themselves as Arabs, regardless of their actual origins. Asrate Kassa, Governor-General of Eritrea, feels that this is a tactical error on the part of the Front and that most Muslim Eritreans could never consider themselves

Arabs. For Asrate the solution to pacifying Eritrea is a vast program of economic development that would end the stagnation and unemployment that have fed the growth of the guerrilla movement; he has also distributed arms to loyalist villagers who in the past had aided the Eritrean Liberation Front out of fear. This may be true, but within Ethiopia the basic causes of dissatisfaction remain: Christian Tigrean distaste for Amhara domination, Christian-Muslim rivalry, the possibility of Pan-Islamic support from abroad (Syria, Saudi Arabia, Sudan, or Somalia), and the resistance of Muslim border tribes to centralized government (the spark that could ever rekindle the flames of separatism in western Eritrea).

To exacerbate the situation, even within the Ethiopian government there is tension between loyal Eritreans and Amhara. Those Eritreans who serve the government faithfully have often been accused of lording it over other Ethiopians; more exposed to European influences, some Eritreans have tended to look down upon other Ethiopians newly introduced to the Europeanizing aspects of modern Ethiopia. A common complaint in Ethiopian government circles is that Eritreans are too clannish and that to place one Eritrean in charge of an office is to introduce the proverbial camel's nose into the tent and end up with an office full of Eritreans.

Haile Selassie's main concern is that a successful separatist movement in any part of the country can endanger the political domination of Ethiopia by the central government that he created. How can there not be the gnawing fear that what has happened in Eritrea might also happen in the Ogaden, Tigre, and Gojjam, or among the Galla or any of the other peoples or regions of the empire?

Far less dramatic than the Eritrean uprising, but of equal concern to a government determined to extend its authority, has been the passive resistance to legal and administrative reform throughout the country. Noncompliance with government regulations increases with the distance from Addis Ababa and provincial administrative centers. Success in resisting the government, however, has depended on other factors equally critical in evaluating the policy of national unity.

Administrative centralization under a unified law that replaces local custom, regional practices, and traditional law has been another means to implement the goal of national unity. Indeed, in Africa Ethiopia has taken the lead in revolutionizing its legal code through a series of sweeping reforms that have given it new civil, commercial, penal, criminal procedure, and civil procedure codes.[8] In promulgating new legal codes and procedures drawn upon the highly varied experiences of France, England, Switzerland, India, Italy, and Australia, the Emperor has declared his intention to modernize the legal framework of the empire's social structure, in other words, to state in legal terms the nature of the modern Ethiopia he wishes to create. This means, of course, that the new codes bear little resemblance to Ethiopian customary law. Critics of such an approach have called this "fantasy law" and have raised doubts about whether the largely untrained judges and administrators will be able to implement the new laws.

In one area, tax reform, attempts at modernization, codification, and unification have only crystallized opposition on the local level to Addis Ababa's tampering with existing practices. Ethiopia's tax structure in the past has favored the landed aristocracy, who have often successfully managed to avoid paying most of the taxes. Land taxes cannot be effec-

[8] J. W. Salacuse, "Developments in African Law," *Africa Report,* March, 1968, p. 43.

tively collected when local officials have a vested interest at stake. Moreover, the Ethiopian Orthodox Church, which in some provinces owns between one-fourth and one-third of the land, pays no taxes whatsoever. In the past, to meet budgetary deficits the imperial government solicited "donations" from the Church and from wealthy landowners, but such a technique hardly suits the exigencies of modern governmental operations. As Peter Schwab has written, "If the Ethiopian tax system remains unchanged, revenue from taxes, though continuing to increase, will actually decrease proportionally, until the political system will be forced either into bankruptcy or reform of the tax policy."[9]

To deal with this situation, in the summer of 1967 the Emperor forced an unwilling Parliament to pass a new tax law, subjecting not only land but also produce to taxation by the central government. The members of the Chamber of Deputies regarded this agricultural income tax as a threat to their local strength, often based on landholdings. The Senate, many of whose members owned vast tracts of land in the provinces, also opposed the legislation, as did the Church. The tax reform was passed only after the Emperor threatened to dissolve Parliament. The real difficulties lay ahead, however, for attempts to collect taxes led to revolts in Gojjam, one of the core Christian provinces of the empire—although long hostile to Shoa and Tigre—and in Bale Province.[10]

[9] P. Schwab, "Modernise Ethiopia's Tax System: A Critical Look into Ethiopia's Structure of Taxation," *East Africa Journal,* February, 1968, p. 31.

[10] A fuller account of the Gojjami rebellion may be found in P. Schwab, "An Analysis of Decision-Making in the Political System of Ethiopia" (Ph.D. dissertation, New School for Social Research, 1969), pp. 198–216.

The Gojjami Amhara have a long history of conflict with the central government and were largely responsible for the failure of land tax reform legislation in 1942 and 1944. They had resisted government attempts to survey their lands in 1951 and again in 1962. When the central government sent tax assessors in May, 1968 across the formidable Blue Nile gorge that more than symbolically separates Gojjam from the rest of Ethiopia, the Gojjami, who at first had ignored the central government's announcement of the new tax measures, refused to allow them on their land. Large landowner, small landowner, and tenant farmer alike resisted the government agents. At issue was the threat to communal land ownership. By accepting government assessment of land taxes, the Gojjami realized that they would become vulnerable to governmental reclassification of all land ownership. Thus, a significant confrontation developed between Addis Ababa and one of the provinces over the basic question of expanding state authority.

When the tax assessors requested the unpopular provincial governor, Dejazmatch Tsehai Inqu Selassie, to use units of the territorial army to protect them, Gojjami farmers decided to resist them with force if necessary. Beginning in May, 1968, the movement spread through five of the seven subprovinces of Gojjam. Local village leaders who served as members of assessment teams were shot, and violence continued unchecked throughout eastern Gojjam. Neither the Emperor nor his Ministers of Defense, Finance, and Interior were willing to challenge the Gojjami, whose rebelliousness against all government had served thirty years earlier as a catalyst for the Ethiopian patriots' resistance against the Italians.

After the rebels, who had formed a loose organization of perhaps three thousand members, threatened to destroy the

Blue Nile bridge, the only link across the Blue Nile gorge between Gojjam and the rest of Ethiopia, unless the assessors *and* the governor were removed from their province, the Emperor ordered nine hundred troops of the regular army into Gojjam. His reasons were twofold: to protect the important bridge, and to prevent the farmers' tax rebellion from turning into a more dangerous political movement. To mollify the rebellious Gojjami, the Emperor called a temporary halt to tax assessment.

When a government investigating committee studied the situation on location in Gojjam, they listened to Gojjami claims against the central government alleging neglect in the construction of schools, roads, and hospitals and demanding the recall of several corrupt provincial and subprovincial officials. Attempts by the government to convince the Gojjami to pay their taxes by sending prestigious churchmen from Addis Ababa also failed, because the Gojjami clergy themselves were averse to the taxation of the land and produce that provided their livelihood. Moreover, the government was unwilling to send in more troops. It found itself in an increasingly difficult predicament, for army officers indicated in no uncertain terms that they could not open fire against their fellow Christians. The Gojjami stubbornly stood their ground, and the Emperor permanently halted tax assessment in Gojjam and dissolved the assessment teams. No arrests were made. On the contrary, on August 3, 1968, the government announced that Tsehai Inqu Selassie was transferred to the governorship of Kaffa Province and that new governors were appointed to three of the rebellious subprovinces.

Thus, the government proved to be powerless in its attempts to collect taxes. Despite the fact that the Emperor had placed his authority behind the tax reforms, the government ran into a situation in which it was opposed at the most basic level by all the traditional elements of a province, spontaneously and successfully mobilized to combat the kind of administrative modernization that is advocated not only by the Emperor but also by his severest critics among the developing political opposition.

Far to the southeast among the Muslim Galla of Bale Province a similar situation arose, but with a very different outcome. There too landowners and nomads objected to tax assessments, and local leaders complained with some reason that their province had been neglected by the government and sometimes exploited by Amhara officials. Schools, roads, and hospitals were demanded as the provincials lamented that tax monies raised in Bale in the past had been spent in other provinces. When the government insisted on the introduction of tax assessors and also sent in the troops, the results differed from those in Gojjam. The army enforced the government's orders against insurgent Galla, and taxes were forcibly collected despite both violent resistance by tribesmen who, like the Gojjami, have never been disarmed by the government, and residual passive resistance. As in Gojjam, the traditional local interests combatted the extension of the authority of the central government, but unlike Gojjam, the province of Bale is Muslim: the army was willing to follow orders to suppress the rebellion with any means at its disposal.

The implications of the Gojjam and Bale tax rebellions for national unity are far from clear. They suggest, however, that the Ethiopian government for many years to come will apparently have greater success in extending the centralizing controls characteristic of the modern state over peripheral provinces like Bale (and perhaps Eritrea and the Ogaden as well) than it will have in those provinces where the Amhara themselves predominate.

CHAPTER 9

The End of
Ethiopian Isolation

Ethiopian foreign policy today rests on the foundations established by Theodore and Menelik in the nineteenth century. Theodore, intent on securing modern arms for his military forces, invited European artisans to Ethiopia. Anticipating modern practices, he insisted that foreign technicians remain subservient at all times to the will of his government, not interfere in the internal affairs of the state, but provide the needed technology. His one failure was not promoting the training of Ethiopians in those skills. Menelik II continued this practice and expanded Ethiopian contacts with the diplomats, as well as the artisans, of European states. He balanced off the aims of Italy, France, and Great Britain with noteworthy skill and clearly foreshadowed contemporary policies of nonalignment. It may very well be that the diplomacy of Theodore and Menelik ensured the continued independence of Ethiopia during the period of greatest European expansion into Africa.

Haile Selassie I has continued these traditional policies and has added two of his own: support of supranational organizations and leadership on the African continent. They have gained for the Emperor international recognition and perhaps enhanced his prestige in his own country. Ethiopia's isolation from the rest of the world has ended, while modernization, state-building, and the development of an African identity have interacted to preserve a modernizing autocracy.

Although the Ethiopian government, as will be seen in the next chapter, has been pursuing an energetic policy in Africa, it has carefully continued its older, more cautious approach to relations with non-African states. Basically, the Ethiopian policy is one of furthering Ethiopian national interests, such as technical assistance and territorial integrity.

The experience of the British military occupation rapidly disillusioned the Emperor about the motives of Great Britain in coming to his aid in World War II. The British at one time briefly toyed with the idea of encouraging Galla separatism, cultivated the Greater Somalia movement, treated Ethiopia as enemy-occupied territory, continued to occupy the Haud and the Ogaden long after the war ended, insisted that the Emperor have British advisers, resisted Ethiopian ambitions in Eritrea, and in general caused the Ethiopians to suspect them of duplicity. Not until 1965, when Queen Elizabeth and the Duke of Edinburgh visited Ethiopia, did the Ethiopian government relax and again manifest interest in Britain. Even then political observers were unsure as to the meaning of the state visit. Some saw it as the Emperor's means of illustrating the stabilizing influence of monarchy; the reigning monarchs of Norway and the Netherlands have also made the long air journey to Addis Ababa. Some foresaw it, rather wishfully, as a prologue to liberalization of the regime, while others viewed it as a shrewd move to attract British investment capital to Ethiopia.

Even before the restoration of full Ethiopian sovereignty in 1945, the Emperor sought to counter British influence. In 1944 he welcomed an economic mission and lend-lease aid from the United States and appointed American and Swedish technical advisers. In February, 1945, Haile Selassie met with President Franklin D. Roosevelt in Cairo, and the foundations of an Ethiopian-American entente were laid. Thus, the

Ethiopians turned to the Americans to offset British influence. It was recalled that the United States had never extended official recognition to the Italian conquest of Ethiopia, and from 1948 American aid increased. When the United States supported the United Nation's resolution in 1951 to create a federation of Eritrea and Ethiopia, the friendship blossomed; Ethiopia in return supported the American initiative in the Korean crisis and sent a battalion of the Imperial Body Guard to the United Nations command in Korea, where they were attached to the Seventh Division of the United States Army. All told, more than five thousand Ethiopians served in Korea, gaining for the Ethiopian army its first experience in modern technical warfare. At that time too Haile Selassie permitted the United States to continue using a former Italian communications base outside Asmara.

In 1953 the United States and Ethiopia signed a mutual defense assistance agreement, which laid the basis for the modernization of the Ethiopian army and the development of an air force to be used "exclusively to maintain its [Ethiopia's] internal security, its legitimate self-defense, or to permit it to participate in the defense of the area, or in United Nations collective security arrangements and measures." Since then a Military Assistance Advisory Group (MAAG) has been attached to the Ethiopian Ministry of Defense. In the first ten years of the agreement, the United States provided Ethiopia with almost $74 million in military assistance; this represented virtually half the United States' military involvement in Africa.[1] The mutual defense assistance agreement, a standard treaty of the Cold War period, enabled the Ethiopian government to build up the necessary military force not only to defend the country but also to ensure the effec-

[1] House of Representatives, *Foreign Assistance Act of 1969: Hearings* (Washington: U.S. Government Printing Office, 1969), pp. 826–828.

tiveness of the government in dealing with rebellious regions like Eritrea, Gojjam, and Bale or troublesome political opposition. It was the army that put down the attempted coup d'état in 1960 and the student riots of 1968 and 1969. It should be noted that although the Ethiopian army came under the extensive influence of the United States, MAAG functions with respect to the air force and navy were confined to logistics and end-use supervision. In this respect the Emperor modified the otherwise enormous influence of the United States on the Ethiopian military by turning to Sweden, Israel, India, and other countries for technical training. Furthermore, the United States was not allowed to train Ethiopian intelligence and security officers; here the Ethiopians looked to Israel, a small state that cannot sway Ethiopian policy, but one that has a highly effective intelligence-gathering network.

The status of the American base near Asmara, renamed Kagnew in honor of the Kagnew Battalion sent by the Emperor to Korea, was regularized by an agreement at the time of the mutual defense treaty. Kagnew is of great strategic importance for tracking space satellites, monitoring radio broadcasts from eastern Europe and the Middle East, and relaying military and diplomatic communications; its specific operations are a closely guarded military secret. The base is a critical link in American telecommunications between Europe and the Far East; its value is enhanced by its location in an area that is relatively free of meteorological interference with radio relay operations.

Relations between Ethiopia and the United States temporarily cooled when the United States gave its tacit approval to Somali aspirations for independence. Dissatisfied with his failure to win British and American support against Somalia, the Emperor increased Ethiopian contacts with Communist bloc nations, gave greater support to Pan-Africanism, and appeared to move toward a neutralist position. In the summer of 1959 he visited the Soviet Union and Czechoslovakia, after which their aid to Ethiopia increased. In time of crisis, however, the Emperor knew he could rely upon the United States.

During the abortive coup in December, 1960, United States Ambassador Arthur L. Richards played a part that one astute observer of Ethiopian politics has described as enigmatic; another expert has asserted that American assistance was instrumental in putting down the revolt.[2] Richards claimed that his role was only humanitarian. On the morning of December 16, 1960, he was called to rebel headquarters, where he agreed to act as an intermediary between the rebels and the loyalist army leaders. Admittedly, the United States also had specific interests to protect in Ethiopia: the Kagnew installation, the military agreement, and the influence of MAAG. Richards' office served as a neutral meeting place for Girmame Neway and loyalist Major Assefa Lemma. Later, the American Ambassador and a military attaché narrowly escaped death when the army attacked rebel headquarters just as they were delivering a message from the loyalists to the leaders of the coup. This indicates a lack of coordination between the American embassy and the loyalist military commanders. On the other hand, when General Merid Mangasha asked Brigadier-General Chester De Gavre, the ranking MAAG officer, to help him plan an operation to regain control of Addis Ababa, in which aerial photography would play a key part, and to lend the loyalists telecommunications equipment, Ambassador Richards approved the

[2] R. Greenfield, *Ethiopia, A New Political History* (New York: Frederick A. Praeger, 1965), pp. 412–413, 425–429; Vernon Mackay, *Africa in World Politics* (New York: Harper & Row, 1963), p. 370.

request. Moreover, the Emperor first received word of the coup via the facilities of Kagnew.

Whether or not the United States was a decisive element in the suppression of the revolt will not be known until scholars have access to classified government reports. This much, however, is certain: the existing regime has been bolstered by American military assistance. From the point of view of Ethiopian critics of Haile Selassie's government, this makes the United States an accomplice of the Emperor. For this reason, as the student demonstrations have grown in size and scope, the United States Information Office in Addis Ababa, the Peace Corps volunteers, and, to a lesser extent, the embassy (which is protected and far removed from the center of Addis Ababa) have been assaulted verbally and physically. For this reason, too, the United States has been accused of giving aerial support to Ethiopian ground operations against rebels in Eritrea and in Bale.[3] Moreover, the United States, which has a vested interest in maintaining stability in Ethiopia and throughout Africa, has developed an even stronger interest in Addis Ababa since that city became the seat of the Organization of African Unity in 1963. Because the United States has no formal link with the Organization of African Unity, it has worked out useful informal relationships with it through the American embassy in the Ethiopian capital, which has thus taken on additional importance.

Haile Selassie made his first visit to the United States in 1956, and seven years later returned in even greater triumph. In February, 1967 the Emperor again visited the United States, at his own request, to discuss world problems, United States regional foreign aid programs which posed a threat to single-nation assistance programs, the Somali question, and

[3] Jack Kramer, "Ethiopia's Unknown War," *The Nation*, August 11, 1969, pp. 104–106.

opportunities for American investment in Ethiopia. It should be noted that after leaving Washington the Emperor flew directly to Moscow to conclude a technical assistance agreement. Three months later he returned to North America to receive an honorary degree from the University of California at Los Angeles and to open the Ethiopian Pavilion at the World's Fair in Montreal.

The importance of American-Ethiopian relations was underscored in July, 1969, when Haile Selassie made still another visit to the United States to confer with President Richard M. Nixon (who had traveled to Ethiopia in 1957 when he was vice-president) to reassure the United States, and to be reassured that the two countries derived mutual advantages from their close relationship despite Ethiopian students' protests taking place in Washington at that very moment. Until then the American public had only briefly glimpsed dissatisfaction with the Emperor when Berhanou Dinke, Ethiopian Ambassador to the United States, dramatically resigned his post in June, 1965 and sought political asylum in the United States. The Ambassador claimed that he resigned because of the failure of his monarch to institute democratic reforms. Quoting Hagos Gebre Yesus, then head of the Ethiopian Students Association in North America, the Ambassador called the Emperor's reforms fraudulent. Berhanou failed to rally about him an opposition party, and after the Ethiopian government accused him of having embezzled embassy funds, the American press lost interest in him.[4]

[4] "Ethiopia Envoy to U.S. Quits, Urges Rights Revolt at Home," *The Washington Post,* June 14, 1965, p. 1; Open letter from Hagos G. Yesus to Berhanou Dinke, December 25, 1966, *Challenge: Journal of the Ethiopian Students Association in North America,* VII, no. 1 (August, 1967), pp. 37–39.

Ethiopia is greatly dependent on the United States for military, as well as economic assistance, and the United States, which has important strategic and political interests in Ethiopia, probably has no stronger friend in Africa than Ethiopia. The Emperor, however, does not think of himself as an American satellite and has tried to keep some freedom of action throughout the relationship; indicative of this was the complete repayment of American lend-lease aid. To counter the excessive influence of any one state, Haile Selassie has encouraged relations with a dozen other nations, many of which can supply technicians and aid in areas of assistance that the United States would prefer to control.

Relations with these other states are characterized by the same eye to advantage and independence seen in Ethiopia's dealings with the major powers. One of Ethiopia's first European friends was France, the nation that supplied the modern arms that helped defeat the Italians at Adowa in 1896. French influence in Ethiopia was strong until the Italian invasion in 1935. The second language of the Emperor and all high officials at one time was French, and the Djibouti-Addis Ababa railway shipped the goods that formerly bound France and Ethiopia in a close commercial relationship. In the years following World War II, however, French influence was minimal. In November, 1959 the Ethiopian government demanded and was accorded a 50 per cent interest in the Franco-Ethiopian Railway Company. To dramatize this move the company was converted into an Ethiopian corporation and transferred its headquarters from Paris to Addis Ababa.

Not until Charles de Gaulle visited Ethiopia in 1966 did French influence begin to revive. In August, 1968 a Franco-Ethiopian cultural convention was signed; the French agreed to provide seventy-five teachers of French to serve in twenty-two Ethiopian secondary schools. In those schools four years of training in the French language became compulsory at the beginning of the 1968/69 academic year. The French also agreed to establish a teachers' training institute to prepare Ethiopians to replace the seventy-five Frenchmen teaching in Ethiopian schools. Today the French *lycée* in Addis Ababa is highly regarded, and government French-language publications, like *Ethiopie d'Aujourd'hui* and *Addis-Soir,* which have excellent editorial staffs, are receiving greater circulation. The visit of de Gaulle and the revised status of the French Territory of the Afar and Issa has drawn the two countries even closer together. In the event that the French should pull out of that territory, it is highly likely that the Ethiopians would be given control of the valuable port of Djibouti and that the action would be justified along strategic and economic lines, as well as ethnic (unification of the Afar). Certainly such a move would exacerbate Ethiopian-Somali relations, but until the development of better transportation facilities, possession of Djibouti would be the only security for Ethiopia's most valuable trade outlet.

A deep suspicion of Italy persists in Ethiopia, even though individual Italians are well received in the country. Nevertheless, Italy has probably had the greatest cultural influence on Ethiopia, for Italians had close contacts with Ethiopia long before Mussolini's decision to invade the country. Ethiopia found the presence of Italy in Somalia as Trust Territory Administrator distasteful, and strong distrust of Italy's motives in supplying economic assistance to the Somali Republic persists. Bad feelings were partly assuaged by the payment of a large sum as reparations in 1957. Only in 1963, however, did the Ethiopian and Italian governments begin to discuss expansion of contacts. Since then trade has expanded enormously, and Italian economic influence is growing. In 1969 the Italian government returned to Ethiopia the statue of the Lion of Judah which commemorated the Ethiopian victory at Adowa. The Italians regarded the return of the statue, which had been removed from Ethiopia by Mussolini's order, as a demonstration of their good faith. The Ethiopians, however, are still waiting for the Italians to return the Axumite stele the Fascists removed at the same time and erected in Rome at the end of the Circus Maximus in front of the Ministry of Italian Africa, a building now housing the United Nations Food and Agricultural Organization. It is ironic that the architect of Africa Hall, the headquarters of the United Nations Economic Commission for Africa, symbol of Ethiopia's commitment to African independence and economic development, is Italian.

When the Emperor first made trips to Czechoslovakia, Yugoslavia, and the Soviet Union in 1959 and concluded aid agreements with Communist states, some American newspapers hastily jumped to the improbable conclusion that Ethiopia had moved to the left. Subsequently, Ethiopia's voting behavior in the United Nations seemed to confirm their assumption as Ethiopia called for the admission of Communist China to the United Nations and support of the use of force on behalf of the African population of Rhodesia. Yet Soviet influence in Ethiopia is minimal. The Ethiopian government has not forgotten Russia's postwar hostility and its condemnation of Ethiopia as a feudal monarchy. Relations between the two countries were for a long time very formal. When the Emperor visited the U.S.S.R. in 1967, before agreeing to the formation of an Ethiopian-Soviet Trading Company he exacted a promise that the Soviet Union would support Ethiopia's territorial integrity. At present the Russians support a hospital established by the tsarist regime and have completed a technical secondary school at Bahr Dar and a large oil refinery at Assab. They offer more than one hundred scholarships for Ethiopians at universities in the Soviet Union. How many of these students and their colleagues at Haile Sellassie I University will become Marxists is subject to conjecture.

For many years it appeared that the Soviet Union was content to exert its influence in Ethiopia by means of its East European allies, and Ethiopia agreed to a number of technical assistance arrangements and cultural exchange programs with Hungary, Bulgaria, Czechoslovakia, Rumania, and Poland. Yet because of Ethiopia's close relationship with the United States and because Ethiopia is far from the Communist model of a modern state, Ethiopia is susceptible to criticism from Eastern European sources. Instances of government repression and of forced labor, common knowledge in Ethiopia, have not been ignored in East Europe as they have been in the United States. One cannot help but wonder how the Ethiopian government reacted to a widely circulated mock travel poster for Ethiopian Air Lines published by *Tricontinental,* a Prague periodical which advertised:

Some of the far away places with charming names that tourists should visit:

    ALEM BEKAGNE, the biggest prison in East Africa

    KAGNEW, U. S. strategic military base for "technical" espionage throughout the world

    ADOLA MINES, where 20,000 men waste away doing forced labor

    MASSAWA, important Ethiopian–U.S.–Israeli naval base for the control of the Red Sea

If the Russians intend to increase their political influence in Ethiopia during the lifetime of Haile Selassie, they will discover, as the Italians, French, and British have, that Ethiopia still intends to limit the influence of all other powers in the Horn of Africa. Indeed, as if to illustrate this, in March, 1969 the Ethiopian government expelled three members of the Czechoslovak embassy and two Soviet journalists alleged to have fomented antigovernment demonstrations among university and secondary-school students.

From time to time the Ethiopian government has also attempted to improve relations with its nearest neighbors to the north, the Arab states. A first effort during the Suez crisis of 1956, which affected Ethiopia's export trade because of the closure of the Suez Canal, did not bring the desired results, but since 1959, in a sharp break with historical tradition, state visits have been exchanged with the United Arab Republic, Saudi Arabia, Jordan, Lebanon, Kuwait, and Yemen. Radio Cairo, which encouraged the Somali Republic in its territorial ambitions, reduced the intensity of its attacks on Ethiopia.

The Ethiopians were still concerned, however, about the extension of Egyptian influence down the Red Sea and into war-torn Yemen, a land that has always had close relations with the Horn of Africa. During the abortive coup of December, 1960 rumors were rife in Addis Ababa that Egyptian aircraft had landed at the capital's airport. Ethiopian distrust of Egypt revived the old fear of Muslim encirclement. The Israeli victory in the Middle East war of June, 1967 allayed Ethiopian fears about the ambitions of a now greatly weakened United Arab Republic. Haile Selassie even offered his services as a mediator in the dispute over the status of Jerusalem, whereas earlier he had assiduously maintained a policy of aloofness from the dispute. Ethiopia's emergence as a leader in the African unity movement has also effectively offset the influence of Nasser in African affairs. Elsewhere in the Arab world, Haile Selassie has tried to build friendships. In state visits to three of the more conservative Arab countries in 1966, he initiated economic relations with Kuwait, an important supplier of oil for the Assab refinery, called attention in Lebanon to Ethiopian Air Lines' new service to Beirut, and in Jordan mentioned the possibility of extending air service to Amman.

Until 1967 the Ethiopian government maintained a discreet silence about its relationship with Israel. Israeli advisers have played a crucial role in the training of Ethiopian security and intelligence officers, and Israelis have aided in military training and in limited economic development projects. Israeli medical personnel have had a strong impact on the Public Health College. The Israeli embassy in Addis Ababa is considered to be Israel's most important diplomatic post on the African continent. The Ethiopian Orthodox Church owns property in Jerusalem, where there have been Ethiopian monks for more than seven centuries, and members of the Emperor's family and Church and government leaders have visited Israel. In many respects Israel is a natural ally of Ethiopia against Arab dominance in the Red Sea; indeed, in August, 1969, the Israeli government proposed a military alliance of the United States, Israel, Iran, Turkey, and Ethiopia to contain radical Arabism.[5] Some Ethiopian officials, enthusiastic about Israeli military prowess, regard Israel as a useful alternative to the United States, whose foreign policy has been known to undergo changes in the Middle East. Yet the Ethiopian government at first moved very cautiously. Direct air links between Ethiopia and Israel did not exist in 1969, despite the interest on both sides. One is tempted to speculate about the romantic aspects of a revival of the three-millennia-old connection between Solomonic Jerusalem and the sons of Sheba.

[5] John K. Cooley, "Mideast Radicals Gain," *The Christian Science Monitor,* December 6, 1969, p. 1.

Although Ethiopia became a charter member of the United Nations Organization on July 28, 1942, the Emperor has not relied unduly on that international organization. For Ethiopia, the United Nations was at first a means to the attainment of national political goals. In this area Ethiopia achieved one notable victory and one noteworthy setback. In November, 1949 the General Assembly appointed a Commission for Eritrea to report back with suggestions for the future of that former Italian colony, then under British administration. Late in 1950 the United Nations adopted a resolution favoring the federation of Eritrea and Ethiopia under the Ethiopian crown. By peaceful diplomacy Ethiopia took the first step; in 1962 the last step was taken when the territory was annexed, as originally desired by Ethiopia twenty years earlier. Although successful in its Eritrean policy, Ethiopia failed in a similar approach to the former Italian Somaliland. Neither federation nor Ethiopian annexation was seriously considered by the United Nations, and the Ethiopian government uneasily watched first the return of Italy to the Horn of Africa as Trust Administrator and then the creation of a hostile, independent Somali Republic.

But for many, Ethiopia is still the symbol of the need for international cooperation. Time and again, as at the session of the United Nations in October, 1963, Haile Selassie has called attention to the failure of the League of Nations to act when Italy invaded Ethiopia in 1935 and has warned the United Nations of the necessity of applying the principle of collective security. For this purpose, in April, 1951 the Ethiopian government gave its backing to United Nations policy and dispatched troops of the Imperial Body Guard to Korea. Again in 1960, when the United Nations faced a serious crisis in the Congo, the Ethiopians were among the nine African states consulted by Dag Hammerskjold to discuss possible African contributions to a program of "technical assistance in the security field." Ethiopians sat on the United Nations conciliation commission that attempted to bring peace to the Congo in November, 1960, and on the commission of investigation charged with studying the death of Patrice Lumumba. When the Congo situation deteriorated, Ethiopian troops were offered to the United Nations. By the end of July, 1961, of a total United Nations force of 8,936 officers and men, 1,160 were Ethiopians, who served mostly in the Congo's Orientale and Equateur Provinces. By November, 1961 the Ethiopian commitment had expanded to more than 3,000 men (only India had a larger contingent), and four Ethiopian Sabre jets joined the small United Nations air force of fourteen planes.[6]

Military involvement inevitably entailed political involvement, and when the secession of Katanga was discussed at the United Nations, the Ethiopian Ambassador forcefully stated that this was not a domestic issue, but a result of meddling from without the Congo. Accusing outside intervention of maintaining the Katangans, the Ethiopian government warned ominously that if the Congolese government were to collapse, the United Nations might well collapse with it. In no uncertain terms the Ethiopians not only supported the United Nations action but advocated the broadening of the UN mandate in the Congo. Thus, the Ethiopians demonstrated both their support of the United Nations action and the newly acquired modern arms and techniques of the Ethiopian army and air force. Continuing this policy of commitment to collective security, in 1964 the Emperor offered to send troops to any state in East Africa threatened by a coup d'état.

[6] Catherine Hoskyns, *The Congo Since Independence* (London: Oxford University Press, 1965), pp. 131, 159, 191, 294, 392.

In the Security Council the Ethiopian representative, Endalkatchew Makonnen, was an eloquent spokesman not only
for the principles of collective security but also for the aspirations of the African bloc. As a member of the Special Committee of 24 on the ending of colonialism, the Ambassador
was an outspoken critic of the last strongholds of foreign
domination on the African continent. In the debate on
Southern Rhodesia in March, 1968 he condemned a desperate colonialism that was trying to push back the frontiers of
independence in southern Africa and was repressing the
black population. "In Southern Africa," he said, "a garrison
State has been created; South West Africa has been usurped;
a colonial war is being waged in the Portuguese Territories;
in Southern Rhodesia, the threat to international peace and
security becomes more obvious every day." Speaking on behalf of the independent African states, Endalkatchew Makonnen urged the United Nations to apply general and
comprehensive sanctions with appropriate and effective
follow-up action with regard to Rhodesia, South Africa, and
Portugal. In June the Ethiopian delegate took the initiative
and proposed a resolution on behalf of Algeria, India, Pakis-
tan, and Senegal urging the United Kingdom to end the
white rebellion in Rhodesia by force if necessary. Later that
same month, on behalf of the Special Committee of 24, Ethiopia introduced another resolution calling on all states, particularly members of the North Atlantic Treaty Organization,
to halt the supply of weapons and military equipment to
Portugal. Again, the Ethiopian Ambassador spoke of the
"evil perpetuation of the status quo of exploitation, oppression and repression."

Not only has Ethiopia become one of the chief spokesmen
for the African bloc in the Security Council, but the Ethiopian Ambassador has also voiced the opinions of the un-

aligned nations in the Middle East crisis, in the aftermath of the Soviet occupation of Czechoslovakia in 1968, and in promoting the ratification of the nuclear nonproliferation treaty. Ethiopia has indeed come a long way since the 1930's when Haile Selassie's speech at the League of Nations in Geneva was like a voice crying in the wilderness.

Ethiopia has also developed important relations with the United Nations in the field of technical assistance. The list of projects in Ethiopia sponsored by United Nations agencies is long and impressive. Some of these projects are joint endeavors of the Ethiopian government, the United States, and the United Nations. UNESCO in 1954 made contributions to a ten-year project for controlled expansion of the Ethiopian educational system and to a training program for teachers in the new community schools. In addition to milk distribution projects in Addis Ababa, UNICEF has sponsored sanitation projects in northwestern Ethiopia and a program for leprosy control. WHO has helped set up a malaria eradication project, tuberculosis control demonstration centers, eye disease clinics, and the promising Public Health College and Training Center at Gondar. In 1968 the United Nations Development Program allocated more than $1.5 million for a five-year work-oriented adult literacy project to establish pilot programs directly linked to economic development. The crowning achievement was the location of the permanent headquarters of the United Nations Economic Commission for Africa in Addis Ababa. Underdeveloped Ethiopia has become the host of innumerable conferences examining the problem of how African governments can best translate their often grandiose development schemes into concrete and realizable projects.

In its dealings with the United Nations, however, the Ethiopian government has maintained the same caution that it exhibits toward foreign states. Africa Hall, the home of the Economic Commission for Africa, has remained the property of the Ethiopian government, and United Nations officials in Ethiopia have reported occasional instances of harassment by lesser Ethiopian officials. Furthermore, although Ethiopia has become the advocate of justice and righteousness in international relations, Ethiopia played no significant role whatsoever in the important International Conference on Human Rights that met in Teheran in April and May, 1968.

Since 1963, Ethiopia has pursued a role of active leadership in African affairs, in the United Nations, and on the world scene in general. But here, as in so many areas of Ethiopian activity, there is a basic paradox. Ethiopia, in so many ways the least African of the African states, has become a major spokesman for Africa. Emperor Haile Selassie, described in 1954 by the Secretary-General of the United Nations as "a symbolic landmark, a prophetic figure in the path of man's struggle to achieve international peace through international action," is now ranged on the same side as African leaders like Sekou Touré, radical leaders who have condemned in their own countries the "feudal" ideas and institutions so much a part of the Ethiopian scene today. The Emperor's leadership in Africa has not been challenged, but there is still a strong feeling that Ethiopia does not wholly belong with the other independent African states which, as they become more attuned to the growing voice of protest emanating from within Ethiopia, cannot ignore the fact that his image at home is very different from that presented abroad.

CHAPTER 10

The Africanization
of Ethiopia

Haile Selassie's policy of enlarging Ethiopia's contacts with the outside world has ended hundreds of years of Ethiopian political isolation. In the past decade Ethiopia, once inaccurately regarded as more Middle Eastern than African because of its Semitic roots and Red Sea connections, has emerged dramatically as a leader on the African continent, as well as a factor in neutralist international politics and an active force in the United Nations.

Historically, Ethiopia was isolated from contact with much of Africa. In an older, smaller context, when attention was not focused on purely Ethiopian affairs, it turned only to its immediate neighbors or across the Red Sea. In the precolonial period Ethiopia was concerned with invasions by Muslims from the Sudan and from the east, from what is now the Ogaden and the Somali Republic. As late as the 1880's Sudanese dervishes raided across the border and put Gondar to the torch. Somali tribesmen have posed a continual threat to security in the Ogaden ever since its conquest during the reign of Menelik II.

Relations with the Sudanese Republic today are tenuous because of the question of refugees from the southern Sudan in Ethiopia and from western Eritrea in the Sudan. The fact that each of the two states has been embarrassed by regional separatist movements drew them together at one time. In August, 1965, Haile Selassie gave Sudanese Premier Muhammad Ahmed Mahgoub a specific commitment to support the Sudanese government by forbidding Sudanese exiles to engage in propaganda against the Khartoum government. The Ethiopians also agreed to call a halt to arms smuggling from the twenty thousand Sudanese refugees at Gambela in southwest Ethiopia to the insurgents in the southern Sudan, who call themselves "Azanians." In return, the Sudanese government agreed to curb the Eritrean Liberation Front, which had been launching raids into Ethiopia from bases on Sudanese soil.

As Ethiopia stepped up its campaign against the Eritrean rebels in 1966 and 1967, relations with the Sudan were complicated by the flight into the Sudan of thousands of Eritrean refugees, who created health and security problems for the Sudanese. When the Ethiopian army crossed the border into the Sudanese province of Kassala in hot pursuit of Eritrean guerrillas in March, 1967, good relations between the two nations were briefly endangered. The two governments hastily reaffirmed their agreement, in the words of Radio Addis Ababa, "to prevent any subversive activity in either country that harmed the security of the other country." Subsequently, after Haile Selassie visited Khartoum in August, 1967, the two governments agreed to demarcate the border between Eritrea and Kassala. At that time the Sudanese government announced plans to resettle more than 100,000 Eritrean refugees at agricultural projects fifty miles west of the border in an effort to reduce frontier incidents, for in 1967 alone more than 28,600 Eritreans crossed into Kassala Province in the biggest influx of refugees in all Africa that year. In other areas the two governments have also made common cause. A branch of the State Bank of Ethiopia has been opened in Khartoum, and both governments have made efforts to increase trade between the two countries. It appeared for a while that there were no outstanding disputes between the two states, and there is some evidence that at one time they had been drawn together by a common apprehension of the expanding influence of Nasser's United Arab Republic.

Evidently the common policy met with a certain modicum of success. A number of Eritrean rebels surrendered to the Ethiopian embassy in Khartoum in return for a grant of amnesty, and the Sudanese government appeared to be less troubled by the Azanian refugees in Illubabor Province. It must be admitted, however, that virtually no information is available about conditions among the Sudanese refugees in that remote area of southwestern Ethiopia. Nevertheless, despite the fact that the Ethiopian and Sudanese governments tried to smooth over their differences, both experienced pressures to pursue a different policy. In the Sudan rightist Islamic elements urged their government not to cooperate with Ethiopia. When those elements criticized the government for turning over eighteen members of the Eritrean Liberation Front to the Ethiopians in September, 1967, the Sudanese Interior Minister publicly denied that Muslim rebels would be turned over to Ethiopian authorities. Similarly, the Sudanese government had to resist pressures to protest against the trial in Asmara of Muhammad Abdel Rahman Saleh, a Sudanese found guilty of espionage on behalf of the Eritrean Liberation Front and sentenced to ten years' imprisonment. In 1968 such pressure mounted, especially after the Governor of Kassala ordered the Eritrean Liberation Front to close its doors in that Sudanese city in accordance with the basic Ethiopian-Sudanese agreement. Whenever Azanian separatists launched raids from Ethiopia and whenever it was felt that Ethiopia's military strength was overshadowing that of its Muslim neighbors, as was the case when part of the Ethiopian fleet (the Sudan has no fleet to speak of) made an official call at Port Sudan, Khartoum's opposition newspapers openly hinted that a different policy was needed.

From the Ethiopian point of view, there were basic conflicts in this choice of policy. The temptation to support a Christian movement like that of the Azanian Liberation Front that would weaken a Muslim neighbor is great, despite the commitment to the Organization of African Unity and the highly publicized principle of noninterference in the affairs of other African states. In 1967 this ambivalence was indicated in the treatment of David Koak Guok and Stephen Ciec Lam, two southern Sudanese nationalists interned at Asosa by the Ethiopians with the original intent of effecting a trade for Eritrean Liberation Front rebels interned in the Sudan. After several months of vacillation, the Ethiopian government, rather than turn the two men over to Sudanese officials, enabled them to fly to Nairobi. The Sudanese press also claimed that within the Sudan Ethiopian consular officials were overstepping their powers, as in the case of the military attaché accused in July, 1968 of having promoted the bombing of houses of Eritreans in Kassala.

Nor can the Ethiopians have been completely happy as they continued to discover caches of arms hidden by the Eritrean Liberation Front in the western Eritrean lowlands. In September, 1968 one such cache of Soviet and Eastern European arms, including light arms, bazookas, and 81mm mortars, was found, together with Arabic documents printed in the Sudan, Syria, and Iraq. An informant, Ibrahim Hamed Muhammad, reported that war matériel of Syrian, Iraqi, Saudi Arabian, Somali, Sudanese, and Chinese origin was usually imported into Eritrea from Saudi Arabia via Port Sudan. In the light of this and other evidence, Ethiopians nursed the suspicion that the Sudanese might some day sponsor the Eritrean Liberation Front's goal of creating another Muslim nation in Eritrea. Finally, as the Ethiopians prepared the diplomatic groundwork for the demarcation of the Ethiopian-Sudanese border, they discovered frontier questions that would inevitably shake any official entente between the two countries.

In May, 1969, a coup d'état toppled the Sudanese government. The Revolutionary Command Council, which engineered the coup, had to face serious internal political and economic problems. To ease the strain, the new government extended an offer of autonomy to the troublesome southerners, who had been in revolt against Khartoum for years. In its initial period of rule the new government could not risk foreign adventures, and in July the Sudanese government sent a high-level ministerial mission to Addis Ababa to reassure its powerful neighbor to the east. Potentially, however, the military government's strong commitment to internal revolution and its rigid support of radical Arab programs for the Middle East could lead to unofficial backing or eventually even open sponsorship of the Eritrean Liberation Front and the disintegration of the tacit agreement between the Sudanese and the Ethiopians.

Relations with the Somali Republic, in sharp contrast to those with the Sudanese Republic, were marked until 1968 by open hostility and the continual threat of a major war in northeast Africa. Somali nationalism has come into direct conflict with Ethiopian state-building policies, and perennial border skirmishes have often attained the proportions of minor battles along the 1,100-mile common border.

The Somali border dispute is the most serious diplomatic problem that Ethiopia has faced since World War II.[1] Somali claims to the Ogaden region, if recognized, would set an

[1] The long and involved background of the dispute is given in J. Drysdale, *The Somali Dispute* (New York: Frederick A. Praeger, 1964).

example that might lead to the disruption of the polyethnic empire. The government does not dare to establish a precedent of regional separatism. The eastern borders of Ethiopia are a result of negotiations with Great Britain and Italy more than a half-century ago. Menelik had expanded Ethiopia's territory into the tribal lands of the Somali after the conquest of Harar at the same time that the Italians made their first tentative efforts along the Indian Ocean coast of what was then called Somaliland. In 1897 the Italian government concluded an agreement with Menelik declaring the boundary to run parallel to the coast 180 miles inland; no relevant documents seem to have survived in the Italian archives, and an authentic map has never been published. The border, unrealistic in terms of the distribution of watering holes and the needs of the population of that arid steppe country, was never delimited and was seldom respected. At one time Ethiopian military units penetrated to the region of Bur Hacaba, less than eighty miles from Mogadishu and the Indian Ocean.[2] In 1908 the matter was renegotiated on the uncertain basis of the earlier treaty, and to the satisfaction of neither party, a provisional line was agreed upon. By then the Somali tribes had been partitioned among the French (Côte des Somalis, or French Somaliland), the British (Somaliland Protectorate and northern Kenya), the Italians (Somalia), and the Ethiopians (the Ogaden region).

Throughout the colonial period the border was an unhappy area of tribal raids between various Somali groups competing for pasturage and water. Somali from the British protectorate were guaranteed dry-season grazing rights in Ethiopia by an 1897 agreement. During the Italian occupation, Italian Somalia and the Somali areas of Ethiopia were

[2] R. L. Hess, *Italian Colonialism in Somalia* (Chicago: University of Chicago Press, 1966), pp. 55–58.

joined under one provincial administration. In the course of the British military occupation that followed, the British continued the Italian administrative divisions, much to the dislike of the Ethiopians. In fact, the Ogaden was not returned to Ethiopian administration until 1948 and the borderland Haud Reserved Area, so important for winter pasturage for the tribes to the north, not until 1955.[3]

In the meantime Somali nationalism had grown, and its leaders appealed to all Somali to join in a struggle for the creation of a Greater Somalia that would include all lands occupied by the Somali. No final border agreement was ever reached by the European governments and the Ethiopian government in the colonial period. When former Italian Somalia and British Somaliland became independent and amalgamated in 1960, the Ethiopians repudiated the Haud grazing agreement as British-imposed and not binding upon an anticolonial African government, and the new Somali Republic inherited the border problem. When the Somali government also denounced existing border arrangements as of colonial inspiration and claimed that the Ogaden rightfully belonged to the Somali Republic, the border became a problem for Ethiopia as well.[4]

In the past twenty years border incidents have continued and occasionally have intensified. The Ethiopians keep a large part of their army on permanent maneuvers in the Ogaden to counter any possible threat from the Somali Republic and to maintain peace among the Somali tribes. Travel is often restricted into the Somali areas of Ethiopia,

[3] D. J. Latham Brown, "The Ethiopia-Somaliland Frontier Dispute," *International and Comparative Law Quarterly*, April, 1956, pp. 245–264.

[4] S. Touval, *Somali Nationalism: International Politics and the Drive for Unity in the Horn of Africa* (Cambridge: Harvard University Press, 1963), pp. 132–146, 160–163.

and little is actually known about the feelings of the Ogaden Somali. It is difficult to gather evidence of Somali nationalism in the region. Many Somali chiefs in the Ogaden apparently owe their offices and allegiance to the Ethiopian government. On the other hand, not many Somali have been absorbed into the national life. Memories of Ahmed Grañ, Muhammad Abdullah Hassan (the protonationalist "Mad Mullah" who overran much of northern Somalia from 1900 to 1920), and past victories of Islam can easily stir the Somali tribes to action. It is debatable whether this represents *Somalia irredenta* or the centrifugal forces of an Ethiopian minority group. Even if Somali nationalism has taken root in the Ogaden, the Somali tribes on either side of the present frontier remain mutually hostile over watering and grazing rights. The age-old pattern of nomadic life has not been altered by political change.

The Ethiopians are content with the *status quo,* it would seem. From time to time, to counter Somali claims, Ethiopian official statements have referred to Somalia as anciently a part of the Solomonic dominions, but there is little historical basis for such an allegation. On more than one occasion, the Emperor has proposed a federation of the Somali Republic and Ethiopia. This unlikely proposal rings hollow in the ears of Muslims who remember the fate of the Eritrean federation. Most recently, there has been talk of resolving the problem through an East African Federation that would include not only Kenya, Uganda, and Tanzania, but also Ethiopia and Somalia. The Somali, however, have never renounced their demands for the Wilsonian right of national self-determination and the creation of a Greater Somalia.

The Somali-Ethiopian border dispute reached a climax in May, 1963, at the Addis Ababa Conference of Heads of State of thirty-two African nations. The ground had been carefully planned for discussion of African unity, but the Somali President, Aden Abdulla Osman, disrupted the atmosphere of solidarity by accusing the Ethiopian government of expansionism and demanded self-determination for all Somali outside the Somali Republic. The Somali leader argued that the problem was unique in Africa. The Somali case could not have been presented at a more inappropriate time, however, and Ethiopian Prime Minister Aklilou Habte Wold, in answering the "unthinkable accusation," accused the Somali themselves of seeking territorial aggrandizement. The sentiments of the other African leaders present were clearly with the Ethiopian Prime Minister when he declared, "It is in the interest of all Africans now to respect the frontiers drawn on the maps, whether they are good or bad, by the former colonizers, and that is the interest of Somalia, too, because if we are going to move in this direction, then we Ethiopians too will have claims to make." [5]

Although the Ethiopians won a great moral victory over the Somali Republic at the Addis Ababa Conference, the matter had a far from happy conclusion. The Ethiopians were uneasy about reports that Russia had offered to supply the Somali Republic with arms. From February through March, 1964 open warfare raged along the border. Continued pressure from the newly created Organization of African Unity compelled the Ethiopian and Somali governments to open negotiations to end the border dispute. After meeting for a week in Khartoum, on March 30, 1964, the two states agreed to stop broadcasting and publishing hostile propaganda and to demilitarize a zone six to ten miles deep on each side of the boundary.

[5] *Proceedings of the Summit Conference of Independent African States* (Addis Ababa: Ministry of Foreign Affairs, 1963), CIAS/GEN/INF/43.

Yet neither government had control of the situation. The Ethiopian army's Third Division was unable to stamp out the rebellion in the Ogaden, and the Somali government at Mogadishu was unable to deter the Ogaden Somali from resisting attempts by the Ethiopians to govern their tribal lands. Muktal Dahir, one of the leaders of the Ethiopian Somali, stated, "My people are under no one's jurisdiction and take orders from no one but me. We have no intention of observing any cease fire. Our fight with Ethiopia has nothing to do with Somalia. We are indifferent to the government position, though we still expect and hope our movement will be recognized both by Somalia and the world."[6] Formerly an Ethiopian government official (district commissioner at Daghabur), Muktal Dahir claimed to lead a movement of twelve thousand guerrilla fighters. Their arguments were very much like those of the Eritrean separatists: they condemned limitations on freedom of speech and of party organization, resisted attempts by the central government to collect taxes in areas that had never paid regular taxes to the Ethiopian treasury, demanded local self-government, and expressed fear for the future of tribal customs and religious traditions in the face of the modernizing and centralizing tendencies of the Ethiopian state. But without large-scale support from abroad the movement evaporated. To the bitter disappointment of the Ogaden Somali, the Ethiopian Governor of Jijiga and the Somali Governor of Hargeisa even cooperated to end border tensions in accordance with the Khartoum agreement. Grievances remained, however, and from time to time there were sporadic outbursts of resistance against the Ethiopian government.

Each March tensions were renewed as the Ethiopian army

[6] "Somali Guerrilla Threatens to Ignore a Truce," *The New York Times,* March 28, 1964, p. 12.

went on maneuvers in the Ogaden and attempts were made to tax its inhabitants. In 1965 the Somali government again raised the question of the Ogaden Somali, and the Ethiopian government withdrew its ambassador from Mogadishu. The Ethiopians also closed the border, ostensibly in reprisal for Somali propaganda, but more likely to force Somali tribesmen in need of pasturage across the border to put pressure on the Somali government to come to terms with Ethiopia. The dispute was tabled for a few months when a joint commission reconvened to examine the demilitarized border. In June, 1965 the Somali government brought the matter to the Organization of African Unity and protested against an Ethiopian attack on Bohodlei, while the Ethiopians gave much publicity to the large amount of arms their army had confiscated from tribesmen entering Ethiopia from northern Somalia. A full-scale barrage of propaganda resumed, and Radio Addis Ababa beamed Somali-language broadcasts to the Ogaden Somali asserting, "The Somali people . . . want to have no more to do with the unrealistic concept of a Greater Somalia. They prefer to see economic development and a solution to the hunger problem." [7]

While the Ethiopian army and Somali nomads fought in the Ogaden, both governments aired their dispute before the world. The Ethiopians took advantage of a state visit by Indian President Radhakrishnan on October, 1965, to promise Ethiopian support of India's claims to Kashmir in return for Indian endorsement of the Ethiopian position on the border question. A joint communiqué declared that traditional and established boundaries of states should be regarded as inviolable and that the principle of self-determination should apply only to colonial territories and not to parts of inde-

[7] "News in Brief," *Africa Report,* October, 1965, p. 17.

pendent sovereign states. Outraged, the Somali government accused the Ethiopians of depriving the "oppressed peoples of Western Somalia [i. e., the Ogaden] occupied by Ethiopia, and the Eritrean peoples annexed by Ethiopia" of their rights.[8] Once again the Organization of African Unity put pressure on the two states, and once again, in an agreement signed by Somali Foreign Minister Ahmed Haji Dualeh and Ethiopian Foreign Minister Ketema Yifru, the two states committed themselves to ending the propaganda war that had inflamed the border dispute.

The détente was short lived, however, when the focus of contention shifted from the Ogaden to French Somaliland in August, 1966. Shortly before French President Charles de Gaulle was to arrive in Ethiopia on a state visit, he was shocked by a rash of anti-French demonstrations in the port of Djibouti. French Somaliland, whose population consisted of Afar tribesmen closely related to the Danakil of Ethiopia and of Issa with close ties to the Somali of both the Ogaden and the Somali Republic, was important as the terminus for the railroad from Addis Ababa, the main exit for Ethiopian exports. Although de Gaulle and Haile Selassie must surely have discussed the fate of Djibouti during the state visit, their public statements mentioned only traditional Franco-Ethiopian amity and avoided the question of French Somaliland's future.[9]

After further public disturbances, de Gaulle conditionally offered the French territory its independence. Alarmed by what appeared to be the abandonment of Djibouti to the prospect of incorporation into Greater Somalia, Haile Selassie unexpectedly countered the French move by a not entirely accurate announcement that Djibouti and its peoples

[8] "News in Brief," *Africa Report,* November, 1965, p. 22.
[9] *The New York Times,* August 30, 1966, p. 2.

historically and ethnically formed an integral part of the Ethiopian Empire. French Somaliland was of vital importance to the Ethiopian economy, and Ethiopia also feared the repercussions of Somali self-determination in Djibouti on the Ogaden. Since Djibouti lay in the part of the territory nearest the Somali Republic, partition was an impossibility.

The outlines of a solution began to take form in the next few months as the Somali Republic accused the French of encouraging Danakil immigration into French Somaliland and stepping up the deportation of Somali from Djibouti to either the Somali Republic, which refused to accept the refugees, or Ethiopia. Perhaps realizing the implication of demographic shifts for the outcome of the proposed referendum, the Ethiopian government bided its time. Haile Selassie announced that the Ethiopian army would not automatically enter Djibouti if the territory voted for independence, although Ethiopian troops were massed at the border.[10]

By the time the referendum took place in March, 1967, its outcome was virtually guaranteed. Once again a French colonial territory voted not to cut its economic as well as political ties with France, and the Ethiopian government appeared relieved that more than 60 per cent of the voters opted for continued association with France. The official returns indicated 22,523 votes for France and 14,734 against. The electorate consisted of 22,024 Afar, 14,689 Somali, 1,408 Arabs, and 923 resident French; yet in 1962 the *total* number of Afar voters and nonvoters was 27,000 and of Issa Somali, 25,000.[11] Evidence of Franco-Ethiopian collusion was indeed strong. In May, Haile Selassie visited de Gaulle in Paris, where his host declared that cooperation between Ethiopia

[10] J. Drysdale, "The Problem of French Somaliland," *Africa Report*, November, 1966, pp. 10–17.

[11] "News in Brief," *Africa Report*, May, 1967, p. 24.

and France was "more useful and necessary now than ever before."

In the aftermath of the referendum a new territorial government was formed; all but two of its ministers were Afar. As the metropolitan and territorial governments consulted about the future of the territory, there was no doubt that the government intended to strengthen the pro-French Afar element and would continue to deport dissident Somali. As a reward for loyalty to France, the territory was granted a $4.4 million credit for the construction of additional port facilities. Then in June, 1967, the territory was officially renamed the French Territory of the Afar and Issa, and the Somali opposition Parti du Mouvement Populaire was banned, a move that inflicted yet another foreign policy setback upon the powerless government of the Somali Republic. For Ethiopia, the new status of Djibouti brought the unexpected benefit of diverting some of the bitterness of Somali attacks from Addis Ababa to Paris. When French gendarmes shot Abdirahman Adola, president of the French Somali Coast Workers' Federation, in the course of a general strike protesting the 1967 referendum, Somali editorials spoke of "the present French atrocities and torture to the inhabitants which connotes their desire to perpetuate the ugly colonialism in the enclave; but, this would never be realized through gun points." [12] All the Somali Republic could do was to observe these events and fume over its helplessness.

Pressure from other African states, the decline of Arab influence in the Horn of Africa and economic setbacks due to the closing of the Suez Canal, and failure to point to any

[12] *Odki Hogsatada: The Voice of the Working Class* (Trade Union Bulletin issued by Confederazione Somala dei Lavoratori/Somali Confederation of Labour), Mogadishu, April, 1967, additional page entitled "Lattest News" (*sic*).

real achievements for Somali irredentism have since led to a Somali-Ethiopian détente. When Muhammad Ibrahim Egal became Prime Minister in July, 1967, he repeated the old formula about the right of all Somali to self-determination, but he also firmly stressed that "we do not covet any territory belonging to Ethiopia or Kenya." [13] Somali policy appeared to change. Subsequently, at meetings of the Organization of African Unity in Kinshasa, Egal met with Haile Selassie to prepare the way for broad negotiations on outstanding issues. Talks continued intermittently from September, 1967, into 1968. In December, 1967, at the inauguration of the East African Community in Arusha, Tanzania, Somali President Abdirashid Ali Shermarke and the Emperor continued discussions. By mid-1968, despite mumblings from within the Somali Republic's political parties, relations between Ethiopia and the Somali Republic had greatly improved.

Prime Minister Egal of the Somali Republic, more than any other man, was responsible for this remarkable *volte-face* in Somali policy, tantamount to a public renunciation of the idea of a Greater Somalia espoused by all politicians since the Somali Republic became independent in 1960. His reasoning was based in part on economic factors, in part on political realities. Virtually alone among Somali politicians, Egal urged the Somali to face the brutally hard realities of their country's economic condition. Dependent for 44 per cent of its exportations on the shipment of bananas to Europe, the Somali Republic was gravely injured by the closing of the Suez Canal in June, 1967. The value of banana exports dropped 60 per cent in one year, a loss of revenue highly damaging to a country with such limited resources. [14] Moreover, the support of irredentist guerrillas in the Ogaden and

[13] "News in Brief," *Africa Report,* October, 1967, p. 33.
[14] *Marchés Tropicaux,* no. 1166 (March 16, 1968), p. 682.

in northeastern Kenya gave the Somali Republic an additional burden of heavy defense expenditures amounting to 60 per cent of the national budget.[15] Somalia, dependent on Italy, the United States, and the Soviet Union for foreign aid monies, had to look for new sources of aid. Great Britain, former ruler of the northern part of the country, could not be approached unless diplomatic relations, broken in 1963 over the question of Somali claims to northern Kenya, could be resumed. Another source of aid would be France, but to approach de Gaulle would first require recognizing the legitimacy of the French Territory of the Afar and Issa. Lastly, Muhammad Egal was also an ardent advocate of Pan-Africanism, an ideology incompatible with the goals of Somali irredentism. For these reasons, Egal had to convince the Somali National Assembly of the need for a complete reorientation of Somalia's foreign policy in the Horn of Africa. In five days of brilliant and impassioned debate Egal won his parliamentary majority.

From September 1 to 5, 1968, Egal and a group of twelve Somali officials conducted a series of important discussions with the Emperor and his Cabinet, and the basis for a settlement was found. Both countries agreed to end the state of emergency along the Somali-Ethiopian frontier. Somali civil airlines would be permitted to fly directly from Mogadishu to Hargeisa over the formerly disputed Ogaden, while new routes would be opened between Addis Ababa and Mogadishu and Hargeisa. Both governments agreed to draft additional agreements regarding cultural and commercial exchanges and, most importantly, to establish a permanent advisory commission on the ministerial level to discuss any major or minor problems between the two countries.

[15] G. Varley, "Avec son nouveau premier ministre (M. Mohamed Egal) la Somalie sort de son isolement," *France Eurafrique* (Paris), no. 191 (January, 1968), pp. 13–14.

Whether or not the settlement would endure was uncertain. Egal's first test was the Somali parliamentary election of March 26, 1969. His policy of reconciliation was ratified by the voters, who elected members of Egal's party, the Somali Youth League, to 73 of the 125 seats in the National Assembly. Five days later, Egal signed the first agreement implementing the détente, a most favored nation trade agreement covering all questions relating to customs, duties, charges, importation and exportation, loading and unloading of goods, shipping, port and harbor facilities, and issuance of import and export licenses. A few weeks later a direct telephone link between Addis Ababa and Mogadishu was inaugurated.

Egal's second test came in June, when he submitted his program to the National Assembly. His main emphasis was on economic development, but he warned the members of the Assembly that there would be difficulties in keeping peace on Somalia's border with Ethiopia. Although the National Assembly gave him an overwhelming vote of confidence (116–1), Egal voiced a warning to the Ethiopians:

At this moment reports are coming to my office from various Regional Governors that the Ethiopian authorities in Ogadenia and elsewhere in the Somali territory are trying to enforce upon the nomadic community the payment of a [head] tax [on animals] called *gibir*. The introduction of this tax has never been even contemplated by the Somali Republic on its own nomadic citizens, neither did the ex-colonial governments of Italy or Britain ever attempt to impose such a tax. This was due to the fact that this kind of tax has always been most odious to nomadic Somali communities. . . .

Secondly, it is not an economically feasible proposition, since the collection of the tax is more expensive than the amount realized. We, therefore, consider that this measure is a mere provocation of the people to rebellion. This measure, coupled with any other malpractices, is now heading toward a destruction of the firm foundations we have been trying to build with the leaders in Addis Ababa. This situation poses a grave threat to the *détente* and the atmosphere of amicable understanding which we have reached since the formation of my government.

The Somali Government cannot be immune to the situation in the territories and the plight of its policy and will seek the intervention of the Emperor and his Government in Addis Ababa.[16]

For the first time in the modern history of this part of Africa peace had been achieved, even if only temporarily, between Ethiopia and the Somali. But the situation was basically unstable. It could change if the Somali Republic should suddenly find itself in possession of hitherto elusive mineral wealth; the exploitation of important deposits of uranium ore begun in 1969 by Italian, West German, and American companies may place the Somali Republic in a different economic, and hence political, position in the future. More important, it could change if the Somali government chose to overturn Egal's highly personal policy of rapprochement with an historical opponent.

Egal's third test came in October, 1969, and he failed it. Shortly after the assassination of President Abdirashid Ali Shermarke on October 15, for apparently nonpolitical reasons, the Somali army seized power, allegedly to save the country from corruption. Prime Minister Egal was placed under house arrest, and it appeared likely that his efforts to attain peace in the Horn of Africa would be undone. Although spokesmen of the army's Revolutionary Council declared that it would honor all legitimate international treaties and obligations of the Somali Republic, it was far from clear whether they regarded the Somali-Ethiopian détente as worthy of their respect.

[16] *Somali News,* June 20, 1969.

For Ethiopia the benefits of an understanding with the Somali Republic were clear. No longer would the Eritrean Liberation Front have Somali support. The threat to the unity of the Empire posed by Mogadishu would come to an end, although it was unknown how the Somali of the Ogaden would react to the gradual and inevitable extension of the administrative apparatus of the Ethiopian state into its poorly known easternmost province. For the new leaders of the Somali Democratic Republic the question could be simply stated: Would they be able, if they so desired, to bank the once ardent fires of Somali nationalism and secure popular agreement to maintaining the *status quo* in the Ogaden, as well as the French Territory of the Afar and Issa, and Kenya?

These same difficulties with the Somali Republic drew Ethiopia and Kenya together in their common opposition to the concept of Greater Somalia. At the 1963 Conference of African Heads of State in Addis Ababa, Jomo Kenyatta strongly condemned the Somali stand. Tribal clashes also frequently occurred along the Ethiopia-Kenya border, but the two parties chose to ignore these skirmishes because of the greater threat from the Somali Republic. From these contacts and others in the Organization of African Unity, Ethiopia developed an interest in the affairs of its black neighbors to the south. During the long and often painful negotiations for the establishment of an East African Common Market, the Ethiopians on several occasions suggested that Kenya, Tanzania, and Uganda consider also the possibility of extending associate status to Ethiopia, and the Somali Republic made a parallel request. At the time of the Ethiopian-Somali rapprochement the Somali also formally abandoned their claims to Somali-inhabited areas of northeastern Kenya and ended five years of hostility. If Egal's policy should prove durable, then Ethiopia and Somalia may both develop their economic and political relations with their southern neighbors. The Horn of Africa and East Africa together might comprise a new geopolitical and economic unit if that should happen.

In the past decade Ethiopia has seen the necessity of playing a major role in Africa. Ethiopia's emergence has been rapid but not entirely unexpected. Haile Selassie has long been openly admired by Jomo Kenyatta, President of Kenya, as a great figure in modern African history. Kwame Nkrumah, one-time President of Ghana and a founder of modern Pan-Africanism, mentions in his autobiography the great respect he had for the last independent nation in Africa, as Ethiopia was often called in the 1930's. Nnamdi Azikiwe of Nigeria and others in their writings poured out their grief at the Italian invasion of 1935, and Ethiopia became a symbol of Africa's struggle for independence. In the postwar years Ethiopia has skillfully played on this reservoir of African sentiments and maintained its prestige, despite its aloofness from the cause of African nationalism and anticolonialism. Nevertheless, until 1955, Ethiopia was isolated from African affairs and did not participate forcefully at the Bandung Conference of Asian and African States. The revolutionary aspect of much of Pan-Africanism disturbed the Emperor, who held back from actively supporting the movement.

Only gradually did Ethiopian policy change. In 1958, the Ethiopian government accepted an invitation to attend the first Conference of Independent African States at Accra, capital of Ghana; the Emperor sent his youngest son, Prince Sahle Selassie, to represent Ethiopia and end Ethiopia's isolation from the rest of Africa. That same year the Emperor proposed the establishment of an African Development Bank, marking one of the earliest attempts to shift the focus of African independence from the realm of revolutionary politics to realistic economic planning. Perhaps Haile Selassie had been alarmed by the condemnation of Ethiopia for its lack of democracy voiced by delegates to the organizing conference of the Pan-African Freedom Movement of East and Central Africa held at Mwanza, Tanganyika, in September, 1958. By the end of that year the United Nations Economic Commission for Africa had been formed, and the awakened Ethiopian interest was rewarded by the location of the Commission's permanent headquarters in Addis Ababa (see Plate 9). At this time too the Emperor made available a number of scholarships for African students to study at the University College of Addis Ababa. There is also evidence that the Emperor privately began to support African political refugees from South Africa and elsewhere, a number of whom were on scholarship at secondary schools in Ethiopia and, later, at the university. Further recognition of the emergence of Ethiopia in African affairs came in 1960 after the Third Conference of Independent African States, still less than a dozen in number, was held in the Ethiopian capital.

After 1960, as the number of independent African states rapidly grew, the Ethiopians quietly stepped up their activities. The Ethiopian delegation to the United Nations strongly supported the condemnation of South African *apartheid,* the investigation of conditions in South-West Africa, the limitation of French nuclear tests in the Sahara, and the cause of the Algerian nationalists. Late in 1962, Haile Selassie finally took the initiative and invited the heads of state of all independent African countries to Addis Ababa for a conference on the subject of African unity. No African leader could refuse such a general invitation. What Nasser or Nkrumah or the Casablanca or Monrovia or Brazzaville grouping could not do, Haile Selassie accomplished with little difficulty.

The conference, held in May, 1963, was a complete success. The Emperor presented his guests with a well-organized and uncontroversial agenda, and the one African state that had operated free of regional or ideological alignments achieved practical results. The Emperor served as an honorary president of the conference, an Ethiopian became provisional secretary-general, and by midsummer Addis Ababa was chosen as the headquarters of the newly formed Organization of African Unity.

The conference had several significant results. First, Haile Selassie eclipsed the more extreme leaders of Africa and gave the Pan-African movement a new and more moderate direction. Second, Ethiopia committed itself to Africa, thus ending its traditional isolation; contacts with Africa had come only after increased contact with the Middle East, Europe, the United States, and Asia. Third, the Ethiopian government has become an important spokesman for Africa not only in the United Nations, but also in diplomatic exchanges with the United States and other countries. There is no indication that Ethiopia's role will diminish in the near future. On the contrary, the creation in Khartoum in August, 1963 of an African Development Bank, a pet project of the Emperor, and the extension of Ethiopian Air Lines service across the continent to West Africa are evidence of increasing leadership. These developments are all the more striking when one considers the history of Ethiopia, the national detachment from African affairs, and the historical cultural prejudice against Negroid peoples.

Equally important has been the impact of the African "Summit Conference" of May, 1963 on Ethiopia. It enabled the Emperor effectively to undercut the opposition of those modernizing elements who had criticized his aloofness from the mainstream of continental politics. The new emphasis on African unity also served to broaden the horizons of loyalty of Ethiopians, who are asked to think of themselves as Africans and Ethiopians, not as Shoans, Tigreans, Eritreans, or Amhara. Admittedly, this appeal does not reach the peasant masses, but it does affect the educated elite and the nobility. The Emperor has acquired new prestige in the view of many who otherwise might have condemned him, and his role as a leader of his people and of the continent, now recognized by all Africa, has enabled him to strengthen his own position in Ethiopia. Lastly, as Ethiopia has become more involved in African matters and as other Africans have come to know the country better, pressures have mounted for the government to come to grips with the immense problems of education and economic development. It is still a source of embarrassment and anger to some young Ethiopians that their country, the symbol of independent Africa, is one of the most backward countries on the continent. Once again a step in the direction of modernization has led in the short run to increased stability of the imperial regime, but, by throwing a spotlight on Ethiopia, it has exposed the regime to sharper criticism and perhaps accelerated the rate of change.

Since the Addis Ababa conference, Ethiopia has vigorously maintained its leadership in African affairs. The Emperor, with his great experience as arbiter of domestic politics, has particularly relished his role as mediator in international politics. From his sudden and successful intervention in the Moroccan-Algerian border dispute of 1963 to his attempt to reconcile the differences between Ghana and Guinea after the fall of Nkrumah and those between Nigeria and Biafra since 1968, the Emperor has put to use his political skills. The Ethiopian delegation to the Organization of African Unity has also placed itself in the forefront of the African attack on colonialism, though most often as a force for moderation. Thus, Haile Selassie urged other African states not to break relations with Great Britain over the Rhodesian crisis in 1965. Yet at that same time the South African Supreme Court sentenced MacDonald Musela to eleven years' imprisonment on charges of having undergone military (guerrilla) training *in Ethiopia* in order to aid the banned African National Congress.

In November, 1960, Ethiopia and Liberia, the only two African members of the League of Nations, instituted separate proceedings against the Republic of South Africa in the International Court of Justice at The Hague. The two states contested the validity of South Africa's presence in South-West Africa, as a mandatory power under the defunct League of Nations, in a highly legalistic attempt to force South Africa to surrender control over South-West Africa. Although in December, 1962 the court rejected preliminary objections by South Africa and thereby upheld its jurisdiction in the matter, the case dragged on for years. Finally, on July 18, 1966, the Court ruled that Ethiopia and Liberia had not established any legal right or interest to speak on behalf of the League of Nations, and the Court rejected their claims—but not on the basis of whether or not the South African mandate was still valid. The status of South-West Africa is still questioned by the African bloc, but the African states are powerless to act against South Africa in this or apparently any other matter. As a rear-guard nuisance action the General Assembly of the United Nations, with Ethiopian support and under the prodding of the African states, adopted a resolution in June, 1968, that proclaimed that henceforth South-West Africa would be known as Namibia and recommended, to no avail, that the Security Council ensure the immediate removal of South Africa from Namibia and secure its independence.

In other African matters, not only has Ethiopia publicly

attacked white racism in Rhodesia, the Republic of South Africa, and Portuguese Africa, but Haile Selassie has extended an offer of brotherhood to the twenty million Americans of African descent, praising them in their struggle for freedom and urging them to lend their talents and skills in Africa's struggle for dignity and progress.[17] Lastly, Haile Selassie has toured African capitals, from Rabat, Cairo, and Khartoum to Nairobi, Kampala, and Dar es Salaam, from Zambia and Malawi to the Congo, Nigeria, and Niger. Certainly he has traveled more widely about Africa than any other African head of state, indefatigably promoting Ethiopia's new and important part in African affairs. Haile Selassie's search for a major role in world diplomacy has made Addis Ababa the capital of Africa.

[17] "Haile Selassie Attacks Racism in South Africa," *London Times,* November 3, 1967, p. 8; A. Morrison, "Selassie's Message to the Negro," *Ebony,* XIX (December, 1963), pp. 29–32.

CHAPTER 11

Negus Kamotu:
When the Emperor Dies . . .

Haile Selassie has been in power longer than any other man on the face of this planet, if one calculates the beginning of his rule from his selection as regent in 1916. Moreover, his actual reign as emperor, which commenced in 1930, has been longer than that of any other monarch in Ethiopian history since the establishment of the Solomonic dynasty in the thirteenth century. Only the greatest kings of the dynasty approach his reign in duration: Zara Yaqob (1433–1467), Sarsa Dengel (1563–1597), and Fasilidas (1632–1667). He has eclipsed the reputation of Menelik II (1889–1913) as a great innovator and modernizer. Because of his great length of tenure most traditional Ethiopians find it inconceivable to speculate what might happen upon the death of their monarch.

The most solemn oath an Ethiopian can utter is *Haile Selassie yimut,* literally, "May Haile Selassie die [if I am not telling the truth]!" In part this reflects the central position of the monarchy in Amhara-Tigrean culture; the concept permeates many aspects of the life of the Ethiopian. It also reflects, however, an awareness of the disaster that might ensue upon the death of the ruler. It is not the individual who would suffer if he is not telling the truth (in English the comparable oath would be "May I be struck by lightning"); the well-being of the country as a whole is at stake here. Indeed, upon the death of the monarch in the past, all

too often Ethiopia disintegrated until a successor could consolidate his hold upon the country; in the meantime, all
suffered. After the death of Theodore in 1868 there followed
three years of civil war. The sudden death of Yohannes in
1889 brought Menelik II to the throne, but it was a matter
of years before he could effectively control Tigre and Gojjam.
The death of Menelik led to still another succession crisis
until the dead emperor's grandson, Lij Iasu, was deposed by
a coup d'état. In not one of these cases did a son succeed his
father to the throne, nor was there a peaceful transfer of
power. Thus, it is obvious that the question of succession is
of paramount importance for the future of Ethiopia. No
study of contemporary Ethiopia can be complete without an
examination of the possible state of affairs after the over-
powering figure of the Emperor disappears from the Ethiopian scene.

The heir apparent to the throne of the Conquering Lion
of Judah is Merid Azmatch (Crown Prince) Asfa Wossen,
the septuagenarian Emperor's first-born and sole surviving
son. Asfa Wossen was born the year his father became regent,
and he has lived his whole life in the shadow of the Emperor.
A quiet and apparently unassuming man, he spends much of
his time with books and has a reputation for being remarkably well informed about literature and politics. Relations
between father and son have always been somewhat strained.
The Emperor's second son, Prince Makonnen (1923–1957),
was generally regarded as his favorite. It is commonly agreed
that Asfa Wossen was not involved in planning the attempted
coup of December, 1960, nor did he have any foreknowledge
of it. Political observers assume that the Crown Prince had
no alternative but to accept his nomination as head of state
by the rebels. No one is certain, however, whether the heir
apparent welcomed this turn of events. Since the abortive

coup Asfa Wossen has continued in the same anomalous position that he occupied before the uprising. On more than
one occasion he has been deliberately slighted in public by
his father, who usually relegates him to a purely ceremonial
status. Because of his seemingly docile temperament it is
assumed that if he were to become monarch he would not
be averse to the development of a constitutional monarchy,
wherein he would be little more than a ceremonial head of
state. It should be pointed out, however, that while past the
proverbial three score years and ten, Haile Selassie is still in
excellent physical condition. In contrast, the Crown Prince,
who has a tendency toward obesity, is diabetic and does not
enjoy the same good health as his vigorous progenitor. Con-
ceivably, the Emperor might outlive Asfa Wossen. To whom
would the succession then pass?

The Emperor has eight grandsons and a number of great-
grandsons who are also possible contenders for the throne.
The eldest grandson, Prince Eskender (Alexander), has served
as commander of the tiny Ethiopian navy. He is the son of
the Emperor's eldest child, Princess Tenagne Worq. Despite
his seniority and his great personal charm, he is not highly
regarded in government circles. Asfa Wossen has one son by
his second wife, but little is known about Prince Zara Yaqob.
Haile Selassie's second son, Makonnen, was survived by five
sons: Paulos, who was educated in Germany, Mikael, Dawit,
Filpos, and Baeda. Paulos, the eldest, is not generally well
liked. Lastly, there is Prince Ermias, son of Sahle Selassie,
the Emperor's youngest son. None of these grandsons has the
political experience or is old enough to have gathered about
him a retinue of possible future supporters. Should any one
of these be nominated successor, he would be greatly dependent upon the military, the Church, and the aristocracy. Not
one of them appears to have the makings of another Haile

Selassie. Yet the vagaries of politics in Ethiopia are such that they might play some crucial role in the future and might even rise to something better than is suspected out of past accomplishments.

Aspirants to the throne are not limited to the ranks of the immediate royal family, for descendants of Theodore, Yohannes, and Lij Iasu also have claims that cannot be lightly dismissed. Among the prominent descendants of Emperor Yohannes IV are Ras Mangasha Seyum, who is married to Princess Tenagne Worq's eldest child, Princess Aida, and Zawde Gabre Selassie, a scholar in residence at Oxford University. The descendants of Lij Iasu at one time posed severe problems for Haile Selassie. Curiously, the three most significant bore the names of the most important Emperors preceding Haile Selassie. Tewodros (Theodore) Iasu led a rebellion based in southwest Ethiopia in 1941; Yohannes Iasu lived "in exile" in Jimma; Menelik Iasu, who styled himself Menelik III, disappeared from sight in the 1930's, and rumors persist that he is still alive in prison. A fourth son was interned in Sidamo Province, and a large number of Lij Iasu's grandchildren also survive.

There is no shortage of candidates for the Ethiopian throne. But will the monarchy itself survive a succession crisis? That will depend on the armed forces. Elsewhere in Africa, as well as in Latin America, the Middle East, and Asia, the military have intervened in politics to give a foundering nation a new sense of direction. Certainly the Ethiopian army and air force are strong enough to tip the balance in favor of the candidate of their choice. More significantly, the military is the only element in Ethiopia that could successfully intervene in national politics; all other groups are too small, too weak, or too fragmented. When the Emperor dies, only the military will have the ability to act on the national level; the alternative to military intervention would be civil war. But the military too reflects the ethnic and regional divisions of Ethiopia and is not free of personal animosities. The Emperor has seen to it that the military has remained semifragmented, but still able to function under his direction. Without him, it is likely that the fragmentation he has encouraged might prove disruptive.

If the military were to support Asfa Wossen, the chances are strong that he would be able to maintain himself on the throne. In such a case, the military would be able to dictate the nature of the monarchy. One can assume that their major task would be to maintain order and internal security, as well as to fend off threats from neighboring Muslim states. In so doing they would probably run counter to the aspirations of the students and intellectuals (the democratizing elements in the Ethiopian political picture) and of the separatist Eritreans and Somali. The military would most likely continue the limitations on individual political freedom found under the present regime; there is no indication that it would do otherwise.

Would the military lean toward a republican constitution? In 1960 the army and the air force were loyal to the Crown. They have remained loyal since then; there is no evidence to the contrary. To answer this question, one would have to consider whether the military would see any real advantages to changing the Constitution. The cement holding Ethiopia together today is not religion or nationalism; the sole bonding element is the monarchy. To do away with the monarchy would be to destroy the very embodiment of national unity without putting forth a suitable substitute. To abolish the monarchy would be to fly in the face of two thousand years of Ethiopian history. To substitute a loose confederation of ethnic groups for the unitary state would be to court disaster from all those groups which have been chafing under the rule of the centralizing government at Addis Ababa. A change in the form of government would not alter the relationship between the capital and the provinces; the basic tensions would persist. Most likely the military would stand behind the monarch, who would have much less power than the present emperor, and would continue the policies of the present regime.

Gradually, the military might be willing to share power in order to maintain political stability. The military could turn to the aristocracy, whose regional interests are basically opposed to those of the modernizing state. In the recent past the aristocracy has accommodated itself to the expansion of the powers of the central government in return for a small degree of participation in the government (the Senate and high ministerial positions). There is no reason to assume that the aristocracy would attempt to seize power itself; it lacks the military and broad popular base to do so as a result of Haile Selassie's long and patient construction of the central government. There is every reason to believe that it would continue its present adaptive political behavior.

The military could also turn to the Ethiopian Orthodox Church for support. Although the Church has little influence on politics at the national level (again as a result of Haile Selassie's policies), its power in the countryside and its influence over the Christian peasantry has abided. There is also the lesson of the past: the Church intervened to cause the downfall of Theodore in 1868 and to legitimize the coup d'état that deposed Lij Iasu in 1916. The Church, perforce staunchly monarchist, would also give the military cause to think before tampering with traditional institutions. Lastly, the military could turn to Parliament. Such an action would enhance the prestige and authority of that relatively feeble institution and further the development of a constitutional monarchy. In essence, the military would be recreating the balance of power within the government that coexisted with the all-pervading power of Haile Selassie.

What future is there for the Ethiopian student movement, whose ultimate goals are incompatible with those of the military? Revolution and order do not come to terms very easily. The students have made a bid for cooperation with the peasants and with the workers. To judge from their annual March-April riots, which have invariably been quelled by the military, to date they have had little success in infiltrating the military. Moreover, after the abortive coup of 1960, the Emperor carefully scrutinized the loyalty of the officer corps. A military regime like the one described above might regard the demands of the students and intellectuals as inimical to their immediate goals of order and internal security. It is even doubtful whether a military regime would permit the formation of political parties in Ethiopia. Abroad, they could argue, parties have been a divisive element. If the students should choose to resist the military, it is doubtful whether they would be able to achieve any of their goals. They would only contribute to political instability.

Even if the military were to permit civilian authorities to exercise political power, it is debatable how smoothly such a government would run. After all, Ethiopia has had little experience in responsible ministerial government. Inefficiency and corruption might be its hallmarks, as they have been throughout the underdeveloped nations. Sooner or later the military will feel bound to intervene directly in the affairs of government.

After politics, the major problem facing the successors of Haile Selassie will be promoting economic development. One accusation often leveled at the present regime is that it has not developed the Ethiopian economy with sufficient rapidity. The present government might respond by questioning whether other means of development would produce speedier results. The basic limiting factor of the country's geography cannot be ignored. The cost of building an adequate network of motor roads cannot be underwritten in any single five- or ten-year plan. Time works against any regime that would promise rapid economic results. Moreover, Ethiopia will remain an agricultural country for the foreseeable future, and its agricultural surpluses will remain locked in its mountain fastnesses until the transportation system is more highly developed. The cost of economic development is enormous, and Ethiopia, like all other developing countries, has already discovered that investment funds from external sources have begun to shrink drastically.

What will become of Ethiopia's ambitions as a leader of Africa and the Third World? The foreign policy of Haile Selassie has been highly personal. His skill as arbiter of conflicting forces in domestic politics has enabled him to assume the role of mediator on the international level. Ethiopia's presence in Africa has been felt not because of the development of a highly talented cadre of professional diplomatists, but because of the hard work and prestige of the little Emperor who once spoke of collective security before the League of Nations. In all probability, Ethiopia will play a much less active role in African politics and at the United Nations in the future. The location in Addis Ababa of the headquarters of both the Organization of African Unity and the United Nations Economic Commission for Africa, however, will ensure that never again will Ethiopia be isolated from contact with the rest of Africa.

In terms of its relations with its immediate neighbors, Ethiopia has few alternatives. Somalia and the Sudan are modern incarnations of the old fear of Muslim encirclement; to this one must add the moral and material support they afford Muslim separatists within Ethiopia. Any future government of Ethiopia will have to cope with these problems. They cannot be ignored lest they establish a precedent for secession by a dozen other groups. The Sudanese and Somali Republics have both recently experienced military coups d'état; it is to be expected that they will take a more rigid stand on the question of the rights of Muslims in Ethiopia. Moreover, the Ethiopians will have the lingering fear that the Sudan might be attracted into a Pan-Arab union, presumably with Egypt, that would sharply alter the balance of power in the Horn of Africa. To counter this, Ethiopia will probably develop even closer relations with Israel. Whether the Ethiopians like it or not, they will have few alternatives for support by the Great Powers in their region other than the United States. Unless a revolutionary military regime should seize power in Ethiopia, which is not likely in the present circumstances, the Ethiopians will probably continue their military arrangements with the United States. National interests limit their freedom of choice in this matter. Needless to say, this will only exacerbate student feelings.

Thus, the choice for Ethiopia will probably be a monarchy backed by a military regime or great instability and perhaps even civil war. Ethiopians are aware of the alternatives; this has been their historical experience on more than one occasion.

"When the Emperor dies, whom can one ask for justice?" The Emperor's justice, for all its repressive aspects, has given Ethiopia a lengthy period of internal security, modernization, economic growth, and political stability. It is an apt proverb with a poignant double meaning for the uncertain future of Ethiopia. Only one thing is certain: when the Emperor dies, all of Ethiopia's problems will live on.

Bibliography

The materials dealing with contemporary Ethiopia are highly limited and vary considerably in quality. In the past fifteen years several studies of a general nature have appeared. George A. Lipsky *et al.*, *Ethiopia, Its People, Its Society, Its Culture* (New Haven: Human Relations Area File, 1962), is a useful compendium of information on all aspects of contemporary Ethiopia based originally on a limited-circulation intelligence report for the Pentagon and later published as *U.S. Army Handbook for Ethiopia* (2nd ed., Washington: Government Printing Office, 1964). Dependent for the most part on secondary sources, the book adds little knowledge to the field, nor is it entirely free of factual errors. Ernest W. Luther, *Ethiopia Today* (Stanford University Press, 1958), written by a man who spent several years in Ethiopia as a financial adviser to the government, is disappointing and strongly biased against the Ethiopians. E. Sylvia Pankhurst, *Ethiopia: A Cultural History* (Woodford Green, Essex: Lalibela House, 1955), is a staunch apologia for Ethiopia. Unfortunately, the quality of the work does not match Miss Pankhurst's enthusiasm and ardor for things Ethiopian. Far more useful are Richard K. P. Pankhurst, *An Introduction to the Economic History of Ethiopia* (London: Lalibela House, 1961) and *Economic History of Ethiopia 1800–1935* (Addis Ababa: Haile Sellassie I University Press, 1968); much of what Mr. Pankhurst says is applicable to traditional rural Ethiopia today. For a work by an expatriate West Indian, strong supporter of the imperial regime, and frequent contributor to the *Ethiopian Herald,* see David A. Talbot, *Contemporary Ethiopia* (New York: Philosophical Library, 1952) and *Haile Selassie I: Silver Jubilee* (The Hague: Van Stockum, 1955). Edward Ullendorff, *The Ethiopians:*

An Introduction to Country and People (2nd ed., London: Oxford University Press, 1965), is an excellent historiographical description of the literature on Ethiopia by a distinguished linguist who, while worshipping at the shrine of dead Ethiopicists, prefers to avoid mention of contemporary politics and ignores the contributions of younger scholars to this expanding field of studies. A recent German work, Ernst Hammerschmidt, *Äthiopien, Christliches Reich zwischen Gestern und Morgen* (Wiesbaden: Otto Harrassowitz, 1967), is also very well done, but it too contains little information of a political nature; its one serious defect is its slight treatment of Ethiopia's considerable Muslim population. In a popular vein, David Buxton, *Travels in Ethiopia* (London: Lindsay Drummond, 1949; revised edition, New York: Frederick A. Praeger, 1968), is an excellent introduction to little known areas of the country, while Jane and Jean Ouannou, *L'Ethiopie, pilote de l'Afrique* (Paris: Maisonneuve et Larose, 1962), and Charles Billon, *L'Ethiopie, du roi Salomon et de la reine de Saba à l'empereur Haile-Selassie Ier* (Marseilles: Brugnot, 1966), are superficial.

The best historical studies of Ethiopia are A. H. M. Jones and Elizabeth Monroe, *A History of Ethiopia* (Oxford: Clarendon Press, 1960) and David Mathew, *Ethiopia: The Study of a Polity, 1450–1935* (London: Eyre and Spottiswoode, 1946). The former is the standard history of Ethiopia, despite the shortcomings of its original publication date (1935) and the fact that the most recent scholarship was not incorporated into the book when it was reissued. The latter is a highly detailed political history of Ethiopia prior to the Italian invasion. The early origins of Ethiopia are dealt with in Sabatino Moscati, *Le antiche civiltà semitiche* (Bari: Laterza, 1958), A. J. Drewes, *Inscriptions de l'Ethiopie antique* (Leiden: Brill, 1962), and F. Anfray, "Excavations in Ethiopia: A Gold Treasure and Light on the Origins of the Ethiopic Civilisation from Matar," in *Illustrated London News*, CCXLV (October 17, 1964), 601–603. Various volumes of the Hakluyt series deal with what might be called the medieval period of Ethiopian history. Luca dei Sabelli, *Storia di Abissinia*, 4 vols. (Leghorn and Florence: Edizioni Roma, 1936–1938), is a useful study by an Italian scholar, Luca Pietromarchi, who chose to write under a pseudonym. For the Italian invasion, G. L. Steer, *Caesar in Abyssinia* (London: Hodder and Stoughton, 1936), is a journalist's excellent account of that time of troubles. Ernest Work, *Ethiopia, A Pawn in European Diplomacy* (New York: Macmillan, 1935) was at one time undeservedly the standard study of European diplomacy relating to Ethiopia. More recent studies include Angelo Del Boca, *The Ethiopian War 1935–1941* (Chicago: University of Chicago Press, 1969), and George W. Baer, *The Coming of the Italian-Ethiopian War* (Cambridge: Harvard University Press, 1967).

In recent years Ethiopian authors have begun to make some contribution to an understanding of their country. Two short histories are particularly useful: Aleqa Tayye, *Ya-Ityopya Hizb Tarik* (A History of the Ethiopian People, in Amharic) (Addis Ababa: Commercial Printing Press, 1963), and Tekle Sadiq Makuria, *Ya-Ityopya Tarik* (A History of Ethiopia) 2 vols. (Addis Ababa: Artistic Printing Press, 1953–1954). Available in English are Kebbede Mikael, *Ethiopia and Western Civilization* (Addis Ababa: Berhanenna Selam, 1949), and Mesfin Wolde Mariam, *The Background of the Ethio-Somalia Boundary Dispute* (Addis Ababa: Berhanenna Selam, 1964).

The most outstanding analysis of Ethiopian politics is Margery Perham, *The Government of Ethiopia* (2nd ed., London: Faber and Faber, 1969). This classic, first published in 1948, is useful not only for the Ethiopia of that era but also for its insights into contemporary Ethiopia. It is complemented by Christopher Clapham, *Haile-Selassie's Government* (New York: Frederick A., Praeger, 1969). In Nathan Marein, *The Ethiopian Empire: Federation and Laws* (Rotterdam: Royal Netherlands Printing and Lithographing Co., 1955), the reader will find an excellent introduction to the modern legal system of Ethiopia by an expert on matters of jurisprudence. Christine Sandford, *The Lion of Judah Hath Prevailed, being the biography of His Imperial Majesty Haile Selassie I* (London: Dent, 1955), is a revised edition of

Ethiopia Under Haile Selassie (1946). Although the book falls
far short of being a definitive biography, the author, an English-
woman long resident in Ethiopia and an admirer of the Emperor, does present some useful information. Leonard Mosley,
Haile Selassie: The Conquering Lion (Englewood Cliffs, N. J.:
Prentice-Hall, 1965), tends to emphasize the more sensationalistic
aspects of recent Ethiopian history. Recent events are better
handled in Richard Greenfield, *Ethiopia, A New Political History* (New York: Frederick A. Praeger, 1965).

Frederick J. Simoons, *Northwest Ethiopia, Peoples and Economy* (Madison: University of Wisconsin Press, 1960), a useful
regional study of one of Ethiopia's most important provinces,
would have been of greater value had it contained more historical and political materials. Simon D. Messing, "The Highland-
Plateau Amhara of Ethiopia" (unpublished Ph.D. dissertation,
University of Pennsylvania, 1957) is a study of the dominant
ethnic group in Ethiopia. Far more helpful, and highly controversial, is Donald Levine, *Wax and Gold: Tradition and Innovation in Ethiopian Culture* (Chicago: University of Chicago
Press, 1965), a study of the traditional culture of the Amhara and
how it both facilitates and impedes Ethiopian efforts to modernize. J. Spencer Trimingham, *Islam in Ethiopia* (London: Oxford
University Press, 1952) complements these works as a scholarly
investigation of an aspect of Ethiopian life and history that is
often considered apart from the history of Christian Ethiopia.
Unfortunately no study is available of contemporary Muslim
Ethiopia.

For a visual image of this magnificent land and its people,
the following works are recommended: Roger Sauter, *Äthiopien*
(Zurich: Silva-Verlag, 1968); Georg Gerster, *L'art éthiopien*
(Zurich: Zodiaque, 1968); Jules Leroy, *La pittura etiopica*
(Milan: Electra, 1964); Max Ursin, *Äthiopien: Impressionen aus
einem altchristlichen Land* (Mannheim: Bibliographisches In-
stitut, 1958).

The following list will supplement this introduction to the
bibliography of Ethiopia.

Government Publications

1. ETHIOPIA

Chamber of Commerce. *Trade Directory and Guide Book to Ethiopia 1967*. Addis Ababa: Artistic Printing Press, 1967.

Ministry of Commerce. *Economic Handbook*. Addis Ababa: Berhanenna Selam, 1958.

Ministry of Commerce and Industry. *Economic Progress of Ethiopia*. Addis Ababa: East African Standard, for the Ministry, 1955.

Ministry of Finance. *Annual Import and Export Trade Statistics, 1962*. Addis Ababa: Customs Head Office Statistics Department, 1963.

Ministry of Finance. Central Statistical Office. *Report on a Survey of Adwa*. Addis Ababa: Central Statistical Office, 1966.

————. *Report on a Survey of Arussi Province*. Addis Ababa: Central Statistical Office, 1966.

————. *Report on a Survey of Bahir Dar*. Addis Ababa: Central Statistical Office, 1966.

————. *Report on a Survey of Debrezeyt*. Addis Ababa: Central Statistical Office, 1967.

————. *Report on a Survey of Desse*. Addis Ababa: Central Statistical Office, 1966.

————. *Report on a Survey of Gojam Province*. Addis Ababa: Central Statistical Office, 1966.

————. *Report on a Survey of Harer*. Addis Ababa: Central Statistical Office, 1967.

————. *Report on a Survey of Jima*. Addis Ababa: Central Statistical Office, 1966.

————. *Report on a Survey of Soddo*. Addis Ababa: Central Statistical Office, 1967.

————. *Report on a Survey of Tigre Province*. Addis Ababa: Central Statistical Office, 1967.

————. *Report on a Survey of Wello Province*. Addis Ababa: Central Statistical Office, 1967.

————. *Statistical Abstract, 1963.* Addis Ababa: Commercial Printing Press, 1963.

————. *Statistical Abstract, 1965.* Addis Ababa: Commercial Printing Press, 1965.

Ministry of Foreign Affairs. *Proceedings of the Summit Conference of Independent African States.* Addis Ababa: Ministry of Foreign Affairs, 1963.

Ministry of Information. *The African Summit Conference.* Addis Ababa: Berhanenna Selam, 1963.

————. *The Ethio-Somalia Frontier Problem.* Addis Ababa: Ministry of Information [1960].

————. *Financial and Fiscal Policy of Ethiopia (Patterns of Progress, Book I).* Addis Ababa: Ministry of Information, 1968.

————. *Selected Speeches of His Imperial Majesty Haile Sellassie I, 1918–1967.* Addis Ababa: Ministry of Information, 1967.

Ministry of Land Reform and Administration. *Report on Land Tenure Surveys.* Addis Ababa: Ministry of Land Reform and Administration, 1967–1968.

Ministry of Pen. *Negarit Gazeta* (Official Gazette).

Planning Board. *Second Five Year Development Plan, 1963–1967.* Addis Ababa: Berhanenna Selam, 1962.

2. GERMANY

Statistisches Bundesamt, Wiesbaden. *Allgemeine Statistik des Auslandes: Länderberichte: Äthiopien 1965.* Stuttgart and Mainz: W. Kohlhammer, 1965.

3. ITALY

Ministero degli Affari Esteri, Comitato per la Documentazione delle Attività dell'Italia in Africa. *L'Italia in Africa.* Rome: Istituto Poligrafico dello Stato, 1955— .

4. SOMALI REPUBLIC

Information Services of the Somali Government. *The Somali Peninsula, A New Light on Imperial Motives.* London: Staples Printers, for the Somali Government, 1962.

Ministry of Information. *The Somali Republic and African Unity.* Somali Government Official Publication 20681/22962. Mogadishu: Stationery Office, 1962.

5. UNITED KINGDOM

Foreign Office. *Agreement and Military Convention Between the United Kingdom and Ethiopia, Addis Ababa, January 31, 1942.* Cmd. 6334. London: H.M.S.O., 1942.

6. UNITED NATIONS

United Nations. *Compendium of Social Statistics: 1963.*
————. *Annuaire Statistique/Statistical Yearbook, 1968.* United Nations: July, 1969.
UNESCO. *Report of Meeting of African Ministers of Education, Paris, 1962.*
————. *La situation actuelle de l'education en Afrique.* UNESCO/EDAF/S/4.
————. *World Illiteracy at Mid-Century.*
————. *World Survey of Education.* Volume III, 1961.

7. UNITED STATES

Department of Agriculture. *The Agricultural Situation in Africa and West Asia.* Washington: U.S.D.A. Economic Research Service, 1969.
Department of Commerce. *Foreign Economic Trends: Ethiopia.* Washington: Bureau of International Commerce, 1968.
————. *Foreign Economic Trends: Ethiopia.* Washington: Bureau of International Commerce, 1969.
————. *Overseas Business Reports: Market Profiles for Africa.* Washington: Bureau of International Commerce, 1969.
Department of Labor. *Labor Law and Practices in the Empire of Ethiopia.* Washington: Bureau of Labor Statistics, 1966.
Department of State. *Agreement Between the Government of the United States of America and the Imperial Ethiopian Government Concerning the Utilization of Defense Installations within the Empire of Ethiopia.* Washington: Department of State Treaties and Other International Acts, Series 2964, 1953.

————. *Background Notes: Empire of Ethiopia.* Washington: Department of State, 1970.

————. *Mutual Defense Assistance Agreement Between the United States of America and Ethiopia.* Washington: Department of State Treaties and Other International Acts, Series 2787, 1953.

House of Representatives. *Foreign Assistance Act of 1969: Hearings Before the Committee on Foreign Affairs, House of Representatives, Ninety-first Congress, First Session, on H. R. 11792.* Washington: U.S. Government Printing Office, 1969.

Books

Abir, Mordechai. *Ethiopia: The Era of the Princes; the Challenge of Islam and the Re-unification of the Christian Empire 1769–1855.* New York: Frederick A. Praeger, 1968.

Beckingham, C. F., and Huntingford, G. B. (trans. and eds.). *The Prester John of the Indies, A True Relation of the Lands of the Prester John, being the narrative of the Portuguese Embassy to Ethiopia in 1520 written by Father Francisco Alvares.* 2 vols. Cambridge: Hakluyt Society, 1961.

————. *Some Records of Ethiopia, 1593–1646 being Extracts from the History of High Ethiopia or Abassia by Manoel de Almeida, together with Bahrey's History of the Galla.* London: Hakluyt Society, 1954.

Barker, A. J. *The Civilizing Mission, A History of the Italo-Ethiopian War of 1935–1936.* New York: Dial Press, 1968.

Bennett, Norman R., ed. *Leadership in Eastern Africa: Six Political Biographies.* Boston: Boston University Press, 1968.

Bentwich, Norman. *Ethiopia, Eritrea and Somaliland.* London: Victor Gollancz, n. d.

Bruce, James. *Travels to Discover the Source of the Nile in the Years 1768, 1769, 1770, 1771, 1772, and 1773.* 7 vols. Edinburgh: Constable, 1804.

Budge, Ernest A. Wallis. *A History of Ethiopia: Nubia and Abyssinia, according to the hieroglyphic inscriptions of Egypt and Nubia, and the Ethiopian Chronicles.* Oosterhout: Anthropological Publications, 1966.

Cerulli, Enrico. *La letteratura etiopica.* 3rd ed., rev. Florence and Milan: Sansoni-Accademia, 1968.

――――. *Studi etiopici.* 4 vols. Rome: Istituto per l'Oriente, 1936–1963.

Cerulli, Ernesta. *Peoples of South-West Ethiopia and Its Borderland.* London: International African Institute, 1956.

Chaîne, Marcel. *La chronologie des temps chrétiens de l'Egypte et de l'Ethiopie.* Paris: Geuthner, 1925.

Chojnacki, S., and Pankhurst, R., eds. *Register of Current Research on Ethiopia and the Horn of Africa.* Addis Ababa: Haile Sellassie I University Institute of Ethiopian Studies, 1963–   .

Conover, Helen F., comp. *North and Northeast Africa, a selected annotated list of writings, 1951–1957.* Washington: Library of Congress, 1957.

Conti Rossini, Carlo. *Storia d'Etiopia.* Milan: A. Lucini, 1928.

Conzelman, William E., trans. and ed. *Chronique de Galawdewos (Claudius) Roi d'Ethiopie.* Paris: Emile Bouillon, 1895.

Coulbeaux, J. B. *Histoire politique et religieuse de l'Abyssinie.* 3 vols. Paris: Geuthner, 1929.

Crawford, O. G. S., ed. *Ethiopian Itineraries circa 1400–1524.* Cambridge: Hakluyt Society, 1958.

Dillmann, August. *Über die Anfänge des Axumitischen Reiches.* Berlin: K. Akademie der Wissenschaften, 1879.

Doresse, Jean. *Ethiopia.* London: Elek, 1959.

Drysdale, John. *The Somali Dispute.* New York: Praeger, 1964.

Ephraim Isaac. *The Ethiopian Church.* Boston: Henry H. Sawyer, 1968.

Ewert, Kurt. *Äthiopien.* Bonn: Deutsche Afrika-Gesellschaft. 1959.

Findlay, Louis. *The Monolithic Churches of Lalibela in Ethiopia.* Cairo: Société d'Archéologie Copte, 1944.

Geiger, Theodore. *TWA's Services to Ethiopia: Eighth Case*

Study of an NPA Series of United States Business Performance Abroad. Washington: National Planning Association, 1959.

Ginzberg, Eli, and Smith, Herbert A. *Manpower Strategy for Developing Countries: Lessons from Ethiopia.* New York: Columbia University Press, 1967.

Girma Beshah ,and Merid Wolde Aregay. *The Question of the Union of the Churches in Luso-Ethiopian Relations (1500–1632).* Lisbon: Junta de Investigaçoes do Ultramar, 1964.

Gorham, Charles. *The Lion of Judah, a life of Haile Selassie I, Emperor of Ethiopia.* New York: Farrar, Straus and Giroux, 1966.

Graven, Philippe. *An Introduction to Ethiopian Penal Law.* Addis Ababa: Haile Sellassie I University Faculty of Law, 1965.

Gross, Ernest A., D. P. de Villiers, Endalkatchew Makonnen, and Richard A. Falk. *Ethiopia and Liberia vs. South Africa: The South West Africa Case.* Los Angeles: African Studies Center, University of California, 1968.

Harris, Brice, Jr. *The United States and the Italo-Ethiopian Crisis.* Stanford: Stanford University Press, 1964.

Hess, Robert L. *Italian Colonialism in Somalia.* Chicago: University of Chicago Press, 1966.

Howard, William E. H. *Public Administration in Ethiopia: A Study in Retrospect and Prospect.* Groningen: Wolters, 1955.

Huffnagel, H. P., comp. *Agriculture in Ethiopia.* Rome: F. A. O., 1961.

Huntingford, G. W. B. *The Galla of Ethiopia; The Kingdoms of Kafa and Janjero.* London: International African Institute, 1956.

Jäger, Otto. *Antiquities of North Ethiopia, A Guide.* Stuttgart: Brockhaus, 1965.

Jesman, Czeslaw. *The Ethiopian Paradox.* London: Oxford University Press, 1963.

Laurens, Franklin D. *France and the Italo-Ethiopian Crisis,
1935–1936.* The Hague: Mouton, 1967.

Lewis, Herbert S. *A Galla Monarchy: Jimma Abba Jifar, Ethiopia, 1830–1932.* Madison: University of Wisconsin Press, 1965.

Lewis, Ian Myrrdin. *Peoples of the Horn of Africa: Somali, Afar and Saho.* London: International African Institute, 1955.

Longrigg, Stephen A. *A Short History of Eritrea.* Oxford: Clarendon Press, 1945.

Ludolf, Job. *Ad suam Historiam Aethiopicam antehac editam Commentarius.* Frankfort: J. D. Zunner, 1691.

Mann, H. S. *Land Tenure in Chore (Shoa): A Pilot Study.* Addis Ababa and Nairobi: Institute of Ethiopian Studies and the Faculty of Law, Haile Sellassie I University in association with Oxford University Press, 1965.

Matthews, Daniel G. *A Current Bibliography on Ethiopian Affairs: A Select Bibliography from 1950–1964.* Washington: African Bibliographic Center, 1965.

———. *Ethiopian Outline: A Bibliographical Research Guide.* Washington: African Bibliographic Center, 1966.

Mengistu Gedamu. *The Psychology of the White Races.* Addis Ababa: Berhanenna Selam, 1960.

Mesfin Wolde Mariam. *Preliminary Atlas of Ethiopia.* Addis Ababa: Department of Geography, University College, 1962.

Nerazzini, Cesare, trans. *La conquista musulmana dell'Etiopia nel secolo XVI.* Rome: Forzani, 1891.

Nicholas, Archbishop of Axum. *Church's Revival: Emancipation from 1600 Years Guardianship: Free Church in Free State achieved by His Majesty Haile Selassie Ist, Emperor of Ethiopia.* Cairo: Costa Tsouma, 1955.

Oriental Orthodox Conference, Interim Secretariat. *The Oriental Orthodox Churches Addis Ababa Conference, January 1965.* Addis Ababa: Artistic Printers, 1965.

Pankhurst, Richard K. P. *Ethiopian Royal Chronicles.* Addis Ababa: Oxford University Press, 1967.

————. *An Introduction to the History of the Ethiopian Army.* [Addis Ababa:] Imperial Ethiopian Air Force, 1967.

————. *State and Land in Ethiopian History.* Addis Ababa: Haile Sellassie I University Press, 1966.

Perruchon, Jules, trans. *Les chroniques de Zara Ya'eqob et de Ba'eda Maryam, Rois d'Ethiopie de 1434 à 1478.* Paris: E. Bouillon, 1893.

Proceedings of the First National Seminar on Social Welfare, Addis Ababa, November 3–7, 1965. Addis Ababa: Ethiopian Council of Social Welfare, 1966.

Proceedings of the Third International Conference of Ethiopian Studies, Addis Ababa, April 1966. Addis Ababa: Institute of Ethiopian Studies, 1970.

Reid, J. M. *Traveller Extraordinary: The Life and Times of James Bruce of Kinnaird (1730–1794).* London: Eyre and Spottiswoode, 1967.

Rennell of Rodd, Lord. *British Military Administration of Occupied Territories in Africa during the Years 1941–1947.* London: H.M.S.O., 1948.

Schwab, Peter. "An Analysis of Decision-Making in the Political System of Ethiopia." Unpublished dissertation, New School of Social Research, June, 1969.

Shack, William A. *The Gurage, A People of the Ensete Culture.* London: Oxford University Press, 1966.

Social Survey of Addis Ababa 1960, Carried out by a Study Group of the University College of Addis Ababa under the Auspices of the Municipality of Addis Ababa and the United Nations Economic Commission for Africa. Addis Ababa: Haile Sellassie I University, n.d.

Sykes, Christopher. *Orde Wingate.* London: Collins, 1959.

Syoum Gebregziabher. *Collection of Labour Laws of Ethiopia.* Addis Ababa: The Federation of Employers of Ethiopia [1967].

Teshome Adera, ed. *Nationalist Leaders of African Unity.* Addis Ababa: Ethiopian National Patriotic Association, 1963.

Thompson, Virginia, and Adloff, Richard. *Djibouti and the Horn of Africa.* Stanford: Stanford University Press, 1968.

Touval, Saadia. *Somali Nationalism: International Politics and the Drive for Unity in the Horn of Africa.* Cambridge: Harvard University Press, 1963.

Trevaskis, G. K. N. *Eritrea, A Colony in Transition, 1941–1952.* London: Oxford University Press, 1960.

Ullendorff, Edward. *Ethiopia and the Bible.* London: Oxford University Press, 1968.

Universal Ethiopian Students' Association. *The Truth About Ethiopia, a Nation Blocked from the Sea.* New York: Universal Ethiopian Students' Association, 1936.

Vanderlinden, Jacques. *An Introduction to the Sources of Ethiopian Law.* Addis Ababa: Haile Sellassie I University Faculty of Law, 1966.

Wohlgemuth, Lennart. *Etiopiens Ekonomi.* Uppsala: Nordiska Afrika-Institutet, 1967.

Wylde, Augustus B. *Modern Abyssinia.* London: Methuen, 1901.

Articles

Beckett, N. G. S. "Ethiopia Beckons British Exporters," *Board of Trade Journal,* CLXXXVII (January 22, 1965), 147–150.

Clapham, Christopher. "Imperial Leadership in Ethiopia," *African Affairs,* LXVIII (1968), 110–120.

————. "The December 1960 Ethiopian Coup d'Etat," *Journal of Modern African Studies,* VI (1968), 495–507.

Ford, Alan. "Russian Attempt to Control Red Sea Behind Eritrean Movement," *National Review,* XVIII (April 5, 1966), 314–315.

Gibson-Smith, W. "Canadian Prospects in Ethiopia," *Foreign Trade,* CXXI (February 22, 1964), 29–30.

Haberland, Eike. "The Influence of the Christian Ethiopian Empire on Southern Ethiopia," *Journal of Semitic Studies,* IX (1964), 235–238.

Hess, Robert L. "The Ethiopian No-Party State," *American Political Science Review,* LVIII (1964), 947–950 (with Gerhard Loewenberg).

———. "Italy and Africa: Colonial Ambitions in the First World War," *Journal of African History,* IV (1963), 105–126.

———. "The 'Mad Mullah' and Northern Somalia," *Journal of African History,* V (1964), 415–433.

———. "Toward a History of the Falasha," *Eastern African History,* D. F. McCall, N. R. Bennett, and J. Butler, eds. (New York: Praeger, 1969), 107–132.

Karsten, Detlev. "Ethiopia: Industrialisation of a Developing Country," *Intereconomics, Monthly Review of International Trade and Development* (Hamburg), I (1968), 22–25.

Kebedew Ashagree. "Some Problems of the Public Service in Ethiopia," *Canadian Public Administration,* VIII (1965), 292–300.

Klassen, Frank. "Teacher Education in Ethiopia," *School and Society,* XCI (February 23, 1963), 96–98.

Korten, David C., and Korten, Frances F. "Ethiopia's Use of National University Students in a Year of Rural Service," *Comparative Education Review,* X (October, 1966), 482–492.

Kotler, Neil G. "Ethiopia: The Over-Present Americans," *Nation,* CCIV (February 20, 1967), 236–239.

Krzeczunowicz, G. "The Ethiopian Civil Code: Its Usefulness, Relation to Custom, Applicability," *Journal of African Law,* VII (1963), 172–177.

Lewis, William H. "Ethiopia: The Quickening Pulse," *Current History,* LIV (February, 1968), 78–82.

Logan, Rayford W. "Ethiopia's Troubled Future," *Current History,* XLIV (January, 1963), 46–50.

Marein, Nathan. "Emperor Challenges Arab Churches?" *The New Middle East,* June, 1969.

Markakis, John, and Asmelash Beyene. "Representative Institutions in Ethiopia," *Journal of Modern African Studies,* V (1967), 193–219.

Mulugeta Wodajo. "Ethiopia: Some Pressing Problems and the Role of Education in their Resolution," *Journal of Negro Education,* XXX (1961), 232–240.

Roberts, E. "Ethiopia Emergent," *Contemporary Review,* CCII (October, 1962), 196–198.

Russell, Franklin F. "The New Ethiopian Penal Code," *American Journal of Comparative Law,* X (1961), 265–277.

Schultz, H. J. "Reform and Reaction in the Ethiopian Orthodox Church," *Christian Century,* LXXXV (January 31, 1968), 142–143.

Schwab, Peter. "Modernise Ethiopia's Tax System: A Critical Look into Ethiopia's Structure of Taxation," *East Africa Journal,* February, 1968, pp. 27–31

Smith, Peter Duval. "No Dawn in Ethiopia," *New Statesman,* LXV (March 29, 1963), 456.

Stauffer, H. S., and Colebrook, M. J. "Economic Assistance and Ethiopia's Foreign Policy," *Orbis,* V (1961), 320–341.

Sterling, Claire. "The Aging Lion of Judah," *Reporter,* XXXVI (February 9, 1967), 28–30.

Von Baudissin, Georg Graf. "Labour Policy in Ethiopia," *International Labour Review,* LXXXVII (June, 1964), 551–569.

Warren, Cline J. "Ethiopia Broadens its Agricultural Base," *Foreign Agriculture,* XXVI (March, 1962), 15–17.

Yakobson, S. "Soviet Union and Ethiopia: A Case of Traditional Behavior," *Review of Politics,* XXV (July, 1963), 329–342.

Zack, Arnold M. "The New Labour Relations Law in Ethiopia," *Bulletin of International African Labour Institute,* XII (1965), 223–233.

———. "Trade Unionism Develops in Ethiopia," *Boston University Papers on Africa: Transition in African Politics,* J. Butler and A. A. Castagno, eds. (New York: Praeger, 1967), 104–114.

Periodicals

Africa Research Bulletin
Challenge, Journal of the Ethiopian Students Association in North America
Ethiopia Information Bulletin
Ethiopia Observer
Ethiopian Trade Journal
Ethiopie d'Aujourd'hui
Ethnological Society Bulletin (University College of Addis Ababa)
JESAME, Journal of the Ethiopian Students Association in the Middle East
Journal of African History
Journal of African Law
Journal of Ethiopian Law
Journal of Ethiopian Studies
Menen
Something, the Literary Magazine of University College
University College Journal
University College Review
Voice of Labour
The Wake, Magazine of the Imperial Ethiopian Navy.

Newspapers

Addis-Soir
Addis Zemen (New Times, in Amharic)
Ethiopian Herald
Giornale dell'Eritrea
Il Mattino del Lunedì
Il Quotidiano Eritreo
Voice of Ethiopia
Ya-Ityopya Dems (Voice of Ethiopia, in Amharic)

Index